CW00957015

THE ART
OF
FRENCH
BAKING

GINETTE MATHIOT

THE ART

OF

FRENCH
BAKING

Φ

FOREWORD

Growing up in a French family, my earliest and fondest kitchen memories involve pastries.

My mother is an excellent cook and an equally gifted baker. Every weekend was an opportunity to exercise her talents, and to satisfy our hunger for simple baked goods. She would serve them for dessert at the end of our meals – perhaps a caramelized *crème renversée* (Crème Caramel, p. 252), a lustrous *tarte aux fraises* (Strawberry Tart, p. 184), or a feather-light *île flottante* (Floating Island, p. 290) – or in the afternoon, with tea – this time a fragrant *gâteau d'orange* (Orange Cake, p. 92), a buttery *quatre-quart* (Pound Cake, p. 105), or an assortment of crisp *sablés* (p. 228).

She was always keen to get the children involved, and my sister and I spent many a joyful hour elbow-deep in flour, breaking eggs, cutting out flower-shaped biscuits, or glazing golden cakes.

As a result of this early exposure, I am not daunted by French baking as some would-be bakers might be, but I do understand this reaction: certainly, anyone looking through the windows of a Parisian bakery and admiring the display of too-beautiful-to-eat pastries is bound to feel in awe.

Ever since the great French chef Antonin Carême set out to modernize pastry in the wake of the French Revolution, inventing the famous towering construction of caramelized choux buns called *croquembouche* and documenting his work in a series of fascinating books, France has fostered generations of extraordinary artisans who have elevated their craft to an art form.

But the truth is, even the most complex French pastry is but a sum of basic techniques, building blocks that can be learnt, mastered in time, and then used to replicate the greatest classics, or come up with your own creations.

This is what Ginette Mathiot's baking bible is all about: teaching you the elemental components of French baking, and putting them into practice to produce delectable desserts that will make you proud and delight your guests.

Ginette Mathiot was a twenty-five-year-old home economics teacher when she published her first book in 1932, *Je Sais Cuisiner,* a monumental compendium of French recipes that was first published in English by Phaidon in 2009, under the title *I Know How To Cook.* She had put it together over the course of several years, enlisting her students to help with the testing.

The result was so wide in scope and so easy to use, that it soon became a best-selling title, and millions of copies have since then found their place in French kitchens.

The success of this volume led Mathiot to write a second one devoted entirely to sweets and desserts, largely expanding the selection she had included in her first book. A few years later, in 1938, she published *Je Sais Faire La Pâtisserie* (*I Know How to Make Pastries*). In it she effectively covers all the basics that make up the French pâtisserie repertoire, from the simplest confections to the most sophisticated, from biscuits and cakes to tarts and custards, so that no baking need should be left unanswered. *The Art of French Baking* draws recipes from both of these classic books.

Seventy years and several editions later, it remains a much-loved book that readers have used as a learning tool – to familiarize themselves with the different techniques, gain experience and develop their confidence – or as a reference book for looking up the recipe for brioche or chocolate soufflé as the occasion arises.

Ginette Mathiot's writing voice is benevolent and practical, and she believes that less is more: the original versions of her recipes are generally quite short, allowing the baker to get a sense of the process at a glance, without losing him in lengthy explanations.

In this English edition, however, our team of editors has striven to flesh out these recipes, adding detail where we felt more was needed, and we have taken the liberty of amending them from time to time, when modern practice demanded an update. For instance, cakes rise best when the baking powder is combined with the flour beforehand, for optimal dispersion in the batter, but the original French recipes did not specify that.

Our goal was always to bring to an English-speaking audience the helpful and comprehensive baking book that the French have known and used for several generations, and to make these wonderful desserts accessible, showing you how simple it can be to create your own gâteaux, sablés and soufflés.

Whether you're a budding baker or an accomplished one, we hope you will find plenty of recipes to tempt your palate and hone your skills, and that this book soon becomes a trusted companion on your kitchen shelf.

Clotilde Dusoulier

A NOTE FROM THE AUTHOR

"Anyone who enjoys cooking also wants to bake. However, all too often the books you consult are disappointing because the recipes in them are complicated and expensive to make. *Je Sais Faire La Pâtisserie*, on the other hand, is an extremely user-friendly book.

Contrary to a long-held belief, baked goods and desserts should not be regarded as a luxury at home. Composed of flour, sugar, fat and eggs, they are made with a few straightforward ingredients. It goes without saying that when you make a dessert or a cake yourself, instead of buying something ready-made and expensive, you are adding to the nutritional value of the meal and reducing its cost, and, of course, you know exactly what has gone into it.

Practical considerations apart, there is such satisfaction to be gained from making and decorating a dessert or even inventing a sweet confection of your own. Encouraged by the success of *Je Sais Cuisiner* (*I Know How to Cook*), I wanted to respond to the many readers who requested pâtisserie and dessert recipes. This is not a recipe collection for professionals, but rather a cookbook intended for everyone who wants to make classic, tasty desserts using good-quality ingredients and a minimum of equipment. All instructions are set out in simple terms. Quantities and cooking times are stated precisely.

First and foremost, the aim of this book is to help home cooks, to satisfy the most dedicated cake enthusiast and to tempt the beginner. "

Ginette Mathiot, *Je Sais Faire la Pâtisserie*, 1991

INTRODUCTION
TO
BAKING

ESSENTIAL EQUIPMENT

Dough scraper
A stiff, flexible scraper, also known as a 'corne' in France, that is used for scraping every last trace of mixture out of bowls. The straight side fits into your palm, the curved side scrapes the bowl clean. You can also use a rubber spatula.

Food processors
A small appliance which enables you to carry out many of the tasks set out in a recipe quickly and without having to use your hands. Although not strictly a requirement for home baking, food processors are excellent for chopping and liquidizing. The larger size food processors are the most useful. These often come with a small interior bowl as well as a larger bowl. The small bowl can be used for grinding and chopping small quantities of nuts and herbs. Choose a model with the bowl sitting over the top of the motor as this design is the most durable. Different models are available in several sizes.

Kitchen scales
All the recipes in this book are very precise. The quantities are given in grams with an imperial conversion. A recipe may well not work if the proportions have not been strictly adhered to. Accurate scales are essential. Follow one set of measurements only.

Mixers
Stand mixers are one of the most helpful pieces of kitchen equipment for home baking. These mixers come with attachments for mixing, whisking and kneading. Additional bowls can be purchased if the volume of baking grows beyond a cake or loaf of bread. Choose the best model you can afford.

Mixing bowls
Stainless steel, earthenware or copper bowls in various shapes and sizes are needed for preparing various mixtures, beating eggs and so on. A selection of different sizes from small to large in a set of at least 3 is recommended. Plastic bowls are not recommended because they are difficult to clean thoroughly. Heatproof bowls should be used for melting chocolate.

Moulds and tins
Start with a few basic moulds and tins and add to your collection as needed. Many of the moulds and tins you can buy nowadays are non-stick, which makes unmoulding easier.

Non-stick pans do not need to be greased, although lining the base is recommended for cakes. Choose heavy, sturdy tins. These are the most useful:

Cake tins. 20 cm (8 inches), to take about 500 g (1 lb 2 oz) of cake mixture; deep springform cake tins, 20 cm (8 inches) and 25 cm (10 inches).

Tart tins with removable base. 15 cm (6 inches) for 2 servings; 25 cm (10 inches) for 6 servings; 30 cm (12 inches) for 8 servings.

Cupcake trays and madeleine tins.

Baking sheet or tray. A rectangular or round metal dish or tray, with a raised edge for baking biscuits, tarts and free-form loaves. Select the largest size that fits in your oven and choose a heavy-duty make for durability.

Rectangular loaf tins. 20 x 10 cm (8 x 4 inches), to take about 500 g (1 lb 2 oz) of cake mixture or dough; 25 x 12 ½ cm (9 x 5 inches) to take 675 g (1½ lb) of cake mixture and dough:

Savarin moulds and baba moulds. 25 cm (10 inches) average size; 5 cm (2 inches) for individual moulds.

Small cake and tart tins in a variety of shapes. Round, oval, barquette, tall, fluted and smooth ones.

Nozzle
A stainless steel or exoglass tip which is placed in a piping bag and used to decorate cakes. It resembles a cut-off cone, with a small opening in various shapes from oval to star-shaped, for different piping effects.

Oven thermometer
The calibration of ovens varies and can change over time. Using an oven thermometer ensures that your oven is preheated to the correct temperature and that the temperature is maintained throughout the baking period.

Palette knife
A thin metal blade about 2 cm (1 inch) wide and usually 20 cm (8 inches) long that is attached to a wooden or plastic handle, either straight or stepped. A palette knife is used for separating pastry from the work surface, removing cakes from tins, and for chopping through certain types of pastry to combine ingredients.

Pastry brush
A brush used to glaze pastry with either a mixture of egg yolk and water, or to glaze confections with syrup or jam. Also used to brush excess flour from pastry.

Pastry cutter
A metal or plastic utensil used for cutting out well-defined shapes. Pastry cutters can come in many different shapes, such as hearts, animals, flowers and so on.

Pastry scraper
A metal implement with a wooden handle used for scraping off any mixture that has stuck to the slab or countertop. A small knife or metal spatula can just as easily be used.

Pastry blender
A small handle with looped cutting blades attached at each end in a hoop used for chopping fat into flour. Two knives or metal palette knives used scissor-fashion can be used for the same purpose.

Pastry slab
A slab made from a naturally cool material such as marble used for mixing and rolling out pastry. Choose a slab with the dimensions of at least 70 x 70 cm (28 x 28 inches). Too small and it will make the preparation of the pastry difficult. Too large and it will be cumbersome to move. A pastry slab can be replaced with an oilcloth on a table, or with the table itself, providing there are no grooves in the wood and the table is spotlessly clean. If you have granite, Formica or Corian countertops you will not need a pastry slab.

Pastry wheel
A small wheel, either plain or fluted, and mounted on a thin, straight handle that enables you to cut pastry dough without tearing it. A sharp knife can be used instead to give straight cuts.

Pincers/crimping tongs
A metal implement with two sections and serrated tips that enables you to seal and decoratively crimp the edges and borders of tarts and pies.

Piping bag
A funnel-shaped bag of coarse plastic-coated fabric. A nozzle is lowered into the small opening. Piping bags can be used to pipe out cake or biscuit mixtures, or to pipe decorative icing onto cakes.

Rack
A round, square, or rectangular utensil made of wire, about 25 cm (10 inches) in diameter or 25 cm (10 inches) square, or 27 x 40 cm (11 x 16 inches). Racks are essential for cooling cakes and biscuits.

Rolling pin
A cylindrical implement for rolling out pastry, usually made of very smooth wood (preferably beech), either with or without handles. A rolling pin without handles is easier to use because it gives you more control, but a rolling pin with handles is more comfortable to use for many people. At a pinch, a rolling pin can be replaced by a bottle that is totally cylindrical in shape. Modern silicone rolling pins are non-stick.

Spatula
A plastic scraping blade attached to a wooden handle. Used to handle uncooked and cooked mixtures without having to touch them with your hands.

Spoon
Large metal spoons are useful to fold mixtures together without knocking out air that has been beaten into them. The thin metal edge cuts through the mixtures.

Sugar thermometer
Modern sugar thermometers measure in degrees centigrade and Fahrenheit to determine the concentration of a sugar syrup. In the past, a hydrometer was used to indicate the density of sugar syrup. These hydrometers are still sometimes used by professional chefs, particularly for sugar work.

Whisk
Several thin wires looped around and attached to a handle used to aerate mixtures, particularly egg whites. There are many different sizes of whisk, but the largest whisk you can hold which still feels comfortable in your hand will be the most useful. Whisks also come in hand-held electric versions.

Wooden spoon
To help you mix various ingredients evenly. You will need several in different sizes.

ESSENTIAL INGREDIENTS

It is extremely useful to be as familiar as possible with the nature of the essential ingredients used in home baking. Home bakers are careful to use only fresh products, the source or origin of which is recognised and regulated.

Cocoa powder
For use in baking, this is made from finely ground fermented cocoa beans. It does not contain sugar.

Chocolate
Block chocolate consists of cocoa solids, cocoa butter and a varying amount of sugar. Sometimes other ingredients are added such as milk solids to make milk chocolate, vanilla for flavour, and lecithin for emulsification. For cooking, it is best to choose plain chocolate with a high proportion of cocoa solids, normally 60–72%, for best flavour. The cocoa butter content gives ease of melting. This is sometimes called *couverture*, meaning coating, because it is often used to coat cakes and biscuits. Choose a chocolate flavour that you like: some chocolate is too bitter.

Eggs
The weight of a medium egg without its shell is 50–60 g (1¾–2 oz). When making cakes and some pastries the whole egg may be used, or just the yolk, or just the white. The yolk, high in fat content, binds various pastries, adds colour to them and imparts a characteristic flavour. Egg white (albumen) has a particular viscosity, which enables it to stiffen when whisked energetically. Beaten egg white is formed of small air bubbles, which make any mixture to which it is added much lighter. When whisking egg whites, start gently and slowly, then gradually increase the speed. To facilitate the process add a drop of lemon juice or a pinch of salt to the egg whites. An electric whisk makes this task a breeze.

Always use a broken egg immediately: the yolk will spoil quickly. You can use this part of the egg immediately in a variety of desserts and cakes and should avoid throwing it away if possible. Unused egg whites may be frozen for later use. It is essential, for the purposes of home baking, to know how fresh an egg is. Egg whites keep up to three weeks in the fridge as they contain a natural antioxidant. To test the freshness of an egg, place it in a bowl of water. A fresh egg will immediately sink to the bottom and lie flat on its side.

A bad egg will float in the water and should be discarded. Old egg whites are also preferred for making meringues because they whip up more easily.

Fats
Cream. Fresh cream should always be used in baking and will have a subtle, very pleasing taste. Whipped, sweetened with sugar or flavoured with vanilla, it is often used to decorate pastries.

Butter. Very high in fat content (about 85%), it plays an important role in pâtisserie. As soon as oxidization begins to take place, butter becomes rancid and gives an unpleasant taste to mixtures. Check its temperature before you use it. Unless otherwise stated, butter should always have the same consistency as the dough or mixture to which it is added. Too much butter in a pastry will make it softer but also much too crumbly.

Oil. Some mixtures and doughs have oil added to them to make them crisper. Use fresh oil of the type specified in the recipe.

Flavourings, extracts, liqueurs and spirits
Among these are fruit and flower extracts, cordials and fortified wines. Their flavour is concentrated, so use sparingly and with discrimination. Choose natural flavourings and extracts for the best flavour.

Vanilla is used widely in pâtisserie to flavour custards, cakes and biscuits. It can be used in the form of an extract or as a whole bean. Always use a natural extract, not a chemical essence. To use a whole vanilla pod, infuse it in the liquid from the recipe, usually milk or cream, for at least 10 minutes, then split it lengthways using a small, sharp knife. Scrape the seeds from the inside the pod and add to the recipe. Discard the pod or add to a container of white sugar to make vanilla sugar.

Flour
Found in practically all pastry, cake and biscuit recipes, flour is the powder obtained by grinding the grains of some cereals, usually wheat. Sometimes you can substitute polenta flour, buckwheat flour, barley flour or chestnut flour.

Wheat flour, however, remains the most popular choice. This is made up of about 75% starch; 10% protein ; 1% fat; 13% water and 1% mineral salts.

Starch is the most nutritious element in flour. There are two proteins in flour, glutenin and gliadin, that when combined with liquid and worked cause the flour to become an elastic, smooth dough. Good flour should be yellowish white in colour, soft to the touch, and have a pleasant smell. It cannot be stored for long, just a few months at most. If you use too much flour in a cake mixture it will have a slightly bitter taste and be very dry in consistency.

Fruit

A very important ingredient in pâtisserie, not least because it adds to the nutritional value (mineral salts, acids, fructose, vitamins). Fruit also enhances the appearance and taste of pâtisserie. It plays a very important decorative role, whether it is fresh or cooked, crystallized or dried, or in the form of jam.

Liquids

Water and milk are often used to moisten doughs and batters. Milk will increase the nutritional value of the dough.

Nuts

Almonds, walnuts, hazelnuts and peanuts, which all have a high nutritional content, make delicious cakes and biscuits, adding both texture and flavour. Ensure nuts are fresh by buying only what you require. Nuts can also be stored in the freezer.

Potato flour

This starch can be used in pastry making. It yields light results and keeps well. However, a dough made with potato flour does not have the same smoothness as one made with ordinary flour. Potato flour can replace ordinary flour in a recipe that does not call for fermentation. Potato flour is very bright white in colour, and very soft to the touch. It makes little squeaking sounds when worked with your fingers.

Raising agents

Leaven or yeast and chemical raising agents are used to make baked products lighter.

Yeast. This contains lactic-acid producing bacteria, fermenting enzymes, and cells of brewer's yeast which need moisture and gentle heat before they can become active. Under the right conditions, the cells react with the various components of dough and produce carbon dioxide. It takes several hours for dough to rise. The carbon dioxide gas bubbles expand in the dough and make it swell so that it increases in volume and becomes lighter in texture. Baker's yeast must be very fresh if it is to work effectively. Dried yeast is available in powdered form and is reconstituted with liquid either directly or by combining first with flour then liquid. Check the use-by date to ensure it is still active.

Baking powder. A white powder made with bicarbonate of soda, cream of tartar, and a small quantity of starch. The release of carbon dioxide is instantaneous upon contact with liquid and continues under heat.

Bicarbonate of soda. Sometimes small quantities of bicarbonate of soda or ammonium bicarbonate are used instead of baking powder; if too much of either is used, the taste can be unpleasant. If too much raising agent or leaven is used, the dough will be so light that the texture will be affected. If the dough has risen excessively, it will sink quickly.

Rice flour or ground rice

Ground white rice is often used in shortbread and gluten-free baking.

Salt

Salt is indispensable in baking. It adds flavour and balances what would otherwise be too sugary, sweet and insipid a taste if sugar alone were used. The salt should be very finely ground, like table salt.

Sugar

Most often beet or cane sugar (sucrose) are used. Sugar comes in many different forms: sugar cubes, granulated sugar, caster sugar, icing sugar. Sugar is differentiated according to the fineness of its grains. Sugar added to pastry dough and other pâtisserie mixtures can add colour and facilitate browning during cooking; it will make it sandier in consistency.

Sugar reacts adversely with iron. It is therefore essential to exclude this metal from all equipment used in pâtisserie or confectionery. Sucrose is capable of crystallization. Very often, glucose is added to a syrup, which will then not crystallize at all. Industrial manufacturers of pastries, cakes and sweets sometimes use glucose, which is three times less sugary than sucrose. Brown sugar, honey, and molasses are also used in cooking. These sweeteners hold moisture, thereby producing moister and softer cakes and biscuits.

ESSENTIAL TECHNIQUES

BASIC RECIPES

With a thorough knowledge of how to make the five main types of pastry, some basic icings and sauces, it is easy to make all sorts of delicious confections. Using the practical experience gained while following the basic recipes, the home cook will be able to create new delicacies, new treats and new masterpieces.

Pastry doughs

Butter, eggs, flour and sugar are nearly always used in pâtisserie. But the different ways in which they are processed and their varying proportions mean that the end products will bear little resemblance to one another.

Each of the basic pastry, cake and other mixtures described in this book has its own characteristics which make it particularly suited to certain recipes.

This book explains how to be successful with the most widely used and easiest recipes. The most common are Shortcrust Pastry (p. 33), Rich Sweet Pastry (p. 35) and Sweet Pastry (p. 32), which form the basis of many pastry creations. They can be used as a basis to create a diverse range of pastries from Jam-Filled Pastry (p. 176) to Tarte Tatin (p. 195). These pastry types are not interchangeable. Each has certain characteristics that are required for different types of pies and tarts.

Shortcrust pastry. Known in French as *pâte brisée*, this pastry can be used as the basis for any baked goods, both sweet and savoury, that are very highly flavoured or which have a considerable amount of filling, including savoury quiches, tarts and pies. Pastry must be made quickly and with a light touch if it is to be tender. The use of butter gives it a particularly delicious crispness. If made 12 hours in advance of baking, it will be even lighter.

Once cooked, this pastry absorbs fruit juices very quickly. It is therefore best baked 'blind', meaning baked through completely before filling. The fruit or filling is often cooked separately, or the pastry is used with fruit that does not release a lot of juice. Shortcrust pastry will not keep well and will lose its crispness. Shops and supermarkets now sell ready-made shortcrust pastry. For the best flavour, look for pastry that lists butter in the ingredients. Rhubarb Tart (p. 193) and Walnut Tart (p. 180) are examples of recipes using shortcrust pastry.

Rich sweet pastry. The French name for this pastry, *pâte sablée*, describes the 'sandy' appearance the mixture has in the earlier stages of preparation. The ingredients include eggs, which make the texture of this pastry more compact than shortcrust pastry, and less crumbly. It also swells less as its cooks, eliminating the need for baking blind, and it can withstand moisture much better. When used for small fruit tarts such as in Strawberry Tartlets (p. 184), the pastry stays firm and crisp for some considerable time.

Sweet pastry dough. This has the same advantages as shortcrust pastry but is sweeter. Known in French as *pâte sucrée*, it is used for tarts and pies such as the Chestnut Tartlets (p. 190) that are going to be filled with sweet mixtures and/or fruit. It is not suitable for savoury fillings. Tarts are made with this pastry in round or square baking tins. They can also be made in very long rectangular shapes. Springform tins are practical, making it easy to take out the cooked tart or pie.

Puff pastry. When cooked, this pastry has many very thin, even layers: this is achieved partly by the way the butter is incorporated into the flour and water dough, and partly by the way in which the dough is folded as it is prepared. For successful puff pastry it is vital to allow the dough to rest for 15–20 minutes after each 'turn' (each series of rolling, folding and turning).

The butter should be of the same consistency as the flour-and-water dough, otherwise they will not layer with one another effectively. The proportions of butter to flour can vary slightly and, predictably, the quality of the pastry will reflect this. The more butter there is, the finer the pastry. It is not advisable, however, to use more butter than flour: the pastry would have too high a fat content. For a fine puff pastry, use the same weight of butter as of flour. For a semi-fine puff pastry, use one-fifth less butter in weight than flour. For an everyday puff pastry, the amount of butter used should be half the weight of the flour.

The edges of raw puff pastry should be trimmed with a very sharp knife when the pastry dough is cold, or the layers will fuse together and it will not rise properly during the cooking process. Dampening the tin very slightly before placing the pastry on it can facilitate rising, as the water creates steam in the hot oven. Do not overdo this: too much water will have the opposite effect, making the pastry soggy.

When most of the puff pastry has been used, some

trimmings will be left over. These can be placed on top of each other and rolled together, keeping the layers horizontal, and used to make pastries that will rise nearly as well as the larger pieces. Any leftovers from this second batch will not rise as well but can be pressed into shape and used to line baking tins. It is possible to buy excellent ready-made puff pastry, both frozen and fresh. Apple Turnovers (p. 159), Pithiviers (p. 164) and Mille-Feuilles (p. 170) are examples of recipes requiring puff pastry.

Choux pastry. This is the only pastry that requires cooking in its preparation. Some cooks claim there can be a slightly tricky stage of the preparation, which entails adding all the flour at once to the boiling liquid. Sometimes it does not mix well to begin with: the solution is to stir the mixture fairly quickly and vigorously to get rid of any lumps that have started to form. Following the recipe accurately should dispel any misgivings you have about making choux pastry.

Once the mixture is smooth, the pan needs to be returned to a low heat to dry out the pastry. Continue stirring the pastry over the heat for 10 seconds. Allow the pastry to cool to room temperature before adding any beaten egg or the egg will cook in the hot dough and lose its elasticity.

Enough egg needs to be beaten into the dough base to give it a soft dropping consistency. Add the beaten egg a tablespoonful at a time.

Choux pastry is piped out in little mounds or other shapes, well spaced out (it puffs up considerably) on a baking tray greased with butter or covered with baking parchment. This same dough can be deep fried to make *beignets soufflés* (choux fritters). Chocolate Éclairs (p. 153), Caramelized Choux Buns (p. 147) and Saint-Honoré (p. 148) are examples of recipes using choux pastry.

If my pastry is greasy
It is best to work in a cool kitchen. You need to work quickly to avoid the ingredients heating up which can make the pastry greasy. If you have hot hands, cool them by running them under the cold tap.

If my pastry has shrunk
With the notable exception of choux, all pastry needs to be chilled until it is hard before it goes into the oven to bake. If not, the butter in the pastry will melt before the flour has had the chance to cook the pastry into its desired shape. The oven must be preheated to the specified temperature in the recipe before any pastry is placed in the oven.

If my pastry is too tough
Too much water may have been added to pastry. Add only as much as you need to bring the dough together. Overworking the pastry may also cause pastry to be tough, so handle pastry gently.

If my puff pastry keeps breaking when I roll it out
Good pastry often breaks around the edges when it is being rolled out. Squeeze it back together with your fingertips. Try using a little less pressure when rolling out and next time add a little more water.

If my puff pastry does not rise well
The pastry may not have been chilled sufficiently between rolling and folding. Also, the pastry may have been rolled too thinly, or the oven temperature may have been too low.

If my choux buns collapse
Make sure you bake the choux buns until they are golden brown. If the buns are taken out of the oven too soon before the sides are firm, the buns could collapse.

If my choux buns do not rise well
The expansive qualities of the egg in choux pastry make the buns rise well in the oven. If you do not add enough egg to the base, the buns will be dense and heavy. Keep beating egg into the base until a small spoonful of the mixture can be dropped with little shake of the wrist on to the baking sheet.

If my choux buns are tough
The base mixture may have been beaten too long or the choux buns may have been overbaked.

If my choux buns are soggy
Choux buns should be returned to the oven with a steam hole in them to dry out. The choux buns may also have been undercooked.

Icings and fillings

When you make a cake or dessert, you will frequently need to make a filling, topping or sweet sauce for it. These preparations play a supporting role in pâtisserie which is nevertheless very important. They often provide an extra layer of flavour and texture that becomes a vital part of the main recipe, as well as adding an attractive the finishing touch to cakes and desserts that will delight your guests.

Some icings such as fondant and ganache may be prepared in advance and can be kept ready for use in the refrigerator. These days fondant icing is rarely home-made. The shop-bought version is now widely available, and used mainly to ice choux pastries, éclairs and mille-feuille pastries.

The toppings, fillings and accompaniments in this book frequently contain just a few ingredients, and therefore it is critical that these ingredients are of the highest quality. Good-quality chocolate and butter have far better flavour, cooking and melting qualities. The butter for the recipes in this book is unsalted, and the chocolate is plain, dark chocolate with a high cocoa content, unless otherwise stated. Always buy the freshest eggs and cream possible.

Syrups and sauces

Sugar plays a very important role in the production of desserts, pâtisserie and confectionery. Sugar syrup can be cooked to various degrees which make it ideally suited for a wide variety of preparations. Fondant (p. 36), Créme Mousseline (p. 43), and Rum-flavoured Syrup for Babas (p. 48) are a few examples.

When sugar mixed with a certain quantity of water is heated, it forms a syrup, which changes in consistency and appearance as the water evaporates. The density of sugar syrup can be measured very accurately with a sugar thermometer.

Very distinct phases in the gradual transformation of sugar syrup can be identified. Modern sugar thermometers measure temperatures in both Celsius and Fahrenheit, and are widely available.

Sugar syrups are easy to make successfully if the following rules are adhered to:
- The pan must be absolutely clean without any trace of grease.
- The sugar and water should be stirred with a wooden spoon until the sugar dissolves.
- The syrup should not be allowed to boil until the sugar has dissolved.
- Once the syrup boils it should not be stirred as this could cause crystals to form, making the finished syrup lumpy and possibly unusable.
- To evenly cook the sugar in the pan without stirring it, the pan can be gently swirled, and a pastry brush dipped in cold water can be used to brush away any sugar crystals forming around the inside of the pan, without touching the boiling syrup itself.
- Any foam that rises to the top of the boiling sugar syrup should be carefully skimmed off using a metal spoon.

To ascertain the stage of the sugar syrup, use a sugar thermometer, or if no measuring instrument is available, the various stages of cooking can be checked manually by texture and appearance. A receptacle containing very cold water is placed near the stove and when the sugar syrup is thought to have reached the required stage, a drop of syrup is dripped into the water. The cook retrieves the syrup which, having cooled and firmed, now exhibits measurable characteristics which demonstrate the degree to which the sugar has been cooked. These characteristics are detailed below:

Coated (105°C/221°F). The syrup coats the surface of a metal spoon with a fairly thin film.

Small thread or small gloss (107°C/224°F). At this stage the sugar syrup can be tested with your fingers, but it is hot. Dip a metal spoon into the syrup then dip your fingers in cold water. Quickly dip your fingers in the sugar syrup on the spoon; on parting the fingers carefully, short threads form which break easily.

Large thread or large gloss (109–110°C/228–230°F). This stage can be tested as for small thread above using your fingers. The thread which forms between the fingers is strong and wide, and range between 2–3 cm (¾–1¼ inches) in length.

Small pearl (111°C/231°F). As the sugar cooks round bubbles or 'pearls' form on its surface. The thread which forms between the fingers measures 4–5 cm (1½–2 inches).

Large pearl or soufflé (114°C/237°F). Round bubbles or 'pearls' are still visible on the surface of the syrup; if you blow on the syrup after plunging the metal spoon into the syrup, bubbles form on the other side of the spoon.

Small ball (115–117°C/239–242.5°F). If you dip a metal spoon into the syrup and blow on the surface of the syrup , bubbles break loose and blow away.

Ball (120°C/248°F). Drip a small amount of sugar syrup

into the ice water. The sugar syrup forms a small, soft ball between the fingers, the size of a pea.

Large ball (120–130°C/250–266°F). Drip a small amount of the syrup into the ice water. If you roll some of this syrup between your fingers, it will form a fairly hard ball the size of a hazelnut.

Soft crack (135–140°C/275–284°F). Drip a small amount of sugar syrup into the ice water. A ball of this syrup pressed between your fingers is hard and will crack. It sticks to the teeth if chewed.

Hard crack (149–150°C/295–300°F). The drops of syrup in cold water become hard and brittle like glass and acquires a pale straw-yellow colour around the edges of the pan.

Light caramel (151–160°C/302–325°F). The syrup begins to change into barley sugar and then caramel, yellow at first, then golden, then amber.

When coating a mould with caramel, first warm the mould in the oven. Remove the caramel from the heat as soon as it has reached the correct colour. Using a cloth to protect your hands from the heat, carefully pour the caramel into the mould then tip the mould this way and that to coat the inside evenly. As it cools, the caramel will thicken and harden, sticking to the inside of the mould. Wait until it is cold before filling the mould with the dessert mixture.

When sugar syrup is to be used to make fondant or to be cooked to the hard crack stage, 50 g (¾ oz) glucose must be added as soon as the water has been added to the sugar. Alternatively, 3 – 4 drops of vinegar or 4 drops of lemon juice or citric acid can be used.

If the sugar syrup has crystallized
The pan may not have been clean. Small pieces of sugar may have fallen into the syrup. Next time wash the sides of the pan down with a pastry brush dipped in water.

If the sugar syrup is too thick
It may have been boiled for too long, but it can be thinned out by adding some water.

If the sugar syrup is too thin
The syrup may not have been boiled for long enough. Boil until it reaches the stage required.

SMALL CAKES

Small cakes are made by the same methods as large cakes. Of course the baking times will be shorter. These small cakes are useful for entertaining because they are already divided into serving portions.

Babas
Babas can be either yeast-raised cakes or creamed sponge mixtures baked in small dariole or timbale moulds. The dough or cake mixture often contains dried fruit, such as currants or candied peel. The cooked cakes are soaked in a sugar syrup flavoured with a liqueur to serve. A classic example is the Kirsch-Flavoured Baba (p. 53). The large version of this cake, called a savarin (p. 106), is baked in a ring mould.

When making a yeast-raised batter for a baba or savairn the mixture needs to be left to rise long enough to make it light in texture. Be sure to follow the instructions in the recipe.

If the baba is dense and heavy
It may not have had enough time to rise sufficiently. Also be careful when soaking it with syrup that you do not use too much syrup.

If the fruit has fallen in the mixture
The mixture may have been too thin.

Petits fours
The term *petits fours* in French means 'small oven'. This refers to the small oven in which these confections were originally baked in France. You do not need a special small oven these days, as any oven will work. Petits fours are bite-sized, often whimsical confections that are served in small fluted paper cups with coffee at the end of the meal. They are made with a whisked cake mixture that has been baked in very tiny tins or are made from a ground nut mixture that is held together with egg white and sugar, flavoured and shaped like fruits or nuts. Biscuit mixtures also can be baked into small sizes. If you do not have petits fours tins you can make a large, shallow cake using a creamed or whisked sponge mixture. The large cake is then cut into small pieces when cool.

Petits fours without icing (plain or 'dry' petit fours) keep very well in airtight containers or tins. 'Fresh' petits fours, embellished with various creams and covered with icing, should be eaten on the day they are made.

The home baker will find it difficult to make a great variety of petits fours: a professional pastry cook will have a considerable range of equipment and an extensive stock of extracts, colourings and decorative ingredients (jams, almonds, crystallized fruits).

Plain or dry petits fours can be made with almond paste, ordinary meringue or Swiss meringue. It can also be made with puff pastry or sweet pastry. Iced fresh petits fours can be made with fresh cream or fruit and are often served in little fluted paper cases.

The almond paste petits fours do not hold together
There may not have been enough oil in the nuts. Try adding a little more egg white to get the petits fours to hold together.

Other small cakes

Small cakes, such as Madeleines (p. 82), are made from whisked sponge mixtures that are spooned or piped into special moulds to give the finished small cakes their characteristic shape. You do not need to have special moulds, however, as you can cut a large cake into smaller pieces either with a serrated knife or with a small biscuit cutter. It is usually a good idea to make a large cake on one day and ice it the following day because the cake is very fragile on the day it is made and is likely to tear. Use a dry pastry brush to remove any crumbs from the surface of the cake before icing.

If my cake was too dry
A dry cake can be caused by adding too much flour or by baking the cake too long.

If my cake was too dense
Some cakes, such as fruit cakes, are meant to be dense. However, if your cake is meant to be light in texture, the oven door may have been opened too soon. Other reasons a cake might be dense is that the raising agent was left out of the cake or that the whisked egg whites were over-folded when added to the mixture.

GÂTEAUX

Different types of cakes can be made from similar ingredients. The results will be determined by the method used. The easiest type of cake to make is one where the dry ingredients are mixed together and the wet ingredients are combined separately. The dry ingredients are then folded into the wet ingredients and the mixture is spread in the cake tin. Germaine's Gâteaux (p. 104) is an example of this method of cake making. These cakes tend to be highly flavoured and keep well.

Fruit cakes

Fruit cakes are popular for special occasions. They often improve on keeping. Many of the fruit cake recipes call for macerating the fruit in a liqueur before adding the fruit to the cake mixture. This process softens the fruit and adds flavour to the cake. If you prefer not to use liqueur you can substitute warm fruit juice or water instead. It is a good idea to wash raisins and currants before using them as their sticky surfaces collect dust. If small dried stems are still attached to the fruit you should remove these before soaking the fruit.

Fruit cakes are cooked at a lower temperature for a longer time than sponge cakes due to the higher sugar concentration in dried fruit, which causes the fruit to burn at high temperatures. If the cake seems to be browning too quickly, cover the cake loosely with a piece of crumpled foil.

Nut cakes

Ground nuts give cakes a wonderful flavour and a moist texture as well as a nutritional boost. Use only the freshest nuts for cakes. Nuts become rancid very quickly. If you live in a hot climate, nuts can be stored in the freezer. It is always best to buy the whole nuts, rather than nuts that have been chopped, sliced or ground.

To enhance the flavour of nuts you can toast them in 180°C/350°F/Gas Mark 4 oven in a single layer on a baking tray for 5–10 minutes or until they are lightly browned. Cool completely before grinding. Examples of nut cakes are Lorraie Gâteau (p. 96) and Hazelnut Gâteau (p. 97).

Spice cakes

Ground spices have been added to cakes for centuries. In addition to making the cake taste delicious, they help preserve the cake. Indeed, most spice cakes such as Orange Spice Cake (p. 113) improve after several days and many will keep for up to a month. As dried, ground spices lose their potency after six months, always use fresh spices when making a spice cake to get the best flavour. Sieve the spices with the flour to ensure that the spices are equally distributed throughout the cake.

When using fresh fruit, such as oranges and lemons, buy unwaxed fruit so you don't have wax and chemicals going into your cake. Always wash the fruit well in hot soapy water, rinse well, then dry thoroughly. To remove the zest from the fruit, use a fine grater or pare thinly then chop the zest. Do not take any of the white pith which can be very bitter.

Sponge cakes

The traditional sponge cake is made by a different method in which softened butter and sugar are beaten together until light in texture and colour. This is called the creaming method. Genoa Cake (p. 101) is an example of this method. This type of cake is a little more difficult to make and takes a bit longer. After the butter and sugar are creamed together the eggs are beaten in a little at a time. Once all the egg has been added the flour is gently folded.

Most cake mixtures contain an ingredient, usually baking powder or stiffly beaten egg whites, that makes the cake rise and become very light as the cake cooks. Each bubble expands as it is heated and increases the volume of the mixture.

A sponge cake always increases in volume as it cooks; the uncooked cake mixture should therefore half-fill the baking tin (unless the recipe specifically indicates otherwise). It is a wise precaution to insert the blade of a knife into the very centre of a cake to check whether it is cooked: the entry point of the knife will not be visible and, if the blade comes out clean, this means the cake can be removed from the oven. If it is not cooked, the blade will be covered with sticky batter. If the cake has browned on top but has not yet cooked through, it can be covered with greaseproof paper or foil lightly brushed with melted butter. This prevents the top of the cake being too browned, or even burnt, by the time the cake is cooked through.

The whisked sponge, a third type of cake, relies primarily on the air beaten into the eggs or egg whites as the mixture is prepared. This is the most difficult type of cake to make as the cake can collapse if the eggs are not beaten sufficiently or if the oven door is opened before the cake is cooked. Savoy Sponge Cake (p. 115) and a Chocolate Log (p. 127) are examples of this type of cake. It is important to follow the recipe very carefully. For a whisked sponge, it is sometimes a good idea to increase the temperature of the oven while the cake is cooking (medium, increasing to hot) to help the cake rise.

The sponge cakes called Genoese are whisked sponge cakes that have melted butter added to the mixture just before baking. These are the most delicate types of cakes to make because the folding in of the butter knocks out much of the volume that has been beaten into the eggs. This folding must be done very gently using a large metal spoon. Génoese Sponge (p. 118) is an example of this method.

Chocolate cakes

Working with chocolate is notoriously tricky. Chocolate melts very quickly when warmed so it is best to treat it gently. Melt it in a double boiler or a heatproof bowl placed over a pan of steaming water. The water should not touch the bowl. If the chocolate gets too hot it can seize (it solidifies into a hardened mass). It can also scorch if it gets too hot. Do not allow any water or steam to get into the chocolate as this can cause it to seize. Once the chocolate has seized it is unusable for making a cake. If adding liquid ingredients to chocolate, the additional ingredients must be stirred in quickly. Small drips of liquid will cause the chocolate to seize. If the chocolate sets in lumps because it has become too cold, reheat it in a heatproof bowl set over but not touching steaming water.

When making a chocolate cake use good quality plain chocolate with a high proportion of cocoa solids and a low amount of sugar and other added ingredients. Chocolate Pound Cake (p. 128) and Tonkin Chocolate Cake (p. 132) are some of the delicious examples of chocolate cakes.

Brioches

Enriched with butter and eggs, a brioche is a sweetened French yeast bread, formed into a roll or a bun and traditionally shaped with a fluted bottom. It is often regarded as a bread more than a cake.

If my brioche crust is lop-sided
The gluten may not be fully developed and this may cause the brioche to collapse. Try reducing the amount of sugar in the recipe. In addition, the oven temperature may be a bit low.

If my cake mixture has curdled
When making a creaming-method cake, the mixture may curdle if the eggs are added too quickly. This means that the liquid eggs separate from the lumps of butter and sugar mixture. If this happens, a spoonful of the flour should be beaten in to make the mixture smooth again.

If my cake does not rise
The oven door may hae been opened or closed too quickly, which can ruin a cake: the displaced colder air rushing into the oven, will blow on to the cake, cooling it and making it sink. It is therefore advisable to open the oven door as seldom as possible and to avoid moving the cake.

If my cake sticks to the mould or tin
Cake tins are usually prepared by coating them with melted butter and sometimes a dusting of flour. Usually the butter can be melted in the cake tin itself and a pastry brush can be used to coat the base, sides and grooves. Non-stick cake tins do not need to be greased, but if the cake is delicate it is a good idea to line the base with baking parchment.

If my cake crumbles or cracks
The cake may have been overbaked or the oven may have been too hot.

If my cake domes in the centre
Although they will still taste good, a peak in the centre makes decorating difficult. An oven that was too hot is likely to be the cause of the cake peaking.

If there are large tunnels or air bubbles in my cake
Tunnels in a cake are usually caused by over mixing the mixture when the flour was added.

If the fruit has dropped to the bottom of the cake
The batter is too thin. Try dusting the fruit with a little flour or add a little more flour to the batter to make the cake mixture thicker.

If the fruit cake is too dark and has a bitter flavour
The cake may have been baked at too high a temperature and/or too long. Try reducing the temperature and amount of baking time.

If my cake is greasy and heavy
Nuts will become oily if they are ground for too long. Mix a little of the sugar in the recipe into the ground nuts. This will make it easier to fold the nuts into the cake batter.

TARTS AND PASTRIES

Pastries are often made of thinly rolled-out doughs with a sweet or savoury filling. Tarts are pastries which consist of a pastry base plus a flavoured filling such as crème pâtissière (p. 41) or fruit.

Tarts

Different kinds of pastry achieve different results when making tarts. For example, a firmer, less absorbent pastry would be used for a tart with a more liquid filling. Be guided by the instructions given and you will achieve the best results for your effort. It is important, when using the basic pastry recipes in this book, to follow the pastry recipe in question closely, and to take note of the preparation time before you start, including the resting time for each pastry dough.

If time is short, you can buy ready-made uncooked fresh or frozen pastry, which only needs to be rolled out and laid in a tin or mould in order to proceed with cooking. Ready-rolled pastry is also available.

If the tart contains crème pâtissière or fruit that does not require cooking, it is always a sensible precaution to bake the dough 'blind', which means cooking the pastry case without any filling. See individual pastry recipes for instructions on how to do this.

Fruit fillings which are not so delicate can be cooked successfully in the oven, such as apples, pears, cherries, prunes and plums. They can therefore be cooked at the same time as the pastry and for the same length of time. Some very delicate fruits – strawberries, raspberries, redcurrants, grapes and peaches – are often not cooked at all.

Choux pastries

See Basic Recipes (p. 15)

Puff pastries

See Basic Recipes (p. 14)

BISCUITS

There are many methods of making biscuits, from the creaming and whisking methods used to make cakes to the rubbing-in method used for pastry. The results vary depending on the method used and the proportions of the ingredients.

Classic biscuits

The mixture can be thick, in which case it is 'worked' in various ways on a pastry board and rolled out with a rolling pin. In the absence of specific instructions, both the pastry board and the rolling pin must always be dusted with flour and, as a general rule, the dough should be ½ cm (¼ inch) thick. The dough sheet can be cut using pastry cutters (in a very wide variety of shapes) or with a pastry cutting wheel. Citron Sablés (p. 227) are made from a stiff mixture which is rolled out and cut with biscuit cutters.

Other types of biscuits – such as Langues de Chat (p. 221) and Hazelnut Tuiles (p. 200) – can be made from a mixture that has a pouring consistency, in which case it will be mixed in a mixing bowl. Usually this sort of mixture spreads out during the cooking process. It is placed on the baking tray in small quantities, using a spoon or a piping bag. If you practise using the piping bag, you will become more skilled and manage to deposit exactly the same quantity of mixture each time, resulting in very even-sized biscuits and cakes. Always leave plenty of space between the little quantities of raw mixture or they may all run into one another as soon as they are placed in the oven.

Drop biscuits such as Soft Macaroons (p. 208) are made from a mixture that is thick enough to hold its shape in a mound. These types biscuits are formed on to a baking sheet using two spoons. Slightly thicker, less sticky mixtures can be rolled into balls before baking. Snowballs (p. 217) are an example of a biscuit that is rolled into a ball before baking.

To make biscuits successfully, measure all ingredients accurately and carefully. Make sure the ingredients are at the specified temperature. The oven must be preheated and the oven rack must be at the correct level in the oven, usually the centre. Make sure the individual biscuits are the same size so that they bake evenly. To ensure even browning, turn the baking sheet halfway through baking.

Sablés

Sablé, meaning 'sandy' in French, perfectly describes these crumbly, shortbread-type biscuits. The recipes require a relatively large amount of butter which needs to be very fresh for the best flavour. If the recipe requires the butter to be softened, it should be the texture of tub margarine. The dough needs to be prepared delicately and gently, with the minimum amount of working. If the mixture seems to be dry, use your finger tips to squeeze it together. To make rolling out the dough easier, chill it in a flattened disc until nearly firm.

Savoury biscuits

Savoury biscuits are made using similar methods to pastry, but without any added sugar. Finely grated strong cheese can be added. A little mustard powder or ground cayenne pepper can be added to the flour to enhance the flavour of the cheese. These biscuits are delicious served with a pre-dinner glass of wine.

If the sablé mixture cracks when rolling out
This is characteristic of this type of dough. Squeeze it together with your fingers but be careful not to overwork it.

If the biscuits come out hard and tough
Like pastry, biscuit mixtures should be handled lightly and gently. Take care not to overwork the mixture or the biscuits may be tough.

If the biscuits spread out too much in the oven
It is always a good idea to test bake one biscuit before baking a whole tray. If there is too much butter or sugar in the mixture the biscuits might spread too much. Correct this by adding a little more flour. Sometimes a low oven temperature causes the biscuits to spread too much.

If biscuits became too brown or burnt at the base
If biscuits burn on the base, the oven temperature may have been too high or the biscuits were overbaked. Always use an oven thermometer and a timer when baking.

If the biscuits are bitter
The biscuits may hae been baked for too long or at too high a temperature. Use an oven thermometer to check the temperature of the oven as well as a timer.

If the biscuits cook unevenly
This often happens because ovens do not heat evenly. Rotate the baking sheets from front to back halfway through baking to ensure even baking.

If the biscuits stick to the pan
All the baking tins should be greased with butter and dusted with flour so that the cooked articles will not stick. It is wise to detach biscuits and biscuits from the baking trays while they are still hot, as soon as they come out of the oven. Where the sugar or egg white content is high, such as Langues-de-chat and Tuiles, they can be particularly tricky to lift off the baking tray.

If the biscuits soften after time
Never place biscuits or cakes on top of one another when you take them out of the oven and while they are still hot: as they cool, they release steam which would be absorbed by any biscuits on top of them, softening them. This is also the reason why cakes should never be stored in cake tins until they are cold.

MILK AND EGG PUDDINGS

The word 'pudding' was originally used to describe a preparation made up of a great many and varied ingredients such as flour, pork fat, beef suet, raisins and crystallized fruit. Traditionally, these puddings were boiled. Gradually, the word 'pudding' has come to mean an almost infinite variety of sweet dishes, many of which contain an ingredient which acquires a very thick consistency when cooked such as bread, rice, semolina, macaroons and sponge cakes. Other ingredients must, of course, be included such as eggs, milk, sugar, fruit and liqueurs or spirits.

These desserts are usually cooked in pudding basins, stoneware dishes or baking tins in the oven, or sometimes in a bain marie (a vessel used for a gentle method of heating in which the dish to be cooked is placed in, or over, a pan of hot water, which is then placed in the oven or simmered very gently on the stove). Their nutritional value depends, predictably, on the ingredients used. Sometimes they are served with stewed fruit or with crème anglaise, which not only enhances their appearance but also improves their flavour, so it is worth going to a little more expense: the pudding will be all the more delectable and wholesome.

Puddings made with milk and eggs range from the classic nursery puddings, such as the Crème Caramel (p. 252) and Tapioca (p. 308) to the sophisticated Vanilla Crème Brûlée (p. 256), Coffee Soufflé (p. 296) and Clafoutis (p. 273). All of these puddings are nutritious and are relatively easy to make. The cooking needs to be done carefully however, as the eggs will form into lumps if overheated.

Custards
Custards are made from milk and/or cream thickened with eggs or egg yolks. They can be cooked either on the stove top over gentle heat or baked in a low oven, usually in a roasting-tin half-filled with hot water. The custard in its dish is placed in the hot water so that the water comes half-way up the side of the dish. This provides a steamy, moist atmosphere in the oven which prevents the eggs from getting too hot. It is important not to overheat the mixture or the eggs will cook into lumps giving the custard a grainy texture.

If my custard is lumpy
The custard mixture probably got too hot. If the custard appears to be thickening into lumps, immediately strain it through a sieve into a cold bowl.

If my custard is not thick enough
The mixture may not have been cooked long enough. Trying returning it to a low heat and cook, stirring, until it thickens sufficiently for the recipe.

If my flan is tough and rubbery and has bubbles in it
The custard was probably overcooked. Egg custards should always be cooked at a low temperature so they set gently.

Meringues
Meringues are made with egg whites and sugar. The end product can vary, depending on the method used. For ordinary (also known as Swiss) meringues, egg whites and sugar are beaten together to form stiff peaks with a wire whisk or whisk attachment in a stand mixer. The beaten egg whites can also be combined with sugar syrup. This is a more delicate process and the result is called Italian meringue. It is used a great deal when making fillings for petits fours. The third method involves cooking the meringue, albeit over a very gentle heat, beating the egg whites and sugar in a bain marie until the meringue has increased to its maximum volume. This is *meringue cuite*, which is seldom used.

A meringue mixture is delicate; it needs to be placed in the oven immediately upon making. The oven temperature should be low and this temperature should be maintained for an hour or more depending on the size of the meringues. The meringue is then allowed to dry slowly, either in the oven or using special professional drying equipment. Meringues should never be made on a rainy or very humid day, as they will not dry out. Once they are firm and dry (they should not brown at all), they can easily be detached from the paper. Store in airtight containers or in tins.

If the egg whites fail to form stiff peaks
The egg whites may have some egg yolk in them or the bowl/whisk may not be free from grease. You will need to begin again with a clean bowl and new egg whites.

If the meringue mixture collapses
The egg whites may have been overbeaten. The sugar may have been added before the egg whites are

entirely stiff or the sugar may have been overfolded when it was added. There is nothing you can do to save a collapsed meringue.

If the cooked meringue has beads of sugar syrup on it
The meringue may have been overbaked. It will still be nice to eat, however.

Soufflés

Soufflés are delicious and delicate desserts that require last-minute attention from the cook, and patiently waiting diners. To get the texture just right, the base of the soufflé must be the thickness of Greek yoghurt and the white must be whisked so that it is just stiff to give them the opportunity to expand to their maximum size. If egg whites are over-whisked they will require too much folding when they are added to the base. This will knock out a lot of the air that has been whisked into the whites.

Although the base of the soufflé may be prepared in advance, the whites must not be whisked until the oven has reached the correct temperature with a baking sheet placed in the centre. Make sure there is enough room for the soufflés to rise in the oven. There is nothing more disappointing than to find your soufflés firmly glued to the oven rack above. The soufflé dishes must be prepared with a smear of butter and a sprinkling of sugar, and then the whites can be whisked and gently folded into the soufflé base. Run the point of a small sharp knife 1 cm (½ inch) down into the mixture around the inside of the soufflé dish. This releases the mixture from the edge of the dish, allowing the soufflés to rise more easily. Place the soufflés on the hot baking sheet. Do not open the oven door again until the soufflés are well risen and nearly cooked through.

If my soufflé falls during cooking
The oven door may have been opened too soon. Try returning the soufflés to the oven for a couple of minutes. They will often rise back up.

If my soufflé does not rise well
The base mixture of the soufflé may be too thick. Too few egg whites may have been used. Also, make sure the egg whites are whisked to the right consistency, and do not overfold the egg whites.

If my soufflé mushroomed out of the dish
The base mixture may have been too thin. There were too many egg whites in the soufflé or the dish was overfilled.

If my soufflé cracked on top
The soufflé may have been overbaked or the oven may have been too hot. Watch the soufflés carefully near the end of cooking. If shaken gently, they should have a slight wobble when they are done.

Fruit puddings

Fruit puddings are very easy to make and a good way of using up a surplus of fruit. Use ripe fruit if possible, as this will have the best flavour. Taste the fruit before starting to cook, as the amount of sugar might need adjusting according to the sweetness of the fruit.

If the fruit is hard
It may not been cooked for long enough. Test the fruit by inserting the point of a sharp knife. If it needs further cooking, return it to the oven.

Starch puddings

Starch puddings are similar to custard puddings, but are easier to make as the starchy ingredients make the preparation more forgiving by stabilizing the texture of the pudding. The starch puddings are often baked in a roasting tin half-filled with hot water to provide a steamy, moist atmosphere in the oven. This helps to ensure that the pudding does not dry out. To check if the pudding is cooked insert the tip of a sharp knife into the centre. No runny mixture should be visible.

If the pudding was too runny
The pudding may not have been cooked long enough or at a high enough temperature. Too few eggs/egg yolks may also have been used. Try cooking it for a bit longer.

If the pudding rose in the oven
The pudding was overcooked. It should be fine to eat, but the texture will be firmer than anticipated. Serve with some extra cream.

If the custard mixture was tough and rubbery
The pudding was overcooked. It should be fine to eat, but the texture will be firmer than anticipated. Serve with some extra cream.

OVENS

It is important to make sure your oven is preheated to the correct temperature. Although it is best to use an oven thermometer, a traditional way of checking the temperature of an oven involves placing a piece of greaseproof paper on a baking tray where the pastry confection is to be cooked. The paper will change colour and darken progressively as the temperature is increased. Here are the successive stages and their corresponding temperatures.

Temperatures

Low oven (100ºC–150ºC /212ºF–302ºF)
The paper is barely coloured. Suitable for biscuits, meringues, large, light cakes, confections with a high sugar content.

Medium oven (150ºC–180ºC /302ºF–356ºF)
The paper is pale yellow. If you put your hand in the oven, you can feel the warmth. Suitable for certain petits fours, small and large cakes, rich Madeira cake, Genoese sponge cake.

Hot oven (180ºC–220ºC /356ºF–420ºF)
The paper turns light brown. If you put your hand into the oven, it immediately feels hot. Suitable for baked goods containing yeast, puff pastry, brioches, fruit cakes. Sugar sprinkled on cakes as a finishing touch will melt.

Very hot oven (220ºC–270ºC /420ºF–518ºF)
The paper turns dark brown. If you put your hand in the oven, it feels extremely hot. Suitable for choux pastry, puff pastry, small baked goods which need to be cooked quickly. If the paper blackens immediately, your oven is too hot for any baking.

Keeping an eye on your baking

Once you are sure that your oven is at the correct temperature to start baking, place your confection in it. In most cases the oven temperature can remain the same throughout the baking process. Sometimes it will need to be increased at a predetermined point: this can either be done by moving the baking sheet or tin to a higher shelf (if you have an ordinary gas oven) or by selecting a higher oven setting. It is reassuring to check on the cooking process from time to time. It is,

however, wise not to do this too often: each time you open the oven door, you allow a certain amount of cold air to penetrate. This slows up the cooking and also risks causing the preparation to 'sink'.

All large baking goods should be cooked for longer and at a lower temperature than small ones. Cakes and other confections can be shielded from a very hot oven floor by using an extra baking sheet. If your baking is browning too quickly, you can cover it with greaseproof paper or foil.

To check whether the middle of a cake is cooked, insert a skewer, cocktail stick or the blade of a thin knife deep into it. This should not be done until the baking time is nearing its end. There will be cake mixture sticking to the metal if the cake is not cooked through.

Where to place your baking in the oven

If you have an ordinary gas oven, preparations such as quiches, deep tarts and soufflés will cook more quickly in the bottom of your oven. Preparations such as gratins should be placed near the top of the oven, as their surfaces brown quickly there. The middle of the oven will, in theory, be a good compromise. Modern fan-assisted ovens are less variable than traditional ovens and the heat will be much the same in all parts of the oven, which is of great benefit to the pastry cook.

Gas cookers

The hot air circulates between the double walls of the oven and then flows into the oven space, eventually discharging through vents in the bottom of the oven. This system means that heat radiates from the entire inner surface of the oven and the systematic circulation of hot air ensures an even temperature surrounds the food being cooked. This means that you do not have to keep a constant watch over your baking to be sure of satisfactory results. It is absolutely necessary to preheat the oven for 15 minutes before you use it. You can then place your confection in the oven, on a rack or on a baking sheet (never directly on to the floor of the oven). Gas ovens are often hotter near the back and sides of the oven.

Electric ovens

Electric ovens usually heat more evenly than gas ovens and therefore are sometimes preferable for baking pâtisserie. In an electric oven there is usually a heating element situated in the roof of the oven, predictably called the upper heating element and, when switched on, this becomes incandescent within 2 or 3 minutes. There is often a similar element, the lower heating element, positioned in the bottom of the oven, often masked by the floor of the oven. These two heating elements may both be controlled by one switch or by two separate switches. The latter allows for greater flexibility and a greater variety of cooking processes. The upper part of the oven can thus be heated very quickly, as can the lower part. Again, the oven must be preheated for 10–15 minutes, depending on the required cooking process. When cooking cakes and pastries, the oven should be preheated for about 15 minutes.

Fan ovens

Many electric ovens, and some gas ones, have a fan at the back of the oven which circulates the hot air throughout the oven. The idea is to even out the heat in all parts of the oven. The fan also helps to brown the food in the oven. In some ovens this can cause the food to appear done when, in fact, it is not cooked underneath the surface. If this occurs in your oven it may be best to turn off the fan during baking. It is also sometimes necessary to cook at a lower temperature in fan-assisted ovens; check the manufacturer's instructions.

THE ART OF AFTERNOON TEA

Entertaining friends and offering them a variety of exquisite homemade delicacies is a real pleasure. It is scarcely necessary to resort to the pâtisserie or cake shop. Culinary know-how notwithstanding, it is important also to plan ahead and organize everything. Preparations should be carried out in a calm frame of mind; everything will be done faster and it will mean that your guests will receive a warmer welcome.

Afternoon tea is one of the most elegant ways of entertaining. Generally, it is intended as a get-together for a few friends over a cup of tea, accompanied – of course – by pastries, cakes and biscuits. A formal afternoon tea can be enjoyed sitting around a table. This should be covered by a tablecloth. The tea things should be placed in the centre of the table, you will need a teapot, strainer, sugar bowl, a small jug of milk, a pot of hot water (a heatproof glass decanter with a stopper or a vacuum jug are very elegant and highly practical), and a plate with lemon slices.

The teapot can be a metal, china or earthenware one. True connoisseurs of tea prefer loose leaf tea that is infused in an earthenware teapot. Depending on your guests' tastes, you can serve either Indian or China tea. Either way, the tea should be very hot and sufficiently fragrant, that is to say well infused!

If the hostess is well acquainted with her guests' preferences, she can offer them hot chocolate, coffee or thirst-quenching cold drinks. However, it is a wise precaution always to serve tea as well, regardless of the other drinks chosen. If the snack is to be taken round the table, small plates should be evenly spaced at each place setting on the tablecloth. The napkins should be placed on the plates, with the cup and saucer on top.

The handle of the teacup should be on the right, and you should place a teaspoon to the right of each cup, on the saucer. A small pastry fork should be placed on the tablecloth, or on each plate. A pastry fork is three-pronged and has one sharp side. It serves as both fork and knife and is particularly useful at teatime.

For afternoon tea, the beverages can be accompanied by:

- Buttered bread or toast
- Cheese biscuits (Savoury Biscuits, p. 239)
- Small biscuits (Classic Biscuits, p. 200)
- Tarts or tartlets (Tarts, p. 172)
- Petits fours (Petits Fours, p. 56)
- Cakes (Gâteaux, p. 88)
- Madeleines (Other Small Cakes, p. 80)

Another way of serving tea is to place the beverages and crockery on a trolley. If this is done, each guest should have a small table next to them. On each table you should place the teacup, pastry plate and small napkin, teaspoon and pastry fork. Serving is more complicated with this option, because you will be obliged to circulate among your guests in order to hand them their cups of tea. Your guests will also have to pass the serving plates to each other. This method of serving drinks and pastries is sometimes used at bridge parties. We would, however, advise against this procedure: the game of bridge will continue while you are eating. This is not practical for the players and it makes serving the tea difficult. In this case, it is better to invite your guests to gather around a buffet table in another room, away from all the card tables.

When your guests for afternoon tea number twelve or over, the atmosphere is no longer intimate. The conversation is no longer general. The guests will split into like-minded groups, and they can partake of refreshments laid out buffet-style on a large table in the dining room. On this you should place a felt undercover and spread a white or embroidered tablecloth, trimmed with lace. If using a lace tablecloth, place a pale-coloured cloth underneath. This makes the pretty embroidery show up more. Set a low-sided plant pot in the centre of the table, fill it with florist's foam and arrange seasonal flowers in it. At the front of the table place the plates, teacups and saucers in a row alongside each other, and place a napkin on each plate

For the cold drinks, arrange glasses – in differing sizes to match the drinks selected – in one corner of the table, but within reach of the person serving. At this sort of tea party, besides tea, one should offer fruit juices (orange, grapefruit) or hot or iced coffee, as well as tea depending on the time of year. When the guest has chosen a drink, the person serving pours some fruit juice into a tall glass and places it on a plate or a small metal server before offering it. The guest only picks up the glass. Iced coffee should be served in a cup or glass, with a teaspoon alongside it. Fruit juices should be served in tall glasses, filled half-full.

The buffet should consist of sandwiches, pâtisserie (including one or two large cakes) and petits fours. Avoid making cakes that are difficult to eat, such as cakes that are accompanied by cream or sauces, or biscuits that are too crunchy and hard to bite into.

BASIC RECIPES

The art of French baking is based upon a simple series of building-block recipes that are easy to prepare and require only minimal equipment and ingredients. These recipes for pastries, icings, fillings and syrups are essential for many of the recipes throughout the book, and once you have mastered them you will have learnt the basics of the French pastry-makers' art.

PASTRY DOUGHS

Flour, butter and eggs are the main ingredients in French pastry making. Various combinations and preparation methods are used to create useful doughs such as shortcrust, puff and choux pastry. The key to making quality home-made pastry is to use the best quality ingredients, and to chill the pastry well.

PUFF PASTRY

pâte feuilletée

Preparation time: 2 hours, plus chilling time
Makes 400 g (14 oz)

200 g (7 oz) plain flour, sifted, plus
   extra for dusting
1 pinch of salt
100 ml (3½ fl oz) ice-cold water
100 g (3½ oz) butter, diced and softened

In a bowl, mix the flour, salt and most of the water to make a smooth, elastic dough, adding the rest of the water if necessary. Flour a work surface and roll the dough out to a square 1.5 cm (¾ inch) thick. Put the butter in the middle of the dough and fold over the 4 corners so that they meet in the middle and the butter is completely enclosed. Allow to chill for 10 minutes in the refrigerator. Roll out again, taking care not to let the butter escape, into a long rectangle 5 mm (¼ inch) thick.

Turn the dough through a right angle and roll out again. Fold both short ends to overlap in the centre, like a business letter, to make a smaller rectangle with 3 layers. Chill again for 15 minutes in the refrigerator. Roll out the dough again and repeat the folds. Rest for 15 minutes in the refrigerator. Do this 6 more times. Each stage is called a 'turn'. After the sixth turn, the pastry is ready, but the more turns you do, the more layers the pastry will have.

Note: Puff pastry is made with butter and flour, a little water and a pinch of salt. The proportion of butter to flour varies, but a good rule of thumb is to use half the weight of butter to that of flour. The butter should be as soft as the dough, or it will tear the carefully constructed layers. Puff pastry should be made in a cool place, with all the ingredients kept as cool as possible.

ROUGH PUFF PASTRY

pâte demi-feuilletée

Preparation time: 1 hour 15 minutes,
   plus 2 hours chilling time
Serves 6

250 g (9 oz) plain flour
1 teaspoon salt
100 g (3½ oz) butter, diced

Put the flour on the work surface in a mound. Make a well in it and into this place the salt, 150 ml (¼ pint) water and the butter. Mix these three ingredients, gradually working the flour and butter into the liquid. Alternatively, this process can be done with a mixer set on slow speed. When the dough is smooth, shape it into a ball, cover with clingfilm and chill for 15 minutes in the refrigerator. Dust a work surface with flour and roll the dough into a wide strip. Fold this in three as for puff pastry (see above) and give it 4 turns at 15-minute intervals. Cover and chill the dough in the refrigerator until you are ready to use it.

CHOUX PASTRY
pâte à choux

Preparation time: 20 minutes,
   plus cooling time
Cooking time: 20 minutes
Makes enough for 16 choux buns

20 g (¾ oz) caster sugar
100 g (3 ½ oz) butter, plus extra
   for greasing
1 teaspoon salt
120 g (4 oz) plain flour
4 eggs, beaten

In a large pan, gently heat 120 ml (4 fl oz) water with the sugar, butter and salt until the butter has melted, then bring to the boil. Quickly add the flour all at once, and beat with a wooden spoon. Reduce the heat and continue to beat the dough for about 1 minute until it comes away easily from the sides of the pan. Grease a plate with butter, turn the mixture out onto it and leave to cool to room temperature. Return the dough to the pan, off the heat, and gradually beat in the eggs until the dough is smooth and glossy.

Variation: To make choux buns, preheat the oven to 220°C/425°F/Gas Mark 7. Butter a baking tray and pipe or spoon egg-sized pieces of choux pastry dough onto it, spaced well apart. Turn the oven down to 200°C/400°F/Gas Mark 6. Bake for 20 minutes until well risen and golden. Fill as required and serve hot or cold.

SWEET PASTRY
pâte sucrée

Preparation time: 10 minutes,
   plus 1 hour chilling time
Cooking time: 25 minutes, if baking blind
Serves 6

250 g (9 oz) plain flour
125 g (4¼ oz) butter, softened
1 small egg
125 g (4¼ oz) caster sugar
1 teaspoon salt

Mix together the flour, butter, egg, sugar and salt until the mixture first resembles fine breadcrumbs, then starts to clump together. Add 1–2 tablespoons of chilled water, or enough to obtain a smooth, supple pastry. Knead very lightly until it just comes together to form a ball. Cover and chill for 1 hour before use. Bring back to room temperature before rolling out. On a lightly floured work surface, roll out the pastry to a 5-mm (¼-inch) thick circle and use to line a 25–35 cm (10–14 inch) round tart tin, preferably with a removable base. The dough may also be used to line small round or boat-shaped (barquette) tins.

To bake the pastry case blind, preheat the oven to 190°C/375°F/Gas Mark 5. Cover the pastry case with greaseproof paper and fill with baking beans or uncooked rice. Bake for 10 minutes, then gently remove the greaseproof paper and baking beans or rice and return the pastry case to the oven for a further 10–15 minutes until light golden brown in colour and cooked throughout.

Note: Sweet Pastry can be used for desserts such as the Pumpkin Tart (p. 186).

Choux Buns

SHORTCRUST PASTRY
pâte brisée

Preparation time: 20 minutes,
    plus chilling time
Cooking time: 20–25 minutes, if baking blind
Makes 400 g (14 oz)

250 g (9 oz) plain flour, plus extra for dusting
1 tablespoon flavourless oil, such as
    sunflower or rapeseed
½ teaspoon salt
125 g (4¼ oz) butter, chilled and diced,
    plus extra for greasing
1–2 tablespoons ice-cold water

Put the flour into a bowl. Make a well in the middle and add the oil, salt and butter. Rub the butter into the flour using your fingertips until it resembles breadcrumbs. Moisten with the water to bring the dough together. Briefly knead the dough by hand; the more quickly this is done, the better the pastry will be. Cover the pastry with clingfilm and leave to chill in the refrigerator for between 30 minutes and 24 hours. Bring it back to room temperature before rolling out. On a lightly floured surface, roll it out to a circle 5 mm (¼ inch) thick and use to line a greased 23-cm (9-inch) tart tin, preferably one with a removable base. The pastry may also be used to line small round or boat-shaped tins (barquettes).

To bake the pastry case blind, preheat the oven to 200°C/400°F/Gas Mark 6. Line the pastry case with greaseproof paper and fill with baking beans or uncooked rice. Bake for 10 minutes, then gently remove the greaseproof paper and baking beans or rice and return the pastry case to the oven for a further 10–15 minutes, until it is light golden brown and cooked throughout.

Note: Keep the ingredients and utensils as cool as possible. This will help the pastry to retain a short, crumbly texture. Any leftover pastry can be frozen. Shortcrust pastry can be used for pastries such as Saint-Honoré (p. 148) or Alsace Tart (p. 184).

RICH SWEET PASTRY
pâte sablée

Preparation time: 10 minutes,
    plus 1 hour chillng time
Cooking time: 20–25 minutes, if baking blind
Makes 500 g (1 lb 2 oz)

125 g (4¼ oz) caster sugar
1 egg
Pinch of salt
250 g (9 oz) plain flour
1 teaspoon vanilla extract
125 g (4¼ oz) butter, chilled and diced

Mix the sugar with the egg in a large bowl with a little salt. Stir in the flour and vanilla extract. When the mixture is grainy and sandy in appearance, work in the butter, using a rounded knife to 'cut' the butter into the flour mixture. When the dough starts to combine, transfer to a work surface dusted with flour and knead lightly to obtain a smooth, supple pastry. Cover and chill for 1 hour before use. Bring back to room temperature before rolling out.

On a lightly floured work surface, roll out the pastry to a 5-mm (¼-inch) thick circle and use to line a round tart tin, 25–35 cm (10–14 inches) in diameter, and preferably with a removable base. The dough may also be used to line small round or boat-shaped tins (barquettes).

To bake the pastry case blind, preheat the oven to 190°C/375°F/Gas Mark 5. Line the pastry case with greaseproof paper and fill with baking beans or uncooked rice. Bake for 10 minutes, then gently remove the greaseproof paper and baking beans or rice and return the pastry case to the oven for a further 10–15 minutes until light golden brown in colour and cooked throughout.

Note: Once baked this pastry will be crisp and will withstand moisture well without going soggy. It can used for tartlets containing raw fruit coated in syrup such as the Pineapple Tart (p. 179).

ICINGS AND FILLINGS

Icings are a sweet glaze made from icing sugar and a liquid such as water, liqueur or milk, and they can be enhanced with chocolate, nuts or fruits. An icing should complement the flavours and texture of the dessert it is used for, and the consistency should be light enough for spreading and adhering to the cake.

WHITE OR ROYAL ICING
glaçure blanche dite glace royale

Preparation time: 10 minutes
Cooking time: 5 minutes, if oven drying
Enough for 1 medium-sized cake

200 g (7 oz) icing sugar
1 small egg white
Few drops of lemon juice

Whisk the sugar, egg white and lemon juice until creamy and thick enough to form a thick ribbon as it falls from the beaters. Adjust if necessary with a little icing sugar or water, one drop at a time. Spread this icing on cakes or gâteaux when they are cold. To dry the icing, preheat the oven to 100°C/200°F/Gas Mark ½. Put the iced cake in the oven, leaving the door ajar. Remove the cake as soon as the icing has dried sufficiently to become opaque. It will also dry out and set hard if left at room temperature for several days.

Note: The icing can be made the day before it is needed and chilled overnight in a sealed container. Stir well before use.

FONDANT ICING
fondant au café

Preparation time: 15 minutes
Cooking time: 10 minutes
Enough for 1 large-sized cake

300 g (11 oz) caster sugar
1 tablespoon glucose
10 drops lemon juice
2 teaspoons coffee extract, rum
   or Kirsch (optional)

In a pan over low heat, dissolve the sugar and glucose in 100 ml (3½ fl oz) water and cook to the large-thread stage (p. 17). Carefully pour the syrup on to a marble slab or baking tray. As soon as it is cold, spread and work the syrup with a wooden or metal spatula until it turns opaque. Add the lemon juice, knead well and form into a ball. Return the icing to the pan and melt over low heat without boiling. If desired, add the coffee extract, rum or Kirsch. Use the icing for a large cake or petits fours.

WATER ICING
glace à l'eau

Preparation time: 5 minutes
Enough for 1 medium-sized cake

200 g (7 oz) icing sugar

Add 2 tablespoons water to the icing sugar and stir well to make icing that is soft but not too runny. If more water is required, add this a drop at a time. When ready to use, spread the icing over a cold cake with a palette knife.

KIRSCH ICING
glace au kirsch

Preparation time: 5 minutes
Enough for 1 medium-sized cake

2 tablespoons Kirsch
200 g (7 oz) icing sugar

Stir the Kirsch into the sugar to make a white icing. When ready to use, spread the icing over a cold cake with a palette knife. Do not over-work, since the icing will settle and level itself once set aside.

CHOCOLATE ICING
glace au chocolat

Preparation time: 20 minutes,
    plus cooling time
Enough for 1 medium-sized cake

60 g (2 oz) chocolate, chopped
60 g (2 oz) butter
2 very fresh eggs, separated

In a small pan, gently melt the chocolate and butter in a double boiler. Remove from the heat, allow to cool and then mix in the egg yolks. Whisk the egg whites to soft peaks and fold into the chocolate mixture. When ready to use, spread the icing over a cold cake with a palette knife. The icing sets as it cools.

COCOA ICING
glace au chocolat

Preparation time: 10 minutes
Enough for 1 medium-sized cake

250 g (9 oz) icing sugar
50 g (1¾ oz) unsweetened cocoa powder
3 tablespoons Kirsch

Stir all the ingredients together with 1 tablespoon water, slowly at first and then beating until smooth to make icing that is soft but not too runny. If more liquid is required, add water a drop at a time. Use for icing cakes or gâteaux once they have cooled. When ready to use, spread the icing over a cold cake with a palette knife.

SWEETENED WHIPPED CREAM
crème chantilly

Preparation time: 10 minutes
Enough for 1 medium-sized cake

250 ml (8 fl oz) chilled thick double cream,
    diluted with 100 ml (3½ fl oz) milk, or
    330 ml (11 fl oz) whipping cream
20–30 g (¾–1¼ oz) caster sugar, to taste
1 teaspoon vanilla extract, to taste

Whisk the cream, which should be very cold, to soft peaks. Take care not to over-whip it. Lightly fold in sugar and vanilla to taste. Do not allow the mixture to become too warm, as the cream may turn to butter. Chill until required.

GANACHE
crème ganache

Preparation time: 20 minutes,
    plus setting time
Cooking time: 10 minutes
Enough for 1 medium-sized cake

200 g (7 oz) chocolate, chopped
125 g (4¼ oz) crème fraîche,
    at room temperature
50 g (1¾ oz) butter, diced
    and at room temperature

Place the chocolate in a heatproof bowl set over a pan of barely simmering water. Heat gently, stirring occasionally until smooth, then remove from the heat. Gradually stir in the crème fraîche and butter, stirring constantly with a wooden spoon or spatula until mixed to a soft cream. Allow to set for a few hours. Use to decorate or fill cakes while still soft, since the ganache will firm up as it cools.

BUTTERCREAM
crème au beurre

Preparation time: 30 minutes
Cooking time: 10 minutes
Enough for 1 medium-sized cake

3 eggs
120 g (4 oz) caster sugar
270 g (10 oz) butter, softened
Grated orange or lemon zest or
    vanilla extract, to flavour (optional)

In a large heatproof bowl set over a pan of simmering water, whisk the eggs and sugar with an electric whisk until thick and creamy. Remove from the heat and continue whisking until the mixture is almost cold. Whisk in the butter, a little at a time, and continue whisking until the cream is thick, glossy and completely cold. If desired, whisk in the chosen flavouring.

EASY BUTTERCREAM
crème au beurre

Preparation time: 20 minutes,
    plus cooling time
Enough for 1 medium-sized cake

250 ml (8 fl oz) milk
2 egg yolks
200 g (7 oz) butter, diced
Flavouring of your choice, such as grated
    lemon zest or vanilla extract

Make a Crème Anglaise with the milk and egg yolks
(p. 49), adding your chosen flavouring. While the crème
anglaise is still lukewarm, gradually stir in the butter
and mix until the cream is very soft and smooth. Allow
to cool completely before using.

CHOCOLATE BUTTERCREAM
crème au beurre, au chocolat

Preparation time: 20 minutes
Cooking time: 10 minutes
Enough for 1 medium-sized cake

125 g (4¼ oz) caster sugar
3 egg whites
30 g (1¼ oz) unsweetened cocoa powder
125 g (4¼ oz) butter, softened

Place the sugar in a small saucepan, add 100 ml (3½ fl oz)
water and heat gently to dissolve the sugar. Raise the
heat and boil until the syrup has reached the small or
soft-ball stage (p. 17). Whisk the egg whites until they
form stiff peaks and continue whisking as you add the
sugar syrup in a thin stream. The syrup should not
touch the blades of the whisk, so that it produces an
evenly blended mixture. Continue whisking as you add
the cocoa powder and finally the butter, adding this
a little at a time. Once the butter has been incorporated,
stop whisking so that the buttercream does not lose
volume. Use as soon as possible to fill and decorate cakes
or gâteaux.

COFFEE BUTTERCREAM
crème au beurre, au café

Preparation time: 10 minutes
Enough for 1 medium-sized cake

200 g (7 oz) butter, softened
200 g (7 oz) icing sugar
3 egg yolks
1 teaspoon coffee essence or 2 teaspoons
instant coffee powder, diluted in
    1 teaspoon hot water

Beat the butter with a wooden spoon or in a mixer until
very soft. Beat in the icing sugar, then the egg yolks,
one at a time to make a very smooth, creamy mixture.
Beat in the coffee essence, to taste.

PRALINE BUTTERCREAM
crème au beurre pralinée

Preparation time: 50 minutes
Cooking time: 30 minutes
Enough for 1 medium-sized cake

For the praline:
100 g (3½ oz) caster sugar
100 g (3½ oz) slivered or coarsely chopped
   skinned almonds or hazelnuts

For the buttercream:
3 eggs
125 g (4¼ oz) caster sugar
270 g (10 oz) unsalted butter, well softened

To make the praline, place the sugar in a heavy-based pan with 2 tablespoons of water. Dissolve the sugar over moderate heat, and then cook to a pale caramel. Add the almonds or hazelnuts and stir until the sugar takes on a darker, golden brown caramel colour and the nuts are toasted. Pour the mixture on to a lightly oiled marble slab or baking tray. When cold, reduce to a fine powder using a pestle and mortar or a food processor.

To make the buttercream, place the eggs and sugar in a heatproof bowl set over barely simmering water and whisk until pale and tripled in volume. Remove from the heat and continue whisking until the mixture is completely cool. Fold the soft butter gently but thoroughly into the cold egg mixture. Fold in the praline powder.

Note: Ready-to-use, finely-powdered praline can be bought in specialist shops and from online suppliers.

MOCHA BUTTERCREAM
crème moka

Preparation time: 25 minutes
Enough for 1 medium-sized cake

200 g (7 oz) butter, softened
150 g (5 oz) caster sugar
1 teaspoon coffee essence or 2 teaspoons
   instant coffee powder, diluted in
   1 teaspoon hot water

Beat the butter with a wooden spoon or in a mixer until pale and creamy. Gradually add the sugar and coffee. Beat until completely smooth.

Note: To make a mocha flavouring which combines chocolate with coffee, add 25 g (1 oz) of unsweetened cocoa powder to the above, beating it in with the sugar and coffee.

PASTRY CREAM FILLING

crème pâtissière à fourrer

Preparation time: 5 minutes,
  plus cooling time
Cooking time: 10 minutes
Enough for 1 medium-sized cake

30 g (1¼ oz) potato flour
25 g (1 oz) plain flour
500 ml (18 fl oz) crème fraîche or 250 ml
  (8 fl oz) milk mixed with 100 ml (3½ fl oz)
  thick cream
2 whole eggs
4 egg yolks
125 g (4 oz) caster sugar
Kirsch, to taste (optional)

In a heavy-based saucepan, stir together the potato flour, plain flour and crème fraîche together until smooth. Whisk in the whole eggs, the egg yolks and the sugar. Mix well. Place in a pan over gentle heat and stir continuously until thickened. Cool before adding the Kirsch, if using. Wait until the mixture has cooled before adding the Kirsch, otherwise the heat will partially destroy its flavour.

Note: If the crème pâtissière is too thick for your chosen recipe, whisk 1 or 2 egg whites until very stiff and fold them into the mixture while it is still hot.

CRÈME PÂTISSIÈRE

crème pâtissière

Preparation time: 15 minutes
Cooking time: 10 minutes
Enough for 1 medium-sized cake

500 ml (18 fl oz) milk
½ vanilla pod, split and seeds removed
50 g (1¾ oz) plain flour
75 g (2½ oz) caster sugar
1 egg
3 egg yolks

Place the milk and the vanilla seeds and pod in a large saucepan and slowly bring to the boil. Beat the flour, sugar and eggs together in a large bowl. Pour the boiling milk over this mixture, a little at a time, stirring constantly. Pour back into the saucepan and cook over gentle heat, stirring constantly. Remove from the heat as soon as the mixture comes to the boil and thickens. Remove the vanilla pod.

Note: Crème pâtissière can be flavoured by adding grated chocolate, instant coffee, Kirsch or rum.

Crème Pâtissière

LIQUEUR CREAM
crème à la liqueur

Preparation time: 5 minutes,
   plus cooling time
Cooking time: 15 minutes
Enough for 1 medium-sized cake

100 g (3½ oz) caster sugar
3 egg yolks plus 2 egg whites
50 g (1¾ oz) plain flour
250 ml (9 fl oz) milk
90 g (3¼ oz) crème fraîche
3 tablespoons liqueur, such as Kirsch,
   or Cointreau

Place the sugar and egg yolks in a heatproof bowl set over a pan of barely simmering water and whisk for 3 minutes until light and frothy. Whisk in the flour, milk and crème fraîche. Continue mixing over low heat until the mixture thickens. Do not allow to boil. Whisk the egg whites to stiff peaks and fold into the custard when it is barely lukewarm, along with your choice of liqueur. Allow to cool before using.

RUM- OR KIRSCH-FLAVOURED MOUSSELINE
crème mousseline, au rhum ou au kirsch

Preparation time: 20 minutes
Cooking time: 20 minutes
Enough for 1 medium-sized cake

3 egg yolks
90 g (3¼ oz) caster sugar
Pinch of salt
40 g (1½ oz) plain flour
750 ml (1¼ pints) milk, lukewarm
180 g (6¼ oz) butter, softened and diced
100 ml (3½ fl oz) rum or Kirsch

In a heatproof bowl, whisk the egg yolks, sugar and salt. Whisk in the flour, followed by the milk. Set the bowl over a pan of barely simmering water and cook over gentle heat to make a thick, creamy mixture. Continue whisking to incorporate more air and add the diced butter one at a time, followed by the rum or Kirsch. As soon as the butter has been incorporated, stop whisking so that the mousseline does not lose volume.

Variation: For a vanilla-flavoured mousseline, omit the alcohol and add the seeds of 1 vanilla pod to the milk mixture.

SAINT-HONORÉ CREAM

crème à Saint-Honoré

Preparation time: 25 minutes
Cooking time: 15 minutes
Enough for 1 medium-sized cake

2 leaves gelatine
3 egg yolks
100 g (3½ oz) caster sugar
20 g (¾ oz) plain flour
250 ml (9 fl oz) milk, warmed
2 teaspoons vanilla extract
5 egg whites

Soak the gelatine leaves in a little cold water 5 minutes before they are to be used to soften them. Place the egg yolks and sugar in a heatproof bowl set over a pan of barely simmering water. Whisk for 2–3 minutes, then add the flour, milk, vanilla and the well-drained gelatine leaves. Continue stirring the custard until it has thickened, without allowing it to boil. Remove from the heat. Whisk the egg whites until they form stiff peaks and fold them gently but thoroughly into the lukewarm custard. Saint-Honoré cream will not keep for more than a few hours.

CHOCOLATE CREAM

crème au chocolat

Preparation time: 10 minutes
Enough for 1 medium-sized cake

180 g (6¼ oz) butter, softened
100 g (3½ oz) caster sugar
2 egg yolks
2 heaped tablespoons cocoa powder
Grated chocolate, to decorate
Slivered almonds, toasted, to decorate

Beat the butter until pale and creamy. Beat in the sugar and egg yolks, followed by the cocoa powder. Continue mixing until very smooth.

ALMOND CREAM

crème frangipane

Preparation time: 5 minutes
Cooking time: 10 minutes
Enough for 1 medium-sized cake

100 g (3½ oz) caster sugar
2 eggs
1 egg yolk
50 g (1¾ oz) plain flour
30 g (1¼ oz) butter, softened
300 ml (½ pint) milk
60 g (2 oz) ground almonds

Mix together the sugar, the whole eggs and egg yolk, flour and butter in a heavy-bottomed saucepan. Bring the milk to the boil and add it to the mixture in a thin stream, stirring constantly. Continue stirring over a gentle heat for about 2–3 minutes, until thickened. Remove from heat and stir in the ground almonds. Allow to cool before using.

ALMOND CUSTARD

crème frangipane

Preparation time. 15 minutes,
    plus cooling time
Cooking time: 20 minutes
Makes approximately 700 g (1½ lb)

300 ml (½ pint) milk
75 g (2½ oz) caster sugar
2 eggs
2 egg yolks
90 g (3¼ oz) plain flour
90 g (3¼ oz) butter, softened
1 teaspoon salt
60 g (2 oz) ground almonds

Bring the milk to the boil in a large pan. In a bowl, mix together the sugar, eggs, egg yolks and flour with 60 g (2 oz) of the butter and the salt. Beat the boiling milk into the egg mixture, then return to the pan and cook over a medium heat, stirring constantly until the mixture thickens. Mix in the remaining butter and the almonds. Stir gently until cool.

Note: Almond custard is used as a filling in many tarts and pastries.

SAUCES AND SYRUPS

*A large variety of hot and cold sauces and syrups
can be drizzled over cakes, fruits and puddings to
enhance the flavour and provide a moist texture.
They can be cream, fruit or liqueur based.*

RUM SAUCE
sauce au rhum

Preparation time: 5 minutes
Cooking time: 10 minutes
Serves 6

125 g (4¼ oz) caster sugar
200 ml (7 fl oz) rum

Place 250 ml (8 fl oz) water and the sugar and rum in
a pan and bring to the boil over low heat. Remove from
the heat as soon as it starts to boil. Stir well and use
immediately, for example poured over a hot rum baba.

SABAYON
sabayon

Preparation time: 10 minutes
Cooking time: 5–10 minutes
Serves 6

200 g (7 oz) caster sugar
5 egg yolks
½ teaspoon vanilla extract
Grated zest of 1 lemon
200 ml (7 fl oz) fortified wine, such
    as port, sherry or Madeira

Whisk the sugar, egg yolks, vanilla and lemon zest in
a large heatproof bowl until the mixture is thick, white
and smooth. Add the wine and place the bowl over a pan
of barely simmering water. Heat the sabayon gently for
5–10 minutes, constantly whisking until very thick and
foamy. Remove from the heat and serve immediately.

MILK SABAYON
sabayon au lait

Preparation time: 15 minutes
Cooking time: 15 minutes
Serves 6

3 egg yolks
60 g (2 oz) caster sugar
Pinch of salt
1 teaspoon vanilla extract
200 ml (7 fl oz) milk

Place the egg yolks, sugar and salt in a heatproof bowl and whisk for 10 minutes until pale and tripled in volume. Add the vanilla and the milk. Set the bowl over a pan of barely simmering water and whisk continuously until the sauce has thickened. Serve at once with the dessert of your choice, using some of the sauce to coat the cake or dessert and handing round the remainder in a jug.

SABAYON SAUCE WITH MADEIRA
sabayon au madère

Preparation time: 10 minutes
Cooking time: 15 minutes
Serves 6

4 egg yolks
125 g (4¼ oz) caster sugar
100 ml (3½ fl oz) sweet Madeira

Place the egg yolks and sugar in a heatproof bowl set over a pan of barely simmering water. Add 1 tablespoon water and whisk for approximately 10 minutes until the mixture is pale and at least tripled in volume. Gradually whisk in the Madeira and serve the sauce warm.

Note: The sweet Madeira can be replaced with a sweet Marsala.

REDCURRANT SAUCE
sauce à la groseille

Preparation time: 1 minute
Cooking time: 5 minutes
Serves 6

Redcurrant jelly
Kirsch, for taste

Spoon sufficient redcurrant jelly for your purpose (such as for a sauce or glaze) into a saucepan and heat with a little water and Kirsch to form a syrup.

APRICOT SAUCE
sauce aux abricots

Preparation time: 10 minutes
Cooking time: 20 minutes
Serves 6

125 g (4¼ oz) apricots, halved and stoned
125 g (4¼ oz) caster sugar
2 egg yolks
200 ml (7 fl oz) good white wine
  (such as white Burgundy)
Few drops of lemon juice

Place the apricots in a pan with 2 tablespoons of water and cook over gentle heat until soft, approximately 5 minutes. Purée the cooked fruit in a blender and set the purée aside. Place the sugar and egg yolks in a heatproof bowl set over a pan of barely simmering water and whisk for 10 minutes until pale and tripled in volume. Gradually whisk in the wine, a little at a time. When the mixture has thickened, stir in the apricot purée and the lemon juice. Continue cooking this mixture in the bowl set over barely simmering water for a few minutes, then remove from the heat and serve warm or at room temperature.

Note: To make a raspberry sabayon sauce, replace the apricots with 250 g (9 oz) raspberries, puréed and then sieved to remove the seeds.

APRICOT & KIRSCH SAUCE
sauce à l'abricot et au kirsch

Preparation time: 10 minutes
Cooking time: 15 minutes
Serves 6

125 g (4¼ oz) apricots, halved and stoned
125 g (4¼ oz) caster sugar
15 g (½ oz) rice flour
100 ml (3½ fl oz) Kirsch
50 g (1¾ oz) butter, cut into cubes

Place the apricots in a pan with the sugar, 2 tablespoons of water and cook over gentle heat until soft, approximately 5 minutes. Purée the fruit in a blender and set aside. Place the rice flour and Kirsch in a pan and stir, off the heat, until smooth. Gradually stir in the apricot purée. Place the pan over moderate heat and stir continuously until the sauce thickens. Gradually add the butter in small pieces, stirring until smooth. Remove the sauce from the heat. If it is to be served hot, keep warm in a bowl set over hot water.

SYRUP FOR BABAS
sirop pour baba

Preparation time: 5 minutes
Cooking time: 10 minutes
Enough for 6–8 babas

250 g (9 oz) caster sugar
½ vanilla pod, split lengthways
Pared zest from ½ unwaxed
  orange or lemon
200 ml (7 fl oz) rum or Kirsch

Place all the ingredients in a saucepan along with 500 ml (18 fl oz) water. Bring slowly to the boil, allowing the sugar to dissolve and vanilla and citrus zest to flavour the syrup. Remove from the heat as soon as the syrup comes to the boil. Remove the vanilla pod and zest from the syrup and sprinkle or brush it over rum babas or other cakes.

CRÈME ANGLAISE
crème anglaise

Preparation time: 5 minutes
Cooking time: 20 minutes
Enough for 1 medium-sized cake

1 litre (1¾ pints) milk
100 g (3½ oz) caster sugar
½ vanilla pod
8 egg yolks

Add the milk, sugar and vanilla pod to a medium saucepan and bring to a boil. In a heatproof bowl, whisk the egg yolks, then add the hot milk. Add to a bain marie and continue to stir the custard with a wooden spoon until thickened. Do not allow it to boil or the albumen in the eggs will coagulate and separate from the milk.

Note: If the custard curdles, pour small quantities of it at a time into a bottle, stuff a clean cloth into the neck of the bottle and shake it vigorously for 3 to 4 minutes. The custard will revert to a smooth consistency. Alternatively, you can make the custard with whole beaten eggs: 4 eggs will be enough for 1 litre (1¾ pints) milk. Allow to thicken over gentle heat.

Variation: To flavour with coffee, add 2 teaspoons of strong coffee when whisking the egg yolks. To flavour with chocolate, melt 60 g (2 oz) chocolate in the milk. Do not add sugar. To flavour with vanilla, add another whole vanilla pod to the milk.

SUGAR SYRUP
firop de sucre

Cooking time: 1 minutes
Makes 800 ml (1 pint 8 fl oz)

500 g (1 lb 2 oz) caster sugar

Boil the sugar in 500 ml (18 fl oz) water for 1 minute.

Note: In addition to the above ingredients, 50 g (¾ oz) glucose must be added to the cold water before heating if the sugar syrup is to be used to make fondant or cooked to the hard crack stage. Alternatively, 3–4 drops of vinegar or 4 drops of lemon juice or citric acid can be used.

SMALL CAKES

*From traditional madeleines to tasty rum-soaked babas,
small cakes can be enjoyed on their own or eaten with tea
or coffee. Regardless of the occasion, they make the perfect
afternoon treats and always impress guests.*

BABAS

Babas are small cakes made with yeast, and usually contain raisins or currants. Babas can be served as a whole ring or prepared as individual servings in special baba moulds. They are then soaked with a delicious rum syrup.

QUICK BABA
baba rapide

Preparation time: 10 minutes
Cooking time: 20 minutes
Serves 6–8

250 g (9 oz) plain flour
80 g (2¾ oz) butter, melted,
 or 4 tablespoons crème fraîche,
 plus extra butter for greasing
4 eggs
2 teaspoons baking powder
½ quantity rum-flavoured Syrup
 for Babas (p. 48)

Preheat the oven to 200°C/400°F/Gas Mark 6. Generously grease 6–8 individual baba moulds with butter. In large bowl, mix together the flour and baking powder. In a separate bowl, mix butter or crème fraîche and eggs together, then pour into flour mixture and mix until smooth. Divide the dough equally between the moulds and bake for 15–20 minutes. While still warm, sprinkle generously with warm rum syrup and allow this to soak in before turning the babas out onto a serving plate.

RUM BABA FROM LORRAINE
baba lorrain au rhum

Preparation time: 20 minutes,
   plus soaking time
Cooking time: 15–20 minutes
Serves 6–8

80 g (2¾ oz) butter, softened,
   plus extra for greasing
250 g (9 oz) plain flour
50 g (1¾ oz) caster sugar
2 teaspoons baking powder
½ teaspoon salt
4 eggs
50 g (1¾ oz) crème fraîche
½ quantity rum-flavoured Syrup
   for Babas (p. 48)

Preheat the oven to 180°C/350°F/Gas Mark 4. Grease 6–8 individual baba moulds with butter. Place the flour, sugar, baking powder and salt together in a bowl. Mix thoroughly, make a well and add the eggs, crème fraîche and butter to the well. Beat for a few minutes until smooth. Bake the babas for 15–20 minutes. While still warm, sprinkle generously with warm rum syrup and allow this to soak in before turning the babas out onto a serving plate.

KIRSCH-FLAVOURED BABA
baba au kirsch

Preparation time: 25 minutes,
   plus 2 hours rising and soaking time
Cooking time: 15–20 minutes
Serves 6–8

60 g (2 oz) currants, washed and dried
60 g (2 oz) sultanas, washed and dried
60 g (2 oz) candied citron peel,
   finely chopped
100 ml (3½ fl oz) Kirsch
250 g (9 oz) plain flour
8 g fresh yeast, or 1 sachet dried yeast
300 ml (½ pint) milk, lukewarm
4 eggs
100 g (3½ oz) butter, softened,
   plus extra for greasing
1 teaspoon salt
50 g (1¾ oz) caster sugar
1 quantity Kirsch-flavoured Syrup
   for Babas (p. 48)

Place the currants, sultanas and candied peel in a small bowl with the Kirsch. Set aside.

Dissolve the yeast in 50 ml (2 fl oz) of warm milk. Sieve the flour, make a well and pour in the dissolved yeast mixture. Add the eggs and beat for a few minutes; the dough should easily come away from the hand or beaters. Add the butter, salt and sugar and beat the dough again. It should be smooth and glossy. Finally stir in the Kirsch-soaked fruit. If the dough is too stiff, add a little more milk.

Generously grease 6–8 individual baba moulds with butter. Divide the dough equally between the moulds to half-fill them. Leave to rise in a warm place for 2 hours. Preheat the oven to 200°C/400°F/Gas Mark 6. Bake the babas for 15–20 minutes. While still warm, sprinkle generously with warm Kirsch syrup and allow this to soak in before turning the babas out onto a serving plate.

BABA WITH RAISINS
baba aux raisins

Preparation time: 25 minutes, plus
   7–10 hours rising and soaking time
Cooking time: 40 minutes
Serves 6

10 g (¼ oz) fresh yeast or 1 sachet dried yeast
250 g (9 oz) plain flour
3 eggs, beaten
65 g (2¼ oz) caster sugar
1 teaspoon salt
75 g (2½ oz) butter, well softened,
   plus extra for greasing
125 g (4¼ oz) raisins
½ quantity rum-flavoured Syrup
   for Babas (p. 48)

Dissolve the yeast in 50 ml (2 fl oz) of warm water. Put 80 g (2¾ oz) flour in a bowl, make a well in it and pour in the dissolved yeast, mixing it into the flour to obtain a small quantity of light dough. Cover and allow to rise in a warm place until tripled in volume, 3–4 hours (or overnight at a cooler temperature). After it has risen, add the remaining flour, the eggs, sugar and salt and beat for 5 minutes in a mixer set on slow speed, or 10 minutes by hand until the dough is very supple and elastic. Finally, incorporate the butter and raisins. Cover the dough with oiled clingfilm and allow to rise in a warm room until doubled in volume, 4–6 hours.

Preheat the oven to 200°C/400°F/Gas Mark 6. Generously grease 6–8 individual baba moulds with butter. Divide the dough equally between the moulds to half-fill them. Bake for 15–20 minutes. While still warm, sprinkle generously with warm rum syrup and allow this to soak in before turning the babas out onto a serving plate.

ECONOMICAL BABA
baba économique

Preparation time: 10 minutes,
   plus 20 minutes resting time
   Cooking time: 20 minutes
Serves 6–8

Butter, for greasing
200 g (7 oz) plain flour
100 g (3½ oz) caster sugar
2 teaspoons baking powder
½ teaspoon salt
2 eggs
4 tablespoons milk
½ quantity rum-flavoured Syrup
   for Babas (p. 48)

Grease 6–8 individual baba moulds with butter. Place the flour, sugar, baking powder and salt together in a bowl. Mix thoroughly, make a well and add the eggs and milk to the well. Beat for a few minutes until smooth. Transfer the mixture to the baba moulds and allow them to rest for 20 minutes.

Preheat the oven to 180°C/350°F/Gas Mark 4. Bake the babas for 15–20 minutes. While still warm, sprinkle generously with warm rum syrup and allow this to soak in before turning the babas out onto a serving plate.

Baba with Currants

PETITS FOURS

Petit fours (meaning small oven in French) are
bite-sized confections served at the end of the meal,
or they can form part of an afternoon tea buffet.
When baking petits fours, it is especially important
to line the baking tray with a sheet of greaseproof
paper so they can then be detached without difficulty.

BASIC PETITS FOURS
pâte de fond

Preparation time: 25 minutes
Cooking time: 20–25 minutes
Makes 50

Butter, for greasing
4 eggs, separated
40 g (generous 1 oz) caster sugar
85 g (generous 2½ oz) plain flour

Preheat the oven to 140°C/275°F/Gas Mark 1 and line a baking tray with buttered greaseproof paper. Use a spatula to beat the egg yolks with the sugar. Stir in the flour. Whisk the egg whites until they form stiff peaks and then fold into the egg yolk mixture. Transfer to a piping bag and pipe out a variety of shapes on to the baking tray or fill a variety of small moulds with it. Bake for 20–25 minutes until pale golden. These little cakes keep well in tins, away from any moisture. Before topping and decorating them, you can scoop out a shallow depression in their surfaces with the tip of a knife.

ALMOND PASTE
pâte d'amandes

Preparation time: 20 minutes
Makes 500 g

250 g ground almonds
250 g caster sugar
3 egg whites

Pound the almonds with the sugar and egg whites in a mortar to form a smooth paste; this can also be done in a food processor.

ALMOND PETITS FOURS
petits fours aux amandes

Preparation time: 20 minutes
Cooking time: 12–15 minutes
Serves 10

Butter, melted, for greasing
250 g (9 oz) caster sugar, plus
    2 extra tablespoons
250 g (9 oz) ground almonds
4 egg whites
1 teaspoon vanilla extract
Glacé cherries or angelica, to decorate
100 ml (3½ fl oz) milk

Preheat the oven to 180°C/350°F/Gas Mark 4. Line a baking tray with greaseproof paper and brush with melted butter. Mix the 250 g (9 oz) sugar and almonds thoroughly in a mixing bowl. In another bowl, whisk the egg whites to soft peaks, then gradually fold them into the almond mixture, together with the vanilla. Mix until smooth. Transfer the mixture to a piping bag fitted with a large star nozzle to pipe small rosettes or longer straight lengths of the mixture on to the baking tray. Decorate with a glacé cherry or a piece of angelica. Bake for 12–15 minutes until pale golden.

Meanwhile, mix the milk with the remaining 2 tablespoons of sugar and set aside. As soon as the biscuits are cooked, brush them generously with the sweetened milk. Place the greaseproof paper on a damp surface to help detach the petits fours easily.

CROQUIGNOLES
croquignoles

Preparation time: 15 minutes
Cooking time: 20 minutes
Serves 6

Butter, for greasing
2 egg whites
175 g (6 oz) caster sugar ·
200 g (7 oz) plain flour
1 tablespoon orange flower water

Preheat the oven to 180°C/350°F/Gas Mark 4 and grease a baking tray with the butter. Mix all the ingredients together and knead to form a stiff dough. Shape into small biscuits the size of a coin. Place on the prepared tray and bake for 20 minutes.

Raisin Petits Fours

RAISIN PETITS FOURS
petits fours aux raisins

Preparation time: 15 minutes
Cooking time: 10–15 minutes
Serves 6

90 g (3¼ oz) butter, softened,
   plus extra for greasing
120 g (4 oz) caster sugar
1 teaspoon vanilla extract
2 eggs
240 g (8½ oz) plain flour
2 teaspoons baking powder
125 g (4¼ oz) raisins

Preheat the oven to 200°C/400°F/Gas Mark 6 and line a baking tray with buttered greaseproof paper. Whisk the sugar and vanilla with the eggs. In a separate bowl, mix the flour and baking powder, and stir into mixture, followed by the softened butter. Mix in the currants. Arrange the mixture in little mounds on the baking tray and bake for 10–15 minutes.

SACHAS
sachas

Preparation time: 25 minutes
Cooking time: 10–15 minutes
Serves 6

Butter, for greasing
100 g (3½ oz) angelica
200 g (7 oz) Almond Paste (p. 57)
1 egg white
60 g (2 oz) unpeeled almonds,
   coarsely chopped

Preheat the oven to 200°C/400°F/Gas Mark 6 and line a baking tray with buttered greaseproof paper. Cut the angelica into 1-cm (½-inch) squares. In a bowl, soften the almond paste by mixing the egg white into it, kneading until it is very smooth. Mould a small piece of paste so that it encloses a piece of angelica in its centre; the petits fours should be the size and shape of a large olive. Roll these in the almonds. Place on the baking tray and bake for 10–15 minutes.

COFFEE PETITS FOURS
fours au café

Preparation time: 30 minutes
Cooking time: 10–15 minutes
Serves 6

Butter, for greasing
160 g (5½ oz) Almond Paste (p. 57)
50 g (1¾ oz) caster sugar
1 egg white
Coffee extract, to taste
60 g (2 oz) almonds, skinned
   and coarsely chopped

Preheat the oven to 160°C/325°F/Gas Mark 3 and line a baking tray with buttered greaseproof paper. Place the almond paste in a mixing bowl and work in the sugar, egg white and coffee extract by hand. Taking walnut-sized pieces of the mixture, shape into slightly flattened and elongated ovals. Sprinkle with the almonds, pressing these gently in place. Place on the baking tray and bake for 15 minutes.

LITTLE CHERRY PETITS FOURS
cerisettes

Preparation time: 25 minutes
Cooking time: 10–15 minutes
Serves 6

Butter, for greasing
100 g (3½ oz) glacé cherries
1 egg white
Red food colouring
200 g (7 oz) Almond Paste (p. 57)

Preheat the oven to 200°C/400°F/Gas Mark 6 and line a baking tray with buttered greaseproof paper. Chop 80 g (2¾ oz) of the cherries very finely. Mix them with the egg white and a few drops of food colouring and work into the almond paste until this is smooth, malleable and evenly coloured. Shape the almond paste into balls, stuffing a whole cherry in the middle of each so that it is hidden inside. Transfer to the baking tray and bake for 10–15 minutes.

ORANGE PETITS FOURS
petits pains à l'orange

Preparation time: 25 minutes
Cooking time: 15–20 minutes
Serves 6

Butter, for greasing
85 g (3 oz) candied orange peel
250 g (9 oz) Almond Paste (p. 57)
1 egg white
60 g (2 oz) apple cheese (see note)
Grated zest of 1 unwaxed orange
Red food colouring

Preheat the oven to 200°C/400°F/Gas Mark 6 and line a baking tray with buttered greaseproof paper. Finely chop 60 g (2 oz) of the candied orange peel. Cut the remaining candied peel into diamond shapes. In a mixing bowl, soften the almond paste by kneading the egg white into it. Mix in with the apple cheese, orange zest, chopped candied peel and add a drop of red food colouring to give the dough a pink colour. Shape into little oval 'cakes'. Decorate these with the remaining diamond shaped candied peel. Transfer to the baking tray and bake for 15–20 minutes.

Note: Fruit preserves that are thick enough to slice are often called 'cheeses'. Fruit cheese can be made with other fruit, such as damsons or quince.

Little Cherry Petits Fours

EUGENIE

eugénie

Preparation time: 25 minutes
Cooking time: 10–15 minutes
Serves 6

Butter, for greasing
100 g (3½ oz) candied orange peel
200 g (7 oz) Almond Paste (p. 57)
Red food colouring
Few drops of orange oil or orange flower
   water, to taste
1 egg white
Icing sugar, for dusting
½ quantity Sugar Syrup (p. 49), to glaze

Preheat the oven to 200°C/400°F/Gas Mark 6 and line a baking tray with buttered greaseproof paper. Finely chop 75 g (2½ oz) of the orange peel. Knead the almond paste, working in a few drops of red food colouring, orange oil to taste, the chopped peel and the egg white. Dust the work surface sparingly with a little icing sugar and roll out the almond paste to a thickness of 1.5 cm (¾ inch). Use a plain round pastry cutter to stamp the almond paste into discs, then cut these into half-moon shapes. Lightly press the remaining candied orange peel on to the petits fours and transfer to the baking tray. Bake for 10–15 minutes. Brush with sugar syrup to glaze.

MIRRORS

miroirs

Preparation time: 25 minutes
Cooking time: 14–15 minutes
Serves 10

4 egg whites
125 g (4¼ oz) ground almonds
125 g (4¼ oz) caster sugar
1 teaspoon vanilla extract

For the filling:
150 g (5 oz) caster sugar
2 egg yolks
50 g (1¾ oz) butter, well softened
150 g (5 oz) ground almonds
1 tablespoon rum
25 g (1 oz) plain flour

For the glaze and icing:
6 tablespoons apricot jam
   (without fruit pieces if possible)
4 tablespoons rum
½ quantity Water Icing (p. 37)

Preheat the oven to 160°C/325°F/Gas Mark 3 and line a baking tray with greaseproof paper. Beat the egg whites until they are very stiff. Fold in the ground almonds, sugar and vanilla. Fill a piping bag with this mixture. Pipe small, shallow oval meringue cases onto the tray.

To make the filling, whisk the sugar with the egg yolks until pale and creamy. Gently but thoroughly mix in the soft butter, ground almonds, rum and flour. Spoon the filling mixture into the mini cases and bake for 14–15 minutes.

To make the glaze and icing, sieve the apricot jam to remove any pieces of fruit and place in a small pan with the rum. Simmer for 5–10 minutes to reduce and thicken slightly. Pour a little of this syrup over the filling in each meringue case while the latter are still hot. Trickle some very liquid water icing over the apricot glaze.

Eugenie

AVELINETTES
avelinettes

Preparation time: 20 minutes
Serves 10

150 g (5 oz) ground walnuts
150 g (5 oz) ground hazelnuts
150 g (5 oz) ground almonds
450 g (1 lb) caster sugar
2 teaspoons coffee extract
1 small egg white (optional)
2 tablespoons cocoa powder, sieved

Place the walnuts, hazelnuts, almonds, sugar and coffee extract in the bowl of a mixer or food processor and stir or process to a smooth paste, adding a little egg white if required. Shape pieces of the paste into little oval petits fours and roll them in the cocoa powder. Do not cook them. Serve in little paper confectionery cases.

IRMANETTES
irmanettes

Preparation time: 30 minutes
Cooking time: 25–30 minutes
Serves 6

100 g (3½ oz) butter, melted,
    plus extra for greasing
4 eggs
125 g (4¼ oz) caster sugar
60 g (2 oz) ground almonds
100 g (3½ oz) rice flour
120 ml (4 fl oz) Anisette, or other
    aniseed-flavoured liqueur
4 tablespoons apricot jam, sieved
1 quantity Water Icing (p. 37)
Pistachio nuts (unsalted), shelled and
    chopped, or angelica, to decorate

Preheat the oven to 180°C/350°F/Gas Mark 4 and grease a 20-cm (8-inch) square, fairly shallow cake tin with butter. Place the eggs with the sugar in a heatproof bowl set over a pan of barely simmering water and whisk continuously until the mixture is pale and at least tripled in volume. Remove from the heat. Melt the butter in a small pan. Fold the almonds into the whisked egg mixture, followed by the rice flour, 2 tablespoons of liqueur and the melted butter. Transfer the mixture to the cake tin and bake for 25–30 minutes.

While the cake is still hot, turn it out and sprinkle with 2 tablespoons of liqueur. Mix the apricot jam with another 2 tablespoons of liqueur, warm in a small pan and brush over all visible surfaces of the cake.

Using the remaining Anisette liqueur instead of water, make the water icing. Ice the cake with this. Cut the cake into 4–5-cm (1½–2 inch) squares. Alternatively, slice the cake diagonally at the same intervals and, without separating these slices, cut diagonally in the opposite direction to yield diamond shapes. Decorate each little cake with angelica or pistachio nuts.

Avelinettes

Pineapples

PINEAPPLES
ananas

Preparation time: 25 minutes
Cooking time: 10–15 minutes
Serves 6

Butter, for greasing
100 g (3½ oz) crystallized pineapple
1 egg white
200 g (7 oz) Almond Paste (p. 57)

Preheat the oven to 200°C/400°F/Gas Mark 6 and line a baking tray with buttered greaseproof paper. Finely chop 75 g (2½ oz) of the pineapple. Mix it with the egg white and work into the almond paste until this is smooth and malleable. Shape into small balls. Decorate each of these with pieces of the remaining pineapple, cut into diamond shapes or discs. Transfer to the baking tray and bake for 10–15 minutes.

SWEET ORANGE CROQUETTES
croquettes orangines

Preparation time: 30 minutes,
    plus cooling time
Cooking time: 10 minutes
Serves 6

125 g (4¼ oz) butter, softened,
    plus extra for greasing
80 g (2¾ oz) candied orange peel
2 tablespoons rum
250 g (9 oz) plain flour, plus extra
    for dusting
150 g (5 oz) caster sugar
2–3 tablespoons milk
3 tablespoons apricot jam
½ quantity Water Icing (p. 37),
    made with orange juice
Red food colouring, optional

Preheat the oven to 200°C/400°F/Gas Mark 6 and line a baking tray with buttered greaseproof paper. Pound the candied orange peel and rum in a mortar until they form a paste. Place the flour, sugar and butter in a mixing bowl and mix until it resembles breadcrumbs, then add sufficient milk to make a smooth dough. Lightly knead in the rum and orange paste.

Dust the work surface with flour and roll the dough out to a thickness of 2 cm (¾ inch) and cut into strips 4 cm (1½ inch) wide. Cut these strips into short lengths. Transfer them to the baking tray and bake for approximately 10 minutes.

Warm the apricot jam in a small pan and sieve it to remove any fruit pieces. When the biscuits have cooled, brush their surfaces with the apricot jam. Make the water icing using orange juice instead of water, and a few drops of red food colouring if desired. Use this to ice the petits fours.

Neapolitans

NEAPOLITANS

napolitains

Preparation time: 40 minutes
Serves 10

375 g (13 oz) ground almonds
4 egg whites
375 g (13 oz) caster sugar
Red food colouring
Green food colouring

Pound the ground almonds with the sugar and egg whites in a mortar to form a smooth paste. This can also be done in a food processor. Divide the paste into three equal portions. Place a few drops of red food colouring in a bowl and combine it with a third of the almond paste by kneading it. Repeat this process, using the green food colouring and another portion of the almond paste. Leave the third portion uncoloured. Roll out all three portions separately to a thickness of 6–8 mm (¼ inch). Place these on top of one another in any order you choose. Roll lightly to make the layers stick to one another and then use a very sharp knife to cut out into squares.

ESPERANCES

espérances

Preparation time: 40 minutes
Cooking time: 25 minutes
Makes 30

1 quantity Basic Petits Fours (p. 56)
1 quantity vanilla-flavoured
   Crème Mousseline (p. 43)
1 quantity Fondant Icing (p. 36)
Green food colouring
60 g (2 oz) unsalted pistachio nuts, chopped

Preheat the oven to 160°C/325°F/Gas Mark 3. Make the basic petits fours and bake them in mini cake tins for 20–25 minutes, until golden brown. Allow them to cool. Make the vanilla-flavoured crème mousseline and cover the petits fours with this, forming little domes of mousseline. Ice with fondant icing, delicately coloured with a drop or two of green food colouring, and sprinkle with the pistachio nuts.

MICHETTES

michettes

Preparation time: 15 minutes
Cooking time: 10 minutes
Serves 6

Butter, for greasing
200 g (7 oz) ground hazelnuts
200 g (7 oz) caster sugar
1 egg white
30 whole hazelnuts
Caramel (p. 17) (optional)

Preheat the oven to 180°C/350°F/Gas Mark 4 and line a baking tray with buttered greaseproof paper. Place the ground hazelnuts and sugar in a bowl and gradually work in some or all of the egg white to make a malleable paste. Shape into small balls, transfer to the baking tray and press a whole hazelnut lightly on top of each biscuit. Bake for 10 minutes. Dip the tops of the cooked biscuits in caramel if desired.

Brazilians

BRAZILIANS
brésiliens

Preparation time: 40 minutes
Cooking time: 20–25 minutes

1 quantity Basic Petits Fours (p. 56)
125 g (4¼ oz) ground walnuts
125 g (4¼ oz) icing sugar
1–2 tablespoons crème fraîche
125 g (4¼ oz) butter, softened
Maraschino liqueur, to taste

Preheat the oven to 160°C/325°F/Gas Mark 3. Make the basic petits fours and put them into mini cake tins. Mix the ground walnuts with the icing sugar, adding just enough crème fraîche to make a fairly moist paste. Stir in the softened butter and Maraschino, to taste. Spread this topping in a dome shape on each petit four. Bake for 20–25 minutes until pale golden.

Note: If you like, top each petit four with a sugared coffee bean and drizzle with coffee icing.

COFFEE AND WALNUT PETITS FOURS
fours au café

Preparation time: 50 minutes
Cooking time: 20–25 minutes
Makes 30

1 quantity Basic Petits Fours (p. 56)
1 quantity Coffee Buttercream (p. 39)
100 g (3½ oz) walnut halves
1 quantity Coffee Fondant Icing (p. 36)

Preheat the oven to 160°C/325°F/Gas Mark 3. Make the basic petits fours and bake them in mini cake tins for 20–25 minutes, until golden brown. Allow them to cool. Make the coffee buttercream. Cover the petits fours with this, smoothing it into a dome shape. Place a walnut half on top of each petit four. Drizzle with coffee-flavoured fondant icing.

Note: These are sometimes known as Don Juan petits fours.

BENJAMINS
benjamins

Preparation time: 40 minutes
Cooking time: 20–25 minutes
Makes 30

1 quantity Basic Petits Fours (p. 56)
125 g (4¼ oz) butter, softened
125 g (4¼ oz) ground almonds
125 g (4¼ oz) icing sugar
1 tablespoon rum
30 sultanas

Preheat the oven to 160°C/325°F/Gas Mark 3. Make the basic petits fours and bake them in mini cake tins for 20–25 minutes, until golden brown. Allow them to cool. To make the filling, beat the butter until pale and creamy and then stir in the almonds, sugar and rum to taste. Use this as topping for the little cakes, heaping it into a pyramid shape. Place a sultana on the top of each petit four.

Note: To decorate, once the cakes are cooked and cooled, you could make fondant icing (p. 36) flavoured with rum. Soften the icing by warming it gently and use a spoon to trickle it over each little cake.

EUDOXIES
eudoxies

Preparation time: 50 minutes
Cooking time: 20–25 minutes
Makes 30

1 quantity Basic Petits Fours (p. 56)
2 quarters of candied orange peel, or
   60 g (2 oz) chopped candied peel
4 tablespoons apricot jam
2 tablespoons rum
1 quantity Fondant Icing (p. 36)
Orange oil or orange flower water, to taste
Orange food colouring, (optional)

Preheat the oven to 160°C/325°F/Gas Mark 3. Make the basic petits fours and bake them in mini cake tins for 20–25 minutes, until golden brown. Allow them to cool. Place the apricot jam in a small pan and heat gently, then sieve back into the pan, removing any pieces of fruit. Chop three-quarters of the candied orange peel finely (saving the remainder for decoration) and mix with the apricot jam. Add the rum and heat this mixture gently, stirring until it has thickened considerably. Top the petits fours with this.

Flavour the fondant icing with orange oil or orange flower water and delicately colour with a few drops of orange food colouring if desired. Drizzle this over the petits fours and decorate with the remaining crystallized orange peel.

Benjamins

CHOCOLATE PETITS FOURS
fours au chocolat

Preparation time: 50 minutes
Cooking time: 20–25 minutes
Makes 30

1 quantity Ganache (p. 38)
1 quantity Basic Petits Fours (p. 56)
Chocolate sprinkles, to decorate

Make the ganache 2 hours in advance. Preheat the oven to 160°C/325°F/Gas Mark 3. Make the basic petits fours and bake them in mini cake tins for 20–25 minutes, until golden brown. Allow them to cool. Cover the petits fours with little domes of chocolate ganache. Scatter with chocolate sprinkles.

Note: Any shape of mini cake tins can be used if square ones are not available.

RUM AND SULTANA PETITS FOURS
petits fours au rhum

Preparation time: 40 minutes, plus
    48 hours macerating time
Cooking time: 20–25 minutes
Makes 30

100 ml (3½ fl oz) rum
100 ml (3½ fl oz) sweet Madeira
125 g (4¼ oz) sultanas
1 quantity Basic Petits Fours (p. 56)
1 quantity rum-flavoured Crème
    Mousseline (p. 43)
1 quantity rum-flavoured Fondant
    Icing (p. 36)

Prepare 2 days in advance. Place the rum and Madeira in a bowl and add the sultanas. Cover and set aside to macerate for 48 hours.

Drain the sultanas well. Preheat the oven to 160°C/325°F/Gas Mark 3. Make the basic petits fours and bake them in mini cake tins for 20–25 minutes, until golden brown. Allow them to cool. Make the rum-flavoured crème mousseline. Cover the petits fours with this, smoothing it into a dome shape. Place 3 sultanas on top of each petit four and ice them with rum-flavoured fondant icing.

PINEAPPLE TREATS
délicieux à l'ananas

Preparation time: 40 minutes
Cooking time: 20–25 minutes
Makes 30

1 quantity Basic Petits Fours (p. 56)
2 slices of crystallized pineapple
2 tablespoons Kirsch
1 quantity Kirsch-flavoured Fondant Icing (p. 36)

Preheat the oven to 160°C/325°F/Gas Mark 3. Make the basic petits fours and bake them in mini cake tins for 20–25 minutes, until golden brown. Allow them to cool. Chop three-quarters of the pineapple very finely and mix it with the Kirsch in a small bowl. Place a spoonful of the pineapple on top of each little cake. Drizzle the petits fours with Kirsch-flavoured fondant icing. Cut the remaining crystallized pineapple into diamond shapes and place a piece on top of each petit four.

Chocolate Petits Fours

Veronicas

VERONICAS

véronique

Preparation time: 40 minutes
Cooking time: 25 minutes
Makes 30

1 quantity Basic Petits Fours (p. 56)
15 glacé cherries, finely chopped
3 tablespoons redcurrant jelly
1 tablespoon Kirsch
1 quantity Kirsch-flavoured Fondant
Icing (p. 36)
Few drops of red food colouring

Preheat the oven to 160°C/325°F/Gas Mark 3. Make the basic petits fours and bake them in mini cake tins for 20–25 minutes, until golden brown. Allow them to cool.

Place the cherries in a small bowl and mix in the redcurrant jelly and Kirsch. Spread this mixture on top of the petits fours. Delicately colour the fondant icing with red food colouring to make it very pale pink and drizzle this over the petits fours.

MARTINIQUES

martiniquais

Preparation time: 50 minutes
Cooking time: 25 minutes
Makes 30

1 quantity Basic Petits Fours (p. 56)
100 g (3½ oz) butter, softened
125 g (4¼ oz) ground almonds
125 g (4¼ oz) caster sugar
Coffee extract, to taste
1 quantity Coffee Fondant
Icing (p. 36)

Preheat the oven to 160°C/325°F/Gas Mark 3. Make the basic petits fours and bake them in mini round cake tins for 20–25 minutes, until golden brown. Allow them to cool.

Make a filling by beating the butter until pale and creamy. Stir in the almonds, sugar and coffee extract to taste. Use this as topping for the little cakes, heaping it up in a pyramid shape. Cover with coffee-flavoured fondant icing.

ARTICHOKES

Artichauts

Preparation time: 30 minutes
Cooking time: 10–15 minutes
Serves 6

Butter, for greasing
200 g (7 oz) Almond Paste (p. 57)
Few drops of green food colouring
1 egg white
1 teaspoon vanilla extract
60 g (2 oz) almonds, skinned and halved
lengthways (1½ for each petit four)

Preheat the oven to 200°C/400°F/Gas Mark 6 and line a baking tray with buttered greaseproof paper. Place the almond paste in a bowl and add the green food colouring, together with 2 teaspoons of egg white and the vanilla. Slowly knead the ingredients, working them to a soft, malleable and evenly coloured paste. Add a little extra egg white if needed. Take walnut-sized pieces of the paste and shape into cones. Press an almond halve on to the three sides of each cone. Place on the baking tray and bake for 10–15 minutes.

Duchesse Petits Fours

DUCHESSE PETITS FOURS
petits fours duchesse

Preparation time: 10 minutes
Cooking time: 25–30 minutes
Serves 6

110 g (3¾ oz) butter, softened,
   plus extra for greasing
200 g (7 oz) caster sugar
2 eggs, separated
300 g (11 oz) plain flour
1 teaspoon baking powder
Almonds or glacé cherries,
   to decorate

Preheat the oven to 180°C/350°F/Gas Mark 4 and grease a baking tray with butter. Beat the butter with 140 g (4¾ oz) of the sugar and the egg yolks. Stir in the flour and baking powder. Knead to form a smooth dough.

Divide the dough into walnut-sized balls. Place on the baking tray and flatten slightly. Beat the egg whites and brush over the biscuits. Sprinkle with the remaining sugar and decorate each petit four with half an almond or half a glacé cherry. Bake for 25–30 minutes, or until golden brown.

POMPADOURS
pompadours

Preparation time: 1 hour
Cooking time: 20–25 minutes
Makes 30

1 quantity Basic Petits Fours (p. 56)
1 quantity Praline Buttercream (p. 40)
Coffee extract, to taste
30 whole skinned almonds
1 quantity Coffee Fondant
   Icing (p. 36)

Preheat the oven to 160°C/325°F/Gas Mark 3. Make the basic petits fours and bake them in mini oval cake tins for 20–25 minutes, until golden brown. Allow them to cool. Make the praline buttercream and flavour it with a little coffee extract. Spread this on top of the petits fours, smoothing it into a dome shape. Top each one with a toasted almond and cover with coffee-flavoured fondant icing.

Note: Any shape of mini cake tins can be used if oval tins are not available.

OTHER SMALL CAKES

*Madeleines and financiers are just two of the most
popular small cakes in the French pastry repertoire.
Often baked in a mould with a traditional shape,
they are perfect for afternoon tea.*

COCONUT MACAROONS
gâteaux à la noix de coco

Preparation time: 10 minutes
Cooking time: 20 minutes
Serves 6

250 g (9 oz) desiccated coconut
250 g (9 oz) caster sugar
3 eggs, separated

Preheat the oven to 120°C/250°F/Gas Mark 1. Line two baking trays with greaseproof paper. Mix the coconut and sugar with the egg yolks. Whisk the whites until they form soft peaks and fold into the coconut mixture. Arrange in small mounds on the baking trays, leaving space between them. Bake for 20 minutes.

CONGOLAIS
congolais

Preparation time: 10 minutes
Cooking time: 30–45 minutes
Serves 6

Butter, for greasing, or edible rice paper
   (optional)
300 g (11 oz) caster sugar
5 egg whites
250 g (9 oz) desiccated coconut
1 teaspoon vanilla extract

Line a baking tray with buttered baking parchment or the rice paper. Preheat the oven to 150°C/300°F/Gas Mark 2. Put the sugar and egg whites in a heatproof bowl set over a pan of barely simmering water, and stir until warm and the sugar is dissolved. Stir in the coconut and vanilla. Put pyramid-shaped piles of the mixture on the prepared tray. Bake for 30–45 minutes, or until golden brown.

MADELEINES
madeleines

Preparation time: 20 minutes,
    plus 2 hours chilling time
Cooking time: 8–10 minutes
Serves 6

125 g (4¼ oz) butter, melted and cooled,
    plus extra for greasing
2 large eggs
150 g (5 oz) caster sugar
150 g (5 oz) plain flour, sifted,
    plus extra for dusting
1 teaspoon vanilla extract, or grated zest
    of 1 lemon
pinch of salt

Preheat the oven to 200°C/400°F/Gas Mark 6. Grease madeleine tins with butter and lightly dust with flour. Whisk the eggs and sugar with an electric whisk for 5 minutes until pale and tripled in volume. Slowly fold in the flour and butter, then the vanilla, lemon zest or pinch of salt. Chill the batter in the refrigerator for 2 hours before baking. Pour into the prepared tins, half-full, and bake for 8–10 minutes.

ALMOND BUNS
petits pains aux amandes

Preparation time: 20 minutes
Cooking time: 30 minutes
Serves 6

100 g (3½ oz) butter, softened,
    plus extra for greasing
125 g (4¼ oz) ground almonds
250 g (9 oz) caster sugar
1 egg
250 g (9 oz) plain flour
1 teaspoon salt

Preheat the oven to 180°C/350°F/Gas Mark 4 and grease a baking tray with butter. Mix the almonds with the sugar. Add the egg, butter, flour and salt and mix to a soft dough. Knead the dough lightly and form into small bun shapes. Place on the prepared tray and bake for 10 minutes, then increase the temperature to 200°C/400°F/Gas Mark 6 and bake for a further 20 minutes.

Madeleines

VISITANDINES

visitandines

Preparation time: 25 minutes
Cooking time: 30 minutes
Serves 6

125 g (4¼ oz) butter, softened,
    plus extra for greasing
5 egg whites
125 g (4¼ oz) plain flour, sifted
250 g (9 oz) caster sugar
100 g (3½ oz) ground almonds
Grated zest of ½ lemon

Preheat the oven to 160°C/325°F/Gas Mark 3. Grease 10-cm (4-inch) barquette moulds with butter. Mix together the flour, sugar, almonds, lemon zest and softened butter. In a separate bowl. whisk the egg whites to soft peaks with an electric whisk, then slowly fold into the mixture. Pour the mixture into the prepared tins. Bake for 30 minutes.

POTATOES

pommes de terre

Preparation time: 35 minutes
Cooking time: 15–20 minutes
Serves 6

60 g (2 oz) butter, softened,
    plus extra for greasing
250 g (9 oz) caster sugar
1 egg, plus 3 egg whites
50 g (1¾ oz) plain flour
2 teaspoons potato flour
1½ teaspoons baking powder
120 g (4¼ oz) ground almonds
1 teaspoon vanilla extract
100 g (3½ oz) cocoa powder
60 g (2 oz) slivered almonds

Preheat the oven to 160°C/325°F/Gas Mark 3 and grease a baking tray with butter. Beat 150 g (5 oz) of the sugar with the whole egg. Stir in the butter, followed by the flour, potato flour and baking powder. Spread this mixture evenly over the baking tray. Bake for 15–20 minutes, then allow to cool. When cold, break into small crumbs and place these into a bowl. Stir in the remaining sugar, the ground almonds, vanilla and half the cocoa powder. Whisk the 3 egg whites until they form stiff peaks and fold into the crumb mixture. Take pieces of the dough and roll into elongated balls so that they look like small potatoes. Roll these around a plate containing the remaining cocoa and insert slivered almonds randomly to look like potato 'eyes'.

Note: As a short cut, you can use slightly stale sponge cakes (Madeleines, p. 82) for the basic cake crumb mixture.

Visitandines

Financiers

FINANCIERS
financiers

Preparation time: 40 minutes
Cooking time: 20 minutes
Serves 6

120 g (4 oz) butter, softened,
    plus extra for greasing
4 egg whites
125 g (4¼ oz) caster sugar
100 g (3½ oz) plain flour, sifted

Preheat the oven to 180°C/350°F/Gas Mark 4. Grease small financier moulds with butter. Whisk the egg whites and sugar with an electric whisk until stiff and glossy, then fold in the flour and butter. Half-fill the prepared moulds with the mixture and bake for 20 minutes.

SMALL SPICE BREADS
petits pains d'épice ronds

Preparation time: 10 minutes
Cooking time: 25 minutes
Serves 6

Butter, for greasing
500 g (1 lb 2 oz) runny honey
200 g (7 oz) thick crème fraîche
60 g (2 oz) caster sugar
½ teaspoon ground black pepper
1½ teaspoons baking powder
500 g (1 lb 2 oz) plain flour

Preheat the oven to 160°C/325°F/Gas Mark 3 and grease a baking tray with butter. Mix the honey, crème fraîche, sugar, and pepper together. In a separate bowl, mix together the flour and baking powder and pour into the other mixture, adding a little extra flour if necessary to make a thick dough. Using a spoon or piping bag fitted with a plain nozzle, place walnut-sized balls of the mixture on the baking tray. Bake for 20–25 minutes until puffed and golden.

GÂTEAUX

Any cake in France may be considered a gâteau, but it often refers more specifically to a sponge cake made with almond flour. From sponge cakes and fruit cakes to nut cakes and brioches, these classic French desserts are often iced and filled with delicious buttercream, and make a splendid conclusion to a meal, or a centrepiece in an afternoon tea.

FRUIT CAKES

Macerating fruit in liqueur before adding it to the cake mixture will soften the fruit and enrich the flavour of the cake. This can be substituted with a warm fruit juice or water.

ORANGE CAKE
gâteau à l'orange

Preparation time: 20 minutes
Cooking time: 40 minutes
Serves 6

Butter, for greasing
3 eggs, separated
125 g (4¼ oz) caster sugar
60 g (2 oz) potato flour
125 g (4¼ oz) ground almonds
Grated zest and juice of 1 orange

Preheat the oven to 160°C/325°F/Gas Mark 3. Grease a 20-cm (8-inch) round cake tin with butter. Beat the egg yolks and mix in the sugar, flour, almonds, and orange zest and juice. Whisk the egg whites to stiff peaks and fold into the cake mixture. Pour into the prepared cake tin and bake for 40 minutes.

VALENCIA CAKE
valencia

Preparation time: 25 minutes
Cooking time: 45 minutes
Serves 6

Butter, for greasing
7 eggs
250 g (9 oz) ground almonds
250 g (9 oz) caster sugar
3 unwaxed oranges
125 g (4¼ oz) potato flour
200 g (7 oz) icing sugar

Preheat the oven to 150°C/300°F/Gas Mark 2 and grease a 23-cm (9-inch) cake tin with butter. Put one whole egg in a bowl together with six egg yolks. Add the ground almonds and the caster sugar. Mix thoroughly, then add the grated zest and juice of one orange and the potato flour. In a separate bowl, whisk the six egg whites until they form stiff peaks, then fold these into the cake mixture. Pour the mixture into the cake tin and bake for 45 minutes, covering with foil if necessary towards the end. Mix the juice of the two remaining oranges with the icing sugar until smooth, then use this to ice the cake once it has completely cooled.

ORANGE DELIGHT
délice d'oranges

Preparation time: 25 minutes
Cooking time: 30 minutes
Serves 6

Butter, for greasing
250 g (9 oz) caster sugar
5 eggs
125 g (4¼ oz) candied orange peel
300 g (11 oz) plain flour, sieved with
   2 teaspoons baking powder
Juice of 2 oranges
200 g (7 oz) icing sugar

Preheat the oven to 200°C/400°F/Gas Mark 6 and grease a 23-cm (9-inch) cake tin with butter. Whisk the sugar and eggs for 10 minutes until pale and tripled in volume. Finely chop half the candied orange peel and add to the egg mixture. In a separate bowl, combine the flour and baking powder and then fold into the wet mixture.

Pour into the cake tin and bake for 30 minutes. Mix the orange juice with the icing sugar until smooth, then use this to ice the cake once it has completely cooled. Decorate with the remaining candied orange peel.

RAISIN CAKE
biscuit aux raisins

Preparation time: 25 minutes, plus 30
   minutes soaking time
Cooking time: 45 minutes
Serves 6

Butter, for greasing
60 g (2 oz) currants
70 g (2½ oz) Muscatel raisins
50 g (1¾ oz) sultanas
50 ml (2 fl oz) rum
5 eggs, separated
125 g (4¼ oz) caster sugar
100 ml (3½ fl oz) Kirsch
65 g (2¼ oz) plain flour
100 g (3½ oz) potato flour

Preheat the oven to 160°C/325°F/Gas Mark 3 and grease a 20-cm (8-inch) cake tin with butter. Soak the currants, raisins and sultanas in the rum for 30 minutes.

Using a spatula, beat the egg yolks with the sugar in a bowl for 5 minutes, until light and fluffy. Add the Kirsch and both types of flour and mix well. Add the raisins, currants and sultanas and their soaking liquid. In a separate bowl, whisk the egg whites until they form stiff peaks, then fold into the mixture.

Pour the mixture immediately into the cake tin and bake for 45 minutes, covering with foil towards the end if necessary.

ORANGE GÂTEAU
gâteau d'oranges

Preparation time: 30 minutes
Cooking time: 35–40 minutes
Serves 6

Butter, for greasing
170 g (5¾ oz) caster sugar
4 small eggs
Grated zest and juice of 2 unwaxed oranges
200 g (7 oz) plain flour
1½ teaspoons baking powder
250 g (9 oz) icing sugar
Candied peel, to decorate (optional)

Preheat the oven to 180°C/350°F/Gas Mark 4 and grease a 20-cm (8-inch) cake tin with butter. Whisk the sugar and eggs for 10 minutes until pale and tripled in volume. Fold in the orange zest, flour and baking powder. Pour the mixture into the cake tin and bake for 35–40 minutes.

Meanwhile, sieve the icing sugar into a bowl and stir in enough orange juice to make a smooth icing. When the cake is cold, ice it with the orange-flavoured icing and decorate with candied peel, if desired.

CAKE WITH CANDIED FRUIT
délicieux aux fruits confits

Preparation time: 20 minutes
Cooking time: 40 minutes
Serves 6

Butter, for greasing
60 g (2 oz) glacé cherries, halved
100 ml (3½ fl oz) Kirsch
200 g (7 oz) plain flour
2 teaspoons baking powder
60 g (2 oz) caster sugar
100 ml (3½ fl oz) milk
2 eggs, lightly beaten
60 g (2 oz) angelica, finely chopped
Grated zest of 1 unwaxed lemon

Preheat the oven to 180°C/350°F/Gas Mark 4 and grease a 20-cm (8-inch) cake tin with butter. Place the glacé cherries and Kirsch in a small bowl and set aside. In a separate bowl, combine the flour and baking powder. Stir in the sugar, followed by the milk, eggs, glacé cherries with their soaking liquid, the angelica and lemon zest.

Pour the mixture into the cake tin and bake for 40 minutes, covering with foil towards the end of the cooking time if necessary.

Orange Gâteau

BANANA GÂTEAU
gâteau de bananes

Preparation time: 30 minutes
Cooking time: 30 minutes
Serves 6

160 g (5¼ oz) butter, softened,
    plus extra for greasing
200 g (7 oz) caster sugar
125 ml (4½ fl oz) milk
2 eggs, beaten
200 g (7 oz) plain flour
3 teaspoons baking powder
1 quantity Kirsch-flavoured Syrup
    for Babas (p. 48) (optional)
4 bananas
250 g (9 oz) Sweetened Whipped
    Cream (p. 38)
Icing sugar, to decorate (optional)

Preheat the oven to 160°C/325°F/Gas Mark 3 and grease an 18-cm (7-inch) square or 20 × 10-cm (8 × 4-inch) loaf tin with butter. Beat the butter and sugar together until pale and creamy. Stir the milk and eggs. In a separate bowl, combine the flour and baking powder, then add to the butter and sugar mixture. Pour the mixture into the tin and bake for 30 minutes.

When the cake has cooled, cut it in half horizontally. If desired, brush the cut surfaces of the cake with Kirsch-flavoured syrup. Peel the bananas and cut lengthways. Arrange these on the bottom layer of the cake, fill with half the whipped cream and replace the top of the cake. You could also spread the whipped cream over the bottom layer of the cake, and then add the banana slices on top. Dust with icing sugar, if desired.

VENETIAN GÂTEAU
gâteau vénitien

Preparation time: 25 minutes,
    plus 1 hour chilling time
Cooking time: 1 hour
Serves 6

250 g (9 oz) butter, softened, plus extra
    for greasing
150 g (5 oz) caster sugar
5 egg yolks
50 ml (2 fl oz) rum
250 g (9 oz) plain flour
2 teaspoons baking powder
200 g (7 oz) apricot jam

Preheat the oven to 140°C/275°F/Gas Mark 1 and grease a baking tray with butter. Put the sugar and 4 egg yolks in a bowl. Whisk them thoroughly, then add the butter and rum. In a separate bowl, combine the flour and baking powder, then add to the mixture. When the mixture is smoothly blended, cover the bowl and chill in the refrigerator for 1 hour.

Dust the work surface with flour. Divide the dough into two equal portions. Roll out one half to form a 23-cm (9-inch) circle and place on the baking tray. Spread with a layer of apricot jam, leaving a 2.5-cm (1-inch) margin around the edge. Roll out the remaining dough to match the first circle and place over the jam. Mix the remaining egg yolk with 1 tablespoon of water and brush to glaze. Bake for 1 hour, or until golden brown and cooked on the base.

ELECTRA GÂTEAU

gâteau electra

Preparation time: 10 minutes
Cooking time: 40 minutes
Serves 6

150 g (5 oz) butter, softened,
    plus extra for greasing
500 g (1 lb 2 oz) plain flour
2 eggs
Pinch of salt
1 teaspoon baking powder
Grated zest of 1 unwaxed lemon
250 g (9 oz) caster sugar
1 jar apricot jam

Preheat the oven to 180°C/350°F/Gas Mark 4 and grease a 23-cm (9-inch) deep tart tin with a removable base with butter. Mix the flour and baking powder in a bowl, then make a well and then add the eggs, salt and butter. Add the lemon zest and the sugar. Mix by hand to obtain a crumbly dough. Place half of the mixture into the tin and lightly press to level the surface. Spread the apricot jam on top. Cover with the remaining dough mixture, leaving it crumbly, and bake for 40 minutes until light golden.

FRUIT CAKE

fruit cake

Preparation time: 25 minutes
Cooking time: 50-60 minutes
Serves 6

40 g (1½ oz) candied fruit
2 tablespoons rum
175 g (6 oz) butter, softened,
    plus extra for greasing
120 g (4 oz) caster sugar
1 teaspoon salt
3 eggs
250 g (9 oz) plain flour
1½ teaspoons baking powder
50 g (1¾ oz) sultanas
50 g (1¾ oz) currants

Set aside 15 g (½ oz) of attractive candied fruit to decorate the cake. Chop the remainder, put in a small bowl with the rum and leave to macerate.

Preheat the oven to 180°C/350°F/Gas Mark 4 and grease a 900-g (2-lb) loaf tin with butter. In a bowl, beat the butter, sugar and salt until pale and creamy. Beat in the eggs, one by one. In a separate bowl, combine the flour and baking powder, then add to the mixture until just combined. Mix in the macerated fruit and rum, sultanas and currants.

Put the cake mixture into the prepared loaf tin. Level the surface and bake for 50-60 minutes, covering with foil if the cake browns too quickly. Decorate the cake with the candied fruit.

NUT CAKES

*Ground nuts complement light cake bases and add
flavour and a moist texture to cakes. Nuts can also
be toasted in an oven until they are lightly browned.*

LORRAINE GÂTEAU
gâteau lorrain

Preparation time: 15 minutes
Cooking time: 50 minutes
Serves 6

160 g (5¼ oz) butter, softened,
   plus extra for greasing
100 g (3½ oz) plain flour
100 g (3½ oz) potato flour
1 teaspoon baking powder
4 eggs
160 g (5¼ oz) caster sugar
60 g (2 oz) almonds, skinned and chopped
40 g (1½ oz) angelica, chopped
60 g (2 oz) nibbed sugar

Preheat the oven to 180°C/350°F/Gas Mark 4 and
grease a 20-cm (8-inch) cake tin with butter. In a bowl
mix together the plain flour, potato flour and baking
powder. Make a well in the centre and add the eggs,
caster sugar, and softened butter. Mix with a spatula
for 10 minutes until smooth and creamy. Pour the
mixture into the cake tin and sprinkle with the almonds
and angelica. Bake for 50 minutes. When the cake is
cool, sprinkle with the nibbed sugar.

FLOURLESS ALMOND GÂTEAU
gâteau aux amandes

Preparation time: 20 minutes
Cooking time: 40–45 minutes
Serves 6

100 g (3½ oz) butter, softened,
   plus extra for greasing
125 g (4¼ oz) caster sugar
200 g (7 oz) ground almonds
3 eggs
100 ml (3½ fl oz) crème fraîche
5 tablespoons Kirsch

Preheat the oven to 200°C/400°F/Gas Mark 6 and grease an 18-cm (7-inch) cake tin with butter. Place the butter and sugar in a bowl and beat until pale and creamy. Beat in the ground almonds, eggs, crème fraîche and the Kirsch. When the mixture is smooth, pour it into the cake tin and place in a roasting tin half-filled with hot water. Bake for 40–45 minutes, until set, covering with foil towards the end if necessary.

HAZELNUT GÂTEAU
gâteau noisette

Preparation time: 15 minutes
Cooking time: 25 minutes
Serves 6

Butter, for greasing
125 g (4¼ oz) caster sugar
3 eggs, separated
125 g (4¼ oz) ground hazelnuts
25 g (1 oz) potato flour
1¼ teaspoons baking powder
50 ml (2 fl oz) rum

Preheat the oven to 160°C/325°F/Gas Mark 3. Grease a 20-cm (8-inch) cake tin with butter and line with greaseproof paper. In a bowl, whisk the sugar and the egg yolks for 10 minutes until pale and tripled in volume. In a medium bowl, combine the ground hazelnuts, potato flour and baking powder. Add this and the rum to the wet mixture. In a separate bowl, whisk the egg whites until they form stiff peaks, then fold these into the cake mixture. Pour into the cake tin and bake for 25 minutes.

COLETTE GÂTEAU
gâteau colette

Preparation time: 15 minutes
Cooking time: 30 minutes
Serves 6

60 g (2 oz) butter, softened,
   plus extra for greasing
125 g (4¼ oz) caster sugar
4 eggs, separated
75 g (2½ oz) plain flour
2 teaspoons baking powder
75 g (2½ oz) ground almonds
100 ml (3½ fl oz) rum

Preheat the oven to 160°C/325°F/Gas Mark 3 and grease a 23-cm (9-inch) cake tin with butter. Whisk the sugar with the egg yolks in a bowl for 10 minutes until pale and tripled in volume. Add the butter. In a separate bowl, combine flour, baking powder and ground almonds together and add to the wet mixture, then add the rum. In another bowl, whisk the egg whites until they form stiff peaks, then fold it into the cake mixture. Pour into the cake tin and bake for 30 minutes.

SPECIALITY CAKES

*Cakes in this category include a Savarin – a rich
yeast cake baked in a ring mold and soaked in a rum
or Kirsch syrup – and a Genoa cake, a light sponge
cake made with butter.*

BRIANÇON GÂTEAU
gâteau briançonnais

Preparation time: 15 minutes
Cooking time: 45 minutes
Serves 6

Butter, for greasing
100 g (3½ oz) caster sugar
5 eggs, separated
50 g (1¾ oz) potato flour
50 g (1¾ oz) rice flour
Pinch of salt
Grated zest of 1 unwaxed lemon
2 teaspoons baking powder

Preheat the oven to 160°C/325°F/Gas Mark 3 and grease
a 23-cm (9-inch) cake tin with butter. Whisk the sugar
with the egg yolks in a bowl for 10 minutes until pale
and at least tripled in volume. In a separate bowl,
combine the potato flour, rice flour, salt, lemon zest
and baking powder and then add to the egg yolk
mixture. In a separate bowl, whisk the egg whites until
they form stiff peaks, then fold these into the cake
mixture. Pour into the cake tin and bake for 45 minutes,
covering with foil towards the end if necessary.

FLEMISH CAKE
biscuit flamand

Preparation time: 15 minutes
Cooking time: 30–35 minutes
Serves 6

Butter, for greasing
100 ml (3½ fl oz) milk
250 g (9 oz) caster sugar
Pinch of salt
4 eggs
250 g (9 oz) plain flour
1½ teaspoons baking powder
125 g (4¼ oz) butter, softened
Flavour the cake mixture, to taste,
   with any of the following:
   125 g (4¼ oz) currants
   or 100 g (3½ oz) cocoa powder
   or 100 g (3½ oz) ground almonds
   or 100 g (3½ oz) ground hazelnuts
   or 1 teaspoon vanilla extract
   or the grated zest of 1 unwaxed
     orange or lemon

Preheat the oven to 160°C/325°F/Gas Mark 3 and grease a 20-cm (8-inch) cake tin with butter. In a bowl mix the milk, sugar and salt. Beat in the eggs. In a separate bowl, combine the flour and the baking powder. Mix the flour and butter into the wet mixture a little at a time, alternating them. Add your chosen flavouring, mixing quickly but thoroughly. Pour the mixture into the cake tin and bake for 30–35 minutes.

PRINCES' GÂTEAU
gâteau des princes

Preparation time: 20 minutes
Cooking time: 30–35 minutes
Serves 6

150 g (5 oz) butter, softened,
   plus extra for greasing
250 g (9 oz) plain flour, plus extra for dusting
2 egg yolks plus 1 whole egg
90 g (3¼ oz) crème fraîche
125 g (4¼ oz) caster sugar
1½ teaspoons baking powder
1 quantity Almond Cream (p. 44)

Preheat the oven to 180°C/350°F/Gas Mark 3 and grease a 23-cm (9-inch) deep tart tin with a removable base with butter. Combine the flour and baking powder in a mixing bowl. Make a well in the centre and into this place the egg yolk, crème fraîche, sugar and butter. Mix thoroughly to form a soft dough. Dust the work surface with flour. Roll out two-thirds of the dough and use it to line the base and sides of the tin, moulding it with your fingers to fit neatly. Spread almond cream on top. Roll out the remaining dough. Cut it into strips 1 cm (½ inch) wide and arrange them on top of the almond cream in a lattice pattern. Beat the remaining whole egg and brush it over the surface of the cake to glaze. Bake for 30–35 minutes or until golden brown.

Lady Cake

LADY CAKE

biscuit de dames

Preparation time: 15 minutes, plus
   30 minutes soaking time
Cooking time: 30 minutes
Serves 6

120 g (4 oz) butter, softened,
   plus extra for greasing
10 g raisins
100 ml (3 ½ fl oz) rum
150 g (5 oz) plain flour
Pinch of salt
1½ teaspoons baking powder
150 g (5 oz) caster sugar
3 eggs
2 teaspoons vanilla extra

Preheat the oven to 160°C /325°F / Gas Mark 3 and
grease a 20-cm (8-inch) cake tin with butter. Soak the
raisins in the rum for 30 minutes. In a large bowl, mix
together the flour, salt and baking powder. In a separate
bowl, beat together sugar and butter. Add the eggs,
vanilla and the strained raisins. Add to the dry mixture
and mix well. Pour the batter into the cake tin and
bake for 10 minutes. Increase the heat to 200°C /400°F /
Gas Mark 6 and bake for another 20 minutes.

GENOA CAKE

pain de gênes

Preparation time: 25 minutes
Cooking time: 45 minutes
Serves 6

125 g (4¼ oz) butter, softened,
   plus extra for greasing
300 g (11 oz) caster sugar
4 eggs
250 g (9 oz) ground almonds
100 g (3½ oz) plain flour
2 tablespoons Kirsch

Preheat the oven to 160°C/325°F/Gas Mark 3. Grease
a 20-cm (8-inch) cake tin with butter and line it with
greaseproof paper. Beat the butter and sugar until
pale and creamy, then beat in the eggs, one at a time.
Stir in the ground almonds, flour and Kirsch. Pour the
mixture into the cake tin and bake for 45 minutes,
covering with foil towards the end if necessary.

ORANGE-FLOWER GENOA CAKE
pain de gênes à l'orange

Preparation time: 30 minutes
Cooking time: 50 minutes
Serves 6

160 g (5½ oz) butter, plus extra for greasing
250 g (9 oz) caster sugar
5 eggs
300 g (11 oz) ground almonds
125 g (4¼ oz) plain flour
Grated zest of 2 unwaxed oranges
1 teaspoon orange flower water
Candied orange, cut into small thin strips,
    to decorate

Preheat the oven to 160°C/325°F/Gas Mark 3. Grease a 23-cm (9-inch) cake tin with butter and line it with greaseproof paper. Beat the butter and sugar until pale and creamy, then beat in the eggs, one at a time, followed by the ground almonds, flour, orange zest and orange flower water. Pour the mixture into the cake tin and bake for 50 minutes, covering with foil towards the end if necessary. Turn out the cake, allow to cool then peel off the paper. Sprinkle the cake with icing sugar and decorate with a few candied orange strips.

ORANGE GENOA CAKE
pain de gênes à l'orange

Preparation time: 25 minutes
Cooking time: 45 minutes
Serves 6

200 g (7 oz) butter, softened,
    plus extra for greasing
6 eggs, separated
Grated zest of 2 unwaxed oranges
100 g (3½ oz) rice flour
250 g (9 oz) caster sugar
250 g (9 oz) ground almonds

Preheat the oven to 160°C/325°F/Gas Mark 3. Grease a 23-cm (9-inch) cake tin with butter and line it with greaseproof paper. Whisk the egg whites until they form stiff peaks, then fold in the egg yolks and grated orange. In another bowl combine the rice flour, caster sugar and ground almonds. Fold this mixture into the egg mixture and finally add the butter. Pour the mixture into the cake tin and bake for 45 minutes, covering with foil towards the end if necessary.

Note: Genoa cake tastes even better the day after it is made.

ANGEL CAKE
gâteau mousseline

Preparation time: 15 minutes
Cooking time: 45 minutes
Serves 6

Butter, for greasing
5 eggs, separated
75 g (2½ oz) caster sugar
125 g (4¼ oz) potato flour
Grated zest of 1 lemon

Preheat the oven to 160°C/325°F/Gas Mark 3 and grease a 23-cm (9-inch) cake tin with butter. Whisk the sugar and egg yolks for 5 minutes until pale and tripled in volume. In a separate bowl and using an electric whisk, whisk the egg whites to stiff peaks. Stir the flour and lemon zest into the sugar and egg mixture, then fold in the egg whites. Pour into the cake tin and bake for 45 minutes, until risen and golden.

Angel Cake

AUVERGNE GÂTEAU
gâteau auvergnat

Preparation time: 10 minutes
Cooking time: 25–30 minutes
Serves 6

Butter, for greasing
200 g (7 oz) plain flour
2 teaspoons baking powder
80 g (2¾ oz) caster sugar
125 g (4¼ oz) crème fraîche
2 eggs, separated
1½ tablespoons rum

Preheat the oven to 160°C/325°F/Gas Mark 3 and grease an 18-cm (7-inch) cake tin with butter. Combine the flour and the baking powder. Beat the sugar with the crème fraîche until smooth, then beat in the egg yolks. Stir in the rum. In a separate bowl, whisk the egg whites until they form stiff peaks and then fold these gently into the cake mixture. Pour into the cake tin and bake for 25–30 minutes.

GERMAINE'S GÂTEAU
gâteau germaine

Preparation time: 15 minutes
Cooking time: 25–30 minutes
Serves 6

125 g (4¼ oz) butter, melted and cooled, plus extra for greasing
250 g (9 oz) caster sugar
1 teaspoon vanilla extract
50 g (1¾ oz) plain flour
1½ teaspoons baking powder
7 egg whites

Preheat the oven to 190°C/375°F/Gas Mark 5 and grease a 23-cm (9-inch) cake tin with butter. Combine the melted butter with the sugar and vanilla. In a separate bowl, sieve the flour and baking powder and add them to the wet mixture. In another separate bowl, whisk the egg whites until they form stiff peaks and fold them into the cake mixture. Pour the mixture into the cake tin and bake for 25–30 minutes.

THE LITTLE DUKE'S GÂTEAU
gâteau petit-duc

Preparation time: 15 minutes
Cooking time: 25–30 minutes
Serves 6

60 g (2 oz) butter, softened, plus extra for greasing
175 g (6 oz) caster sugar
Grated zest of 1 unwaxed lemon
100 g (3½ oz) plain flour
6 egg whites

Preheat the oven to 200°C/400°F/Gas Mark 6 and grease a 23-cm (9-inch) cake tin with butter. Beat the sugar, butter and lemon zest together first, then stir in the flour. In a separate bowl, whisk the egg whites until they form stiff peaks and fold into the mixture. Pour the mixture into the cake tin and bake for 25–30 minutes.

NORWEGIAN LAYERED GÂTEAU

gâteau fourré norvégien

Preparation time: 35 minutes
Cooking time: 45 minutes
Serves 6

Butter, for greasing
300 g (11 oz) caster sugar
6 eggs
250 ml (8 fl oz) Kirsch
250 g (9 oz) plain flour
2 teaspoons baking powder
1 quantity Crème Pâtissière (p. 41)
250 g (9 oz) icing sugar
Glacé cherries, halved

Preheat the oven to 180°C/350°F/Gas Mark 3 and grease a 23-cm (9-inch) cake tin with butter. Whisk the sugar and eggs for 10 minutes until pale and at least tripled in volume. Fold in 150 ml (¼ pint) of the Kirsch. In a separate bowl, combine the flour and baking powder, then add to the wet mixture. Pour the mixture into the cake tin and bake for 45 minutes.

Once cooled, turn the cake over so the smooth surface is uppermost and cut it horizontally in 3. Brush the remaining Kirsch over the cut surfaces of the cake and spread crème pâtissière between the three layers. Cover with the top cake layer. Beat the icing sugar with 2 tablespoons of cold water until smooth, adding more water a drop at a time if necessary. Spread over the top layer of the cake and decorate with glacé cherries.

Note: The cake can be made and decorated a day in advance of eating if desired.

POUND CAKE

quatre-quarts

Preparation time: 20 minutes
Cooking time: 30–40 minutes
Serves 6

Butter, about 150 g (5 oz),
    plus extra for greasing
3 eggs
Plain flour, about 150 g (5 oz)
Caster sugar, about 150 g (5 oz)
Grated zest of 1 lemon

Preheat the oven to 160°C/325°F/Gas Mark 3. Grease a 23-cm (9-inch) round cake tin with butter. Weigh the eggs and measure out equal quantities of the flour, sugar and butter. Melt the butter and allow to cool. Separate the eggs and whisk the yolks with the sugar for 5 minutes using an electric whisk, until pale and tripled in volume. Gradually fold in the flour and butter in alternating spoonfuls. Add the lemon zest. Whisk the egg whites to stiff peaks and fold into the cake mixture. Fill the prepared cake tin two-thirds full. Bake for 30–40 minutes.

SAVARIN
savarin

Preparation time: 30 minutes,
     plus rising and cooling time
Cooking time: 30 minutes
Serves 6

15 g (½ oz) fresh yeast
50 ml (2 fl oz) lukewarm milk
250 g (9 oz) plain flour
3 eggs
125 g (4¼ oz) butter, softened,
     plus extra for greasing
30 g (1¼ oz) caster sugar
1½ teaspoons salt
½ quantity Rum Sauce (p. 46)

Prepare 6 hours in advance. Add the yeast to the milk and stir to dissolve. Sieve the flour into a bowl, make a well in the centre and pour in the yeast and milk. Add the eggs and beat for a few minutes; the dough should come away easily from the hand or beaters. Cover the bowl and leave the dough to rise at room temperature until doubled in volume.

Preheat the oven to 200°C/400°F/Gas Mark 6 and grease a large ring or savarin mould with butter. Beat the butter, sugar and salt into the dough until very smooth. Place the dough evenly into the mould, filling it two-thirds full. Bake for 30 minutes. While the savarin is still warm and in the mould, pour over the rum sauce. Leave to soak and cool before turning out.

ORANGE SAVARIN
savarin à l'orange

Preparation time: 10 minutes
Cooking time: 30 minutes
Serves 6

Butter, for greasing
90 g (3¼ oz) plain flour
1 teaspoon baking powder
100 g (3½ oz) caster sugar
6 tablespoons light-flavoured vegetable oil
4 eggs
Juice and grated zest of 3 unwaxed oranges
1 unwaxed orange

Preheat the oven to 160°C/325°F/Gas Mark 3 and grease a 20-cm (8-inch) ring or savarin mould with butter. Combine the flour, baking powder and sugar in a bowl, make a well and pour the oil into this, together with 2 eggs and the orange zest. Beat well to make a smooth batter. Beat in the remaining 2 eggs. When the mixture is smooth, pour it into the mould, filling it only two-thirds full.

Bake for 20 minutes, or until golden brown, then increase the temperature to 200°C/400°F/Gas Mark 6 and continue cooking for a further 10 minutes. Brush the savarin, while still in the mould, with the orange juice. Turn out and decorate with orange slices or segments cut from the whole orange.

Orange Savarin

SUPERFINE SAVARIN
savarin surfin

Preparation time: 15 minutes
Cooking time: 20–25 minutes
Serves 6

70 g (2½ oz) butter, melted,
   plus extra for greasing
160 g (5¼ oz) plain flour
1 teaspoon baking powder
4 eggs, separated
200 g (7 oz) caster sugar
Pinch of salt
4 tablespoons milk
125 g (4¼ oz) currants
150 ml (¼ pint) Rum-Flavoured
   Syrup (p. 49)

Preheat the oven to 200°C/400°F/Gas Mark 6 and grease a 23-cm (9-inch) savarin mould with butter. Sieve together the flour and baking powder. In a separate bowl, whisk the egg yolks, sugar and salt in a bowl. Whisk in the milk to make a smooth batter, then stir in the flour mixture, melted butter and currants. Whisk the egg whites until they form stiff peaks and fold these into the batter. Transfer the mixture to the savarin mould and bake for 20–25 minutes. While still warm and in the tin, brush the savarin generously with rum-flavoured syrup.

CRUMBLY SHORTCAKE
gâteau de sable

Preparation time: 15 minutes
Cooking time: 35 minutes
Serves 8

125 g (4¼ oz) butter, softened,
   plus extra for greasing
Icing sugar, for dusting
250 g (9 oz) caster sugar
250 g (9 oz) plain flour
125 g (4¼ oz) potato flour
Pinch of salt
1 teaspoon vanilla extract
5 eggs

Preheat the oven to 180°C/350°F/Gas Mark 4 and grease a 23-cm (9-inch) shallow cake tin with butter. Dust the inside of the tin with a little icing sugar. Beat the butter until pale and creamy, then mix in the sugar, plain flour, potato flour, salt and vanilla. Beat in the eggs, adding them one at a time. Transfer the mixture to the tin and bake for 35 minutes. Allow to cook and dust with icing sugar.

RUM CAKE
cake au rhum

Preparation time: 25 minutes
Cooking time: 45–50 minutes
Serves 6

160 g (5½ oz) butter, softened,
   plus extra for greasing
40 g (1½ oz) candied fruit
50 g (1¾ oz) sultanas, chopped
50 g (1¾ oz) currants, chopped
20 ml (scant 1 fl oz) rum
125 g (4¼ oz) caster sugar
Pinch of salt
3 eggs
250 g (9 oz) plain flour
2 teaspoons baking powder

Preheat the oven to 180°C/350°F/Gas Mark 4. Grease a 20 × 10-cm (8 × 4-inch) loaf tin with butter and line with greaseproof paper. Reserve some of the candied fruit, if you wish, to decorate the cake, and finely chop the remainder. Place in a small bowl with the sultanas, currants and rum.

Beat the butter with the sugar until pale and creamy, then beat in the salt and the eggs, one at a time. In a separate bowl, combine the four and baking powder, then add to the mixture and beat again. Stir in the fruit and its soaking liquid.

Pour the mixture into the tin and bake for 45–50 minutes, covering with foil towards the end if necessary. Decorate the finished cake with the reserved candied fruit if liked.

RUM CAKE WITH CITRON
cake fin

Preparation time: 25 minutes
Cooking: 50–60 minutes
Serves 6

250 g (9 oz) butter,
   plus extra for greasing
60 g (2 oz) candied fruit
60 g (2 oz) candied citron peel
125 g (4¼ oz) currants
50 g (1¾ oz) sultanas
40 ml (scant 2 fl oz) rum
250 g (9 oz) caster sugar
6 eggs
300 g (11 oz) plain flour
2 teaspoons baking powder

Preheat the oven to 180°C/350°F/Gas Mark 4. Grease a 23 × 13-cm (9 × 5-inch) loaf tin with butter and line with greaseproof paper. Reserve some of the candied fruit and citron peel, if you wish, to decorate the cake, and finely chop the remainder. Place in a small bowl with the currants, sultanas and rum. Beat the butter with the sugar until pale and creamy, then beat in the eggs, one at a time. In a separate bowl, combine the flour and baking powder, then add to mixture. Stir in the fruit and its soaking liquid.

Pour the mixture into the tin and bake for 50–60 minutes, covering with foil towards the end if necessary. Decorate the finished cake with the reserved candied fruit if liked.

Kugelhopf

KUGELHOPF
kouglof

Preparation time: 30 minutes,
    plus 6 hours rising time
Cooking time: 1 hour
Serves 6

100 g (3½ oz) butter, diced,
    plus extra for greasing
8 whole almonds, skinned and cut
    lengthwise in half
200 ml (7 fl oz) milk
25 g (1 oz) fresh yeast, or 1 sachet
    of dried yeast
500 g (1 lb 2 oz) plain flour
Pinch of salt
3 eggs, beaten
150 g (5 oz) caster sugar
125 g (4¼ oz) Muscatel raisins
Icing sugar, to serve

Grease a 23–25-cm (9–10-inch) Kugelhopf mould generously with butter, then arrange the almond halves evenly around the bottom of the mould. Heat the milk in a pan until lukewarm, adding the butter to melt it. Add the yeast to the lukewarm milk, stirring it to dissolve. Combine the flour and salt in a large bowl and make a well in the centre. Add the eggs, sugar and milk mixture to the well. Mix the dough until it leaves the sides of the bowl and then knead for 5 minutes, adding the Muscatel raisins towards the end.

Place the dough in the mould; it should half-fill it. Cover with a cloth and allow to rise for 6 hours in a warm room, or until doubled in volume. Preheat the oven to 160°C/325°F/Gas Mark 3. Transfer the mould gently to the oven and bake for 1 hour. Dredge with icing sugar before serving.

LIGHT KUGELHOPF
kouglof fin

Preparation time: 40 minutes,
    plus 10 hours rising time
Cooking time: 40 minutes
Serves 6

125 g (4¼ oz) butter, cut into cubes,
    plus extra for greasing
60 g (2 oz) almonds, skinned and cut
    lengthwise in half
500 g (1 lb 2 oz) plain flour
Pinch of salt
4 eggs
350 ml (12 fl oz) milk, lukewarm
150 g (5 oz) caster sugar
20 g (¾ oz) fresh yeast, or 1 sachet
    of dried yeast
150 g (5 oz) Muscatel raisins
Icing sugar, to serve

Grease a 23–25-cm (9–10-inch) Kugelhopf mould generously with butter, then arrange the almond halves evenly around the bottom of the mould. Put the flour in a bowl with a little salt, make a well and break the eggs into it. Melt the butter in 200 ml (7 fl oz) of the lukewarm milk and add this to the mixture, together with the sugar. Combine the ingredients, then knead the dough for 20 minutes (or 5–10 minutes by machine); it should become very light. Meanwhile, mix the yeast with the remaining lukewarm milk and when it has dissolved, add to the dough and knead again for 5 minutes, adding the raisins for the last minute. Place the dough in the prepared mould. Cover with a cloth and allow to rise for about 10 hours in a warm room.

Preheat the oven to 200°C/400°F/Gas Mark 6. Transfer the mould gently to the oven and bake for 40 minutes. Dredge with icing sugar to serve.

SPICE CAKES

*Spice cakes often keep well due to the
addition of honey or syrups. Always use fresh spices
for the best flavour, as dried spices lose their flavour
after six months.*

SPICE CAKE
pain d'épices

Preparation time: 30 minutes
Cooking time: 50–60 minutes
Serves 6

Butter, for greasing
150 g (5 oz) honey
60 g (2 oz) caster sugar
100 ml (3½ fl oz) milk
2 egg yolks
250 g (9 oz) plain flour
2 teaspoons baking powder
Spices and flavourings of your choice:
orange zest, ground aniseed, cinnamon
  or mixed spice

Preheat the oven to 160°C/325°F/Gas Mark 3 and
grease a 21 × 11-cm (8½ × 4½-inch) loaf tin with butter.
Place the honey, sugar and milk in a pan and heat
gently to dissolve, without allowing to boil. Allow to
cool to lukewarm before pouring half of the
sweetened milk mixture into a bowl and whisking in
the egg yolks. Combine the flour, baking powder, and
spices and gradually add them to the egg yolk mixture,
alternating with additions of the remaining milk. Add
the flavourings to taste.

Place the mixture in the prepared tin and bake for
50–60 minutes, covering with foil towards the end if
necessary. The tin should sound hollow when tapped
on the bottom once the cake is cooked.

ORANGE SPICE CAKE
pain d'épice à l'orange

Preparation time: 10 minutes
Cooking time: 50–60 minutes
Serves 6

Butter, for greasing
1 unwaxed orange
1 unwaxed lemon
500 g (1 lb 2 oz) plain flour
120 g (4 oz) caster sugar
2 teaspoons ground aniseed
2 teaspoons baking powder
200 ml (7 fl oz) milk
240 g (9 oz) runny honey

Preheat the oven to 160°C/325°F/Gas Mark 3 and grease a 21 × 11-cm (8½ × 4½-inch) loaf tin with butter. Wash and dry the orange and lemon. Pare off the zest (rind with no pith) from them and chop it finely. In a bowl combine the flour, sugar, citrus zests, aniseed and baking powder. Stir in the milk and honey and beat to make a smooth batter. Place in the tin and bake for 50–60 minutes, covering with foil towards the end if necessary. The tin should sound hollow when tapped on the bottom once the cake is cooked.

CLAUDINE'S SPICE CAKE
pain d'épices claudine

Preparation time: 15 minutes
Cooking time: 1 hour
Serves 6

50 g (1¾ oz) butter, softened,
    plus extra for greasing
125 g (4¼ oz) honey
125 g (4¼ oz) caster sugar
250 g (9 oz) plain flour
2 teaspoons baking powder
60 g (2 oz) angelica, finely chopped
Grated zest of 1 unwaxed lemon
1 teaspoon ground aniseed

Preheat the oven to 140°C/275°F/Gas Mark 1 and grease a 21 × 11-cm (8½ × 4½-inch) loaf tin with butter. Melt the honey and sugar in 200 ml (7 fl oz) hot water. Combine the flour and baking powder in a bowl, then make a well. Pour the sweetened water into it, followed by the angelica, lemon zest, aniseed and butter, stirring these to make a smooth batter. Place in the loaf tin, cover with a double thickness of foil and bake for 1 hour. The tin should sound hollow when tapped on the bottom once the cake is cooked.

SPONGE CAKES

Unlike butter cakes, sponge cakes include little fat. To make a classic sponge cake, whole eggs should be beaten with caster sugar until the mixture is very pale and doubled in volume, which can take up to 10 minutes. A sponge cake will always increase in volume as it cooks, so allow plenty of space in the tin.

SAVOY GÂTEAU
gâteau de savoie

Preparation time: 20 minutes
Cooking time: 25–30 minutes
Serves 6

Butter, for greasing
4 eggs, separated
200 g (7 oz) caster sugar
40 g (1½ oz) plain flour
60 g (2 oz) potato flour
Vanilla extract or grated
    lemon zest, to taste

Preheat the oven to 180°C/350°F/Gas Mark 4 and grease a 23-cm (9-inch) cake tin with butter. Using an electric whisk, whisk the egg whites to stiff peaks. In a separate bowl, whisk the sugar and egg yolks for 5 minutes until pale and tripled in volume. Fold in the plain flour, potato flour and the vanilla or lemon zest. Fold in the egg whites. Fill the prepared cake tin two-thirds full with the mixture. Bake for 25–30 minutes.

SAVOY SPONGE CAKE
biscuit de savoie

Preparation time: 20 minutes
Cooking time: 30 minutes

Butter, for greasing
4 eggs, separated
200 g (7 oz) caster sugar
175 g (6 oz) potato flour
Grated zest of 1 unwaxed lemon
1 teaspoon baking powder

Preheat the oven to 180°C/350°F/Gas Mark 4 and grease a 20-cm (8-inch) cake tin with butter. Whisk the egg yolks and sugar until smooth then gradually whisk in small quantities of the potato flour. Add the lemon zest. In a separate bowl, whisk the egg whites until they form stiff peaks, then fold into the mixture with the baking powder. Pour into the tin and bake for 30 minutes.

VANILLA OR LEMON SAVOY SPONGE CAKE
biscuit de savoie

Preparation time: 20 minutes
Cooking time: 20 minutes
Serves 6

Butter, for greasing
4 eggs, separated
200 g (7 oz) caster sugar
100 g (3½ oz) plain flour
1 teaspoon vanilla extract,
    or grated lemon zest

Preheat the oven to 180°C/350°F/Gas Mark 4 and grease a 25-cm (10-inch) cake tin with butter. Whisk the egg whites to stiff peaks. In a separate bowl, use an electric whisk to beat the sugar and egg yolks until pale and foamy, about 5 minutes. Fold in the flour and vanilla or lemon zest, followed by the egg whites. Pour into the cake tin, level the surface and bake for 20 minutes.

Sandwiched Savoy Sponge Cake

SANDWICHED SAVOY SPONGE CAKE

gâteau de savoie fourré à la confiture

Preparation time: 30 minutes
Cooking time: 25 minutes
Serves 6

1 quantity Savoy Sponge Cake (p. 115)
6 tablespoons Kirsch-Flavoured Syrup (p. 49)
    Redcurrant or raspberry jam or jelly
100 g (3½ oz) slivered almonds, toasted

Make the sponge cake and allow to cool. Turn the cake over so the smooth surface is uppermost and cut the cake in two horizontally. Moisten the cut surfaces with Kirsch-flavoured syrup. Spread the redcurrant or raspberry jelly over the bottom half and sandwich the cake halves together. Glaze the top and sides of the cake with jam or jelly, and decorate with toasted slivered almonds.

Note: Red fruit jam can be replaced with apricot jam.

SAVOY SPONGE CAKE WITH STRAWBERRIES

biscuit de savoie aux fraises

Preparation time: 45 minutes,
    plus 5 hours chilling
Cooking time: 25– 30 minutes
Serves 6

For the Savoy Sponge cake:
Butter, for greasing
3 large eggs
150 g (5 oz) caster sugar
30 g (1¼ oz) plain flour, sifted,
    plus extra for dusting
50 g (1¾ oz) potato flour

For the filling and topping:
700 g (1½ lb) strawberries
50g (1¾ oz) caster sugar
Juice of 2 oranges
200 g (7 oz) Greek-style yogurt
100 ml (3 ½ fl oz) crème fraîche
2 teaspoons vanilla extract
3 tablespoons redcurrant jelly

Preheat the oven to 160°C/325°F/Gas Mark 3. Grease a 24-cm (9½-inch) cake tin (with straight or sloping sides) with butter and dust with flour. Make a Savoy Sponge Cake (p. 115), using the quantities given here. Transfer the cake mixture to the tin and bake for 25–30 minutes. Turn out the cake and allow to cool.

For the filling, rinse, hull and quarter 550 g (1¼ lb) of the strawberries and place them in a bowl. Sprinkle them with the caster sugar and the orange juice. Cover and chill for 1 hour in the refrigerator. Beat the yogurt with the crème fraîche and vanilla.

When the cake is completely cold, cut it horizontally into 2 discs of exactly the same thickness. Place the lower half on a serving plate. Drain the liquid from the strawberries and use half of it to sprinkle all over the lower half of the cake. Spread the bottom half of the cake with half of the cream filling, then the layer of strawberries, then the other half of the cream filling. Sprinkle the remainder of the liquid over the cut surface of the upper layer and place it, cut side downwards, on top of the filling. Cover the cake tightly in clingfilm and chill for 4 hours.

Just before serving, cut the remaining strawberries into slices of even thickness and arrange them attractively over the top of the cake. Gently heat the redcurrant jelly until melted and brush over the surface of the cake to glaze.

ORANGE SPONGE CAKE

biscuit aux oranges

Preparation time: 25 minutes
Cooking time: 30–40 minutes
Serves 6

Butter, for greasing
75 g (2½ oz) plain flour, plus extra for dusting
2 eggs, separated
100 g (3½ oz) caster sugar
1 teaspoon vanilla extract
1 large unwaxed orange
50 g (1¾ oz) cornflour
1 teaspoon baking powder

Preheat the oven to 160°C/325°F/Gas Mark 3 and grease an 18-cm (7-inch) cake tin (with straight or sloping sides) with butter and dust with flour. In a bowl, beat the egg yolks with the sugar and vanilla in a bowl, using a wooden spoon. Grate the zest of half an orange. Stir this into the egg yolk and sugar mixture, followed by the juice of the orange.

In a separate bowl, whisk the egg whites until very stiff. Fold them into the sugar mixture. Sift in the flour, cornflour and baking powder and fold in very gently to avoid crushing the air out of the egg whites.

Transfer the mixture carefully to the cake tin and bake for at least 30–40 minutes. Allow to cool for 10 minutes before turning the cake out.

Note: To prevent the cake sticking to the bottom of the tin, line the base with a disc of greaseproof paper.

GÉNOESE SPONGE

génoese

Preparation time: 30 minutes
Cooking time: 30–40 minutes
Serves 6

30 g (1¼ oz) butter, melted,
    plus extra for greasing
5 eggs
150 g (5 oz) caster sugar
Grated lemon zest or
    vanilla extract, to taste
130 g (4½ oz) plain flour

Preheat the oven to 180°C/350°F/Gas Mark 4. Grease a 23-cm (9-inch) cake tin with butter and line the base with buttered greaseproof paper. Set a heatproof bowl over a pan of barely simmering water, not allowing the bowl to touch the water. Place the eggs and sugar in the bowl and whisk over a low heat for 5 minutes, or until the mixture is light, creamy and greatly increased in volume. Add the lemon zest or vanilla, then sift over the flour and fold in gently with a spatula. Fold in the melted butter. Pour the mixture into the prepared tin. Bake for 30–40 minutes. The cake is cooked when the centre remains firm if pressed lightly.

Note: Do not use an aluminium bowl, as the mixture will discolour.

KIRSCH GÉNOESE SPONGE
génoese au kirsch

Preparation time: 30 minutes
Cooking time: 35–40 minutes
Serves 6

40 g (1½ oz) butter, melted and cooled,
   plus extra for greasing
4 eggs
125 g (4¼ oz) caster sugar
2 tablespoons Kirsch
125 g (4¼ oz) plain flour
Flavoured icing (p. 36–37) or Buttercream
   (p. 38) (optional)

Preheat the oven to 180°C/350°F/Gas Mark 4 and grease a 23-cm (9-inch) cake tin with butter. In a large heatproof bowl set over a pan of just simmering water, whisk the eggs and sugar for 10 minutes, whisking slowly to begin with then increasing the speed.

When the mixture is lukewarm, remove the bowl from the heat and continue whisking until the mixture has cooled and greatly increased in volume. Fold in the Kirsch, flour and butter. Pour into the tin and bake for 35–40 minutes. If desired, ice the cold cake with a flavoured icing or fill and decorate with buttercream.

RUM SPONGE CAKE
biscuit manqué

Preparation time: 20 minutes
Cooking time: 40 minutes
Serves 6

100 g (3½ oz) butter, melted and cooled,
   plus extra for greasing
250 g (9 oz) caster sugar
1 teaspoon vanilla extract
6 eggs, separated
250 g (9 oz) plain flour
2 teaspoons baking powder
50 ml (2 fl oz) rum

Preheat the oven to 180°C/350°F/Gas Mark 4 and grease a 23-cm (9-inch) cake tin with butter. Whisk 200 g (7 oz) of the sugar with the vanilla extract and the egg yolks for 10 minutes until white and at least tripled in volume.

Sieve the flour and baking powder in a bowl. Fold it into the egg mixture along with the rum and melted butter. In a separate bowl, whisk the egg whites and remaining sugar until stiff and glossy, then fold into the cake mixture. Pour into the cake tin and bake for 40 minutes.

MOCHA CAKE WITH ALMONDS
moka aux amandes

Preparation time: 50 minutes
Cooking time: 25–30 minutes
Serves 6

1 quantity Savoy Sponge Cake (p. 115)
6 tablespoons Rum-Flavoured Syrup (p. 49)
1½ quantities Coffee Buttercream (p. 39)
100 g (3½ oz) slivered almonds

Prepare the Savoy sponge cake, the syrup and buttercream. Toast the slivered almonds evenly in a hot oven. When the cake has cooled, cut it horizontally in two halves and brush the cut surfaces with rum-flavoured syrup . Spread a third of the buttercream over the bottom half and sandwich the cake together again. Spread the top and sides of the cake with the remaining buttercream and sprinkle the surface and sides with toasted almonds.

PORTUGUESE CHARLOTTE
charlotte portugaise

Preparation time: 1 hour 30 minutes
Cooking time: 1 hour
Serves 6

1 quantity Savoy Sponge Cake (p. 115)
125 g (4¼ oz) candied fruit,
   finely chopped
3 tablespoons Kirsch
1 quantity Crème Pâtissière (p. 41)
1 quantity Italian Meringue (p. 286)
Icing sugar

Make the sponge cake. Allow to cool on a rack. Place the candied fruit in a small bowl with the Kirsch and leave to macerate. Turn the cake over so the smooth surface is uppermost and cut it horizontally into three. Place the bottom part of the cake on a rack. Mix the candied fruit and Kirsch into the crème pâtissière. Spread some of this over the lower half of the cake. Place the next cake layer on top. Spread the remainder of the crème pâtissière over it. Place the top of the cake on top of this filling.

Preheat the oven to 200°C/400°F/Gas Mark 6. Place a third of the meringue into a piping bag fitted with a large star nozzle. Spread the remaining meringue over the cake to cover it completely. Pipe whatever meringue decorations you wish. Dredge with icing sugar. Place the cake in the oven for 5 minutes, or just long enough to lightly colour the meringue.

Note: This charlotte can be served with Crème Anglaise (p. 49).

Mocha Cake with Almonds

Swiss Roll

ROULADE
biscuit roulé

Preparation time: 20 minutes
Cooking time: 8–10 minutes
Serves 6

Butter, melted, for greasing
4 eggs, separated
120 g (4 oz) caster sugar
Pinch of salt
100 g (3½ oz) plain flour
4 tablespoons Syrup for Babas
    (p. 48) (optional)
1 quantity Buttercream (p. 38), to decorate

Preheat the oven to 200°C/400°F/Gas Mark 6. Grease a Swiss roll tin with melted butter. Line it with a sheet of greaseproof paper the same size. Brush this paper with melted butter. Whisk the egg yolks in a bowl with 100 g (3½ oz) sugar and a pinch of salt for 10 minutes until pale and tripled in volume. Sift in the flour in two or three batches, folding it gently into the whisked egg mixture. Beat the egg whites with the remaining sugar until they form stiff peaks. Gently mix in a third of the beaten egg whites into the cake mixture to lighten it, then fold in the remaining egg whites using a figure-of-eight motion with the spoon.

Spread the mixture evenly in the tin and bake for 8–10 minutes. Turn out while still hot on to a clean tea towel and then use this to help you roll up the cake, starting with one long edge: the towel holds it securely and prevents any splits or cracks. Allow to cool. Unroll, peel off the paper and if desired, brush the roulade with the syrup. Spread buttercream and roll it up. Cover with more buttercream.

SWISS ROLL
biscuit roulé à la confiture

Preparation time: 15 minutes
Cooking time: 8–10 minutes
Serves 6

Roulade (above)
150 g (5 oz) redcurrant jelly, warmed
100 g (3½ oz) almonds, skinned and toasted

Prepare the roulade, and once cooked and cooled spread a layer of redcurrant jelly over the cake. Roll it up once again. Trim both ends evenly. Cover the outside and ends with jelly. Sprinkle with toasted almonds.

Note: You can brush a little alcohol- or liqueur-flavoured syrup (p. 48) on the Swiss roll before covering with redcurrant jelly, if desired.

CHOCOLATE CAKES

A moist and decadent chocolate cake is a classic dessert.
When making a chocolate cake, use good-quality plain
chocolate with a high proportion of cocoa solids and
a low amount of sugar.

CHOCOLATE GÂTEAU
gâteau au chocolat

Preparation time: 20 minutes
Cooking time: 50 minutes
Serves 6

70 g (2½ oz) butter, plus extra for greasing
140 g (4¾ oz) chocolate, chopped
4 eggs, separated
90 g (3¼ oz) plain flour
140 g (4¾ oz) sugar
1 teaspoon rum, Kirsch or orange-flower
    water, for flavouring
1 quantity Chocolate Icing (p. 37)
Candied fruit, such as cherries, oranges
    and angelica, to decorate (optional)

Preheat the oven to 150°C/300°F/Gas Mark 2. Grease a 23-cm (9-inch) cake tin with butter. In a pan, melt the chocolate with the butter over a very low heat. Remove from the heat and stir in the egg yolks, one by one, followed by the flour and sugar. In a separate bowl, whisk the egg whites and flavouring to stiff peaks. Fold into the chocolate mixture, ensuring everything is evenly incorporated. Pour into the prepared cake tin and bake for 50 minutes. When the cake comes out of the oven, allow to cool, then cover with the chocolate icing. If you like, decorate with candied fruit.

GÂTEAU FROM NANCY
gâteau nancéen

Preparation time: 25 minutes
Cooking time: 35 minutes
Serves 6

Butter, for greasing
250 g (9 oz) plain chocolate, chopped
100 ml (3½ fl oz) milk
1 teaspoon vanilla extract
125 g (4¼ oz) caster sugar
100 g (3½ oz) potato flour
Pinch of salt
125 g (4¼ oz) ground almonds
6 eggs, separated

Preheat the oven to 160°C/325°F/Gas Mark 3 and grease a 23-cm (9-inch) cake tin with butter. Place the chocolate, milk and vanilla in a pan set over very gentle heat, stirring continuously until the chocolate has melted. Remove from the heat and allow to cool to lukewarm. Mix in the sugar, potato flour and salt, then the ground almonds and the egg yolks. Whisk the egg whites until they form stiff peaks and fold these gently into the chocolate mixture, ensuring everything is evently incorporated. Spread into the cake tin, smooth the surface and bake for 35 minutes, or until the cake is firm around the edges but still moist in the centre. Serve cold.

Chocolate Gâteau

Chocolate Log

CHOCOLATE LOG
bûche au chocolat

Preparation time: 20 minutes
Cooking time: 15–20 minutes
Serves 6

Butter, melted, for greasing
4 eggs
160 g (5½ oz) caster sugar
Pinch of salt
160 g (5½ oz) plain flour
2 teaspoons baking powder
1 teaspoon vanilla extract
1 quantity Chocolate or Coffee
   Buttercream (p. 39)

Preheat the oven to 160°C/325°F/Gas Mark 3. Grease a Swiss roll tin with butter. Line it with a sheet of greaseproof paper the same size. Brush this paper with melted butter. In a bowl, whisk the eggs and sugar for 10 minutes until pale and tripled in volume. Fold in the salt, flour, baking powder and vanilla.

Pour the mixture into the tin and bake for 15–20 minutes. The mixture should be slightly springy to the touch, but firm. Turn out while still hot on to a clean tea towel and then use this to help you roll up the cake, starting with one long edge: the towel holds it securely and prevents any splits or cracks. Allow the cake to cool, still rolled up in the tea towel. Ensure the buttercream is soft and at room temperature.

Carefully unroll the cake and spread the inner surface with half of the buttercream. Roll up again and place on a serving plate. Spread or pipe the remaining buttercream onto the outside of the cake, covering all surfaces.

RUY-BLAS CAKE
ruy-blas

Preparation time: 10 minutes
Cooking time: 45 minutes
Serves 6

60 g (2 oz) butter, diced,
   plus extra for greasing
250 g (9 oz) plain chocolate, chopped
250 g (9 oz) caster sugar
125 g (4¼ oz) ground almonds
90 g (3¼ oz) potato flour
6 eggs, separated

Preheat the oven to 160°C/325°F/Gas Mark 3 and grease a 23-cm (9-inch) cake tin with butter. Place the remaining butter and chocolate in a heatproof bowl set over a pan of barely simmering water and heat very gently until melted, stirring occasionally. Remove from the heat and add the sugar, ground almonds and potato flour, then the egg yolks, one by one. Whisk the egg whites to firm peaks and fold these into the chocolate mixture, ensuring everything is evenly incorporated. Pour into the cake tin and bake for 45 minutes.

MARBLED GÂTEAU
gâteau marbré

Preparation time: 20 minutes
Cooking time: 1 hour
Serves 6

100 g (3½ oz) butter, plus extra for greasing
200 g (7 oz) caster sugar
3 eggs, separated
200 g (7 oz) plain flour
100 ml (3 ½ fl oz) milk
1 teaspoon baking powder
60 g (2 oz) chocolate, grated
Vanilla extract or grated
   lemon zest, to taste

Preheat the oven to 150°C/300°F/Gas Mark 2 and grease a 21 × 11-cm (8½ × 4½-inch) loaf tin with butter. Beat the butter and sugar until pale and creamy, then add the egg yolks and milk. In a separate bowl, combine the flour and baking powder and add to mixture. In a another bowl whisk the egg whites until stiff, then fold into the cake mixture, ensuring everything is evenly incorporated.

Divide the mixture into separate bowls. Fold the chocolate into one half and the vanilla or lemon zest into the other. Put alternating spoonfuls of the white and chocolate mixtures into the prepared tin, filling it two-thirds full. Bake for 1 hour.

CHOCOLATE POUND CAKE
quatre-quarts au chocolat

Preparation time: 15 minutes
Cooking time: 30 minutes
Serves 6

125 g (4¼ oz) butter, diced,
   plus extra for greasing
125 g (4¼ oz) plain flour, plus extra
   for dusting
125 g (4¼ oz) chocolate, chopped
125 g (4¼ oz) caster sugar
5 eggs
10 drops lemon juice

Prepare the day before to allow the flavour of the cake to develop. Preheat the oven to 200°C/400°F/Gas Mark 6. Grease a 23-cm (9-inch) cake tin with butter and dust with flour. Place the chocolate and butter in a heatproof bowl set over a pan of barely simmering water and heat very gently until melted. Remove from the heat.

Whisk the sugar and 4 egg yolks for 10 minutes until pale and at least tripled in volume, adding the lemon juice and the remaining whole egg in the final minute. Fold the melted chocolate and butter into the whisked egg yolk mixture, followed by the flour. Whisk the 4 egg whites until they form stiff peaks and fold into the cake mixture with a spatula as delicately as possible so as not to knock air out. Pour into the cake tin and bake for 30 minutes.

Marbled Gâteau

CHOCOLATE CAKE
biscuit au chocolat

Preparation time: 10 minutes ,
    plus cooling time
Cooking time: 40 minutes
Serves 6

Butter, for greasing
225 g (8 oz) caster sugar
5 eggs
200 g (7 oz) plain flour
1 quantity Chocolate Buttercream (p. 39)

Preheat an oven to 160°C /325°F/ Gas Mark 3 and grease a 20-cm (8-inch) cake tin with butter. Put the sugar in a heatproof bowl. Add the eggs and whisk the mixture in the bowl set over a pan of barely simmering water until light and fluffy. Allow to cool. Gradually add the flour, fold in lightly and pour into the cake tin. Bake for 40 min. Once the cake is cooled, slice it into 2 or 3 layers. Ice a layer with the Chocolate Buttercream, then place the next layer on top. Repeat with the second and third layer and finish the cake with more icing. The icing can be smoothed with a knife dipped in warm water.

CHOCOLATE CAKE WITH COFFEE CUSTARD
chocolat et café

Preparation time: 10 minutes
Cooking time: 30 minutes
Serves 6

50 g (1¾ oz) butter, plus extra for greasing
225 g (8 oz) plain chocolate, chopped
350 ml (12 fl oz) milk
4 eggs, separated
30 g (1¼ oz) rice flour
1 quantity coffee-flavoured Crème Anglaise (p. 49)

Preheat the oven to 160°C/325°F/Gas Mark 3 and grease a 20-cm (8-inch) cake tin with butter. Place the chocolate in a pan with the milk and heat gently until the chocolate has melted. Remove from the heat and whisk in the butter, egg yolks and rice flour. Whisk the egg whites until they form stiff peaks and fold them into the mixture. Pour this into the tin and bake for 30 minutes. Turn the cake out when cold and serve surrounded by coffee-flavoured crème anglaise.

DARK CHOCOLATE GÂTEAU
gâteau au chocolat noir

Preparation time: 20 minutes
Cooking time: 25–30 minutes
Serves 6

180 g (6¼ oz) butter, diced,
    plus extra for greasing
4 eggs, separated
180 g (6¼ oz) caster sugar
250 g (9 oz) dark chocolate, chopped
180 g (6¼ oz) plain flour
2 teaspoons baking powder

Preheat the oven to 160°C/325°F/Gas Mark 3 and grease a 23-cm (9-inch) cake tin with butter. Whisk the egg yolks and the sugar for 10 minutes until pale and at least tripled in volume. Place the butter and chocolate in a heatproof bowl set over a pan of barely simmering water and heat very gently until melted. Fold the chocolate and butter into the egg yolk mixture. In a separate bowl, combine the flour and baking powder, then add to the mixture. Whisk the egg whites until they form stiff peaks and fold them gently into the mixture. Pour into the tin and bake for 25–30 minutes.

Chocolate Cake

CHOCOLATE AND ALMOND GÂTEAU

gâteau au chocolat aux amandes

Preparation time: 10 minutes
Cooking time: 45–50 minutes
Serves 6

125 g (4¼ oz) butter, diced,
    plus extra for greasing
250 g (9 oz) chocolate, chopped
250 g (9 oz) caster sugar
125 g (4¼ oz) ground almonds
75 g (2½ oz) plain flour
4 eggs, separated

Preheat the oven to 140°C/275°F/Gas Mark 1 and grease a 20-cm (8-inch) cake tin with butter. Place the chocolate and butter in a heatproof bowl set over a pan of barely simmering water and heat very gently until melted. Remove from the heat and stir in the sugar, ground almonds and flour, then add the egg yolks and mix thoroughly. Whisk the egg whites to stiff peaks and fold into the chocolate mixture. Pour into the cake tin and bake for 45–50 minutes. The cake should still be moist in the centre when cool.

TONKIN CHOCOLATE CAKE

tonkinois

Preparation time: 20 minutes
Cooking time: 25–30 minutes
Serves 6

100 g (3½ oz) butter, diced,
    plus extra for greasing
125 g (4¼ oz) plain chocolate, chopped
125 g (4¼ oz) caster sugar
65 g (2¼ oz) crème fraîche
3 eggs, separated
50 ml (2 fl oz) rum
100 g (3½ oz) whole almonds, ground,
    with the skin left on
65 g (2¼ oz) plain flour
1½ teaspoons baking powder
1 quantity Chocolate Icing (p. 37)

Preheat the oven to 200°C/400°F/Gas Mark 6 and grease a 20-cm (8-inch) cake tin with butter. Place the chocolate and butter in a heatproof bowl set over a pan of barely simmering water and heat very gently until melted. Remove from the heat and stir until smooth. Stir in the sugar, crème fraîche, egg yolks, rum and ground almonds, mixing until thoroughly incorporated.

In a separate bowl, combine the flour and baking powder and fold into the chocolate mixture. Whisk the egg whites until they form stiff peaks and fold these gently into the cake mixture. Pour into the tin and bake for 25–30 minutes. Allow to cool and cover with chocolate icing.

Chocolate and Almond Gâteau

Reve

RÊVE
rêve

Preparation time: 20 minutes
Cooking time: 10 minutes
Serves 6

150 ml (¼ pint) milk
1 vanilla pod, split lengthways
50 g (1¾ oz) caster sugar
1 whole egg plus 1 egg yolk
250 g (9 oz) plain chocolate, chopped
150 g (5 oz) butter, diced
200 g (7 oz) sponge fingers

Prepare the day before. Place the milk, vanilla pod and sugar in a pan and slowly bring to simmering point. In a bowl, lightly beat the whole egg and the egg yolk. Pour the hot milk onto the eggs, then return to the pan and heat gently stirring all the time to make a custard (Crème Anglaise, p. 49). Place the chocolate and butter in a heatproof bowl set over a pan of barely simmering water and heat very gently until melted. Gradually add the custard to the chocolate mixture, stirring until smooth.

Use the sponge fingers to line the base and sides of an 18-cm (7-inch) charlotte mould or straight-sided dish. Pour the chocolate custard into the sponge-lined mould and cover with more sponge fingers. Cover the top with a small plate and set a weight on top of it. Chill the charlotte in the refrigerator overnight. Unmould it the following day.

CHOCOLATE PAVÉ
pavé au chocolat

Preparation time: 25 minutes, plus
  chilling time
Serves 6

250 g (9 oz) plain chocolate, chopped
250 g (9 oz) butter, diced
2 eggs
200 ml (7 fl oz) Kirsch
375 g (13 oz) Petit Beurre Biscuits (p. 215)
1 quantity Vanilla Buttercream (p. 38)
  or Chocolate Buttercream (p. 39)

Melt the chocolate in a heatproof bowl set over a pan of barely simmering water. Mix in the butter and then the eggs. Remove from the heat and stir until very smooth. Place the Kirsch in a bowl with 75 ml (3 fl oz) of water and dip each of the Petit Beurre biscuits in it. Place 4 of the biscuits in a single layer on a flat serving plate and spread with a layer of the chocolate mixture.

Alternate layers of Kirsch-dipped biscuits and chocolate until all the ingredients have been used up. Cover the top and sides of the cake with Petit Beurre biscuits and a coating of vanilla or chocolate buttercream. Refrigerate until ready to serve.

COCOA GÂTEAU

gâteau au cacao

Preparation time: 15 minutes
Cooking time: 45 minutes
Serves 6

Butter, for greasing
1 egg
150 g (5 oz) caster sugar
250 ml (8 fl oz) double cream
240 g (8¾ oz) plain flour
80 g (2¾ oz) cocoa powder
Scant 2 teaspoons baking powder
1 quantity Chocolate Buttercream (p. 39)
   or Sweetened Whipped Cream (p. 38)
1 quantity Chocolate Icing (p. 37)

Preheat the oven to 160°C/325°F/Gas Mark 3 and grease a 20-cm (8-inch) cake tin with butter. Whisk the egg and sugar in a bowl, then add the cream. In a separate bowl, sift together the flour, cocoa and baking powder and stir to incorporate. Pour the mixture into the tin and bake for 45 minutes.

Once cooled, cut the cake in half horizontally. Spread chocolate buttercream or whipped cream over the bottom layer. Sandwich the cake halves together and ice with chocolate icing.

CHOCOLATE AND CANDIED FRUIT GÂTEAU

gâteau au chocolat et fruits confits

Preparation time: 20 minutes
Cooking time: 50 minutes
Serves 6

70 g (2½ oz) butter, diced,
   plus extra for greasing
140 g (4¾ oz) plain chocolate, chopped
4 eggs, separated
90 g (3¼ oz) plain flour
140 g (4¾ oz) caster sugar
1 tablespoon rum, Kirsch or orange
   flower water
1 quantity Chocolate Icing (p. 37)
85 g (3 oz) candied fruit, to decorate

Preheat the oven to 140°C/275°F/Gas Mark 1 and grease a 20-cm (8-inch) cake tin with butter. Place the chocolate and butter in a pan and heat very gently until melted. Remove from the heat and allow to cool.

Stir in the egg yolks, one at a time, then the flour and sugar. Whisk the egg whites until they form stiff peaks and fold into the chocolate mixture along with the rum or other chosen flavouring. Pour into the cake tin and bake for 50 minutes. Once cooled, cover it with chocolate icing and decorate with candied fruit.

BRIOCHES

Half way between bread and cake, brioches are light, buttery and delicious. The ingredients should be very cold and the dough should rest overnight in the refrigerator. You can make large or small brioches; if you don't have traditional brioche pans any loaf tin or muffin tin can be substituted.

BRIOCHE
brioche

Preparation time: 15 minutes,
   plus 3–4 hours rising time
Cooking time: 30–40 minutes
Serves 6

15 g (½ oz) fresh yeast, or 1 sachet
   of dried yeast
2 tablespoons milk, lukewarm
100 g (3½ oz) butter, softened,
   plus extra for greasing
250 g (9 oz) plain flour
4 eggs
1 teaspoon salt
50 g (1¾ oz) caster sugar

Dissolve the yeast in the milk. Grease a 20-cm (8-inch) brioche mould or deep cake tin with butter. Place the flour in a bowl, make a well in the centre and pour in the yeast and milk mixture, 3 eggs, the salt, butter and sugar. Mix by hand for 10 minutes or by machine set on slow speed for 5 minutes, until the dough is glossy and elastic.

Place in the tin, cover loosely with oiled clingfilm and allow it to rise for 3–4 hours in a warm room. Preheat the oven to 200°C/400°F/Gas Mark 6. Beat the remaining egg and brush gently over the brioche to glaze, then bake for 30–40 minutes, until golden brown and the tin sounds hollow when tapped underneath.

CLASSIC BRIOCHE
brioche

Preparation time: 15 minutes,
 plus 8–12 hours rising time
Cooking time: 30–40 minutes
Serves 6

10 g (¼ oz) fresh yeast,
 or ½ sachet of dried yeast
2 tablespoons milk, lukewarm,
 plus extra for glazing
125 g (4¼ oz) butter, softened,
 plus extra for greasing
250 g (9 oz) plain flour
4 eggs plus 2 egg yolks
1 teaspoon salt
15 g (½ oz) caster sugar

Prepare the day before. Dissolve the yeast in the milk. Grease a 23-cm (9-inch) brioche mould or deep cake tin with butter. Place the flour in a bowl, make a well in the centre and pour in the yeast and milk mixture, the whole eggs and yolks, the salt, butter and sugar. Mix by hand for 10 minutes or by machine set on slow speed for 5 minutes, until the dough is glossy and elastic. Cover the dough in oiled clingfilm and allow it to rise in a warm room for 4–6 hours, until doubled in size.

Dust a work surface with flour. Take two-thirds of the dough and shape into a ball. Place in the tin and make a depression in the top of the dough. Shape the remaining one third of the dough into a smaller ball and place this on top of the first one in the tin, fitting it snugly in the depression. Cover the dough in oiled clingfilm and allow it to rise once more in a warm room for 4–6 hours, until doubled in size.

Preheat the oven to 200°C/400°F/Gas Mark 6. Take a floured wooden spoon handle and press this deep into the centre of the brioche, making a depression in the two balls of dough and forming the classic brioche shape. Brush gently with milk to glaze and bake for 30–40 minutes until golden brown and the tin sounds hollow when tapped underneath.

RICH BRIOCHE
brioche

Preparation time: 15 minutes,
 plus 6 hours rising time
Cooking time: 30–40 minutes
Serves 6

10 g (¼ oz) fresh yeast, or ½ sachet
 of dried yeast
50 ml (2 fl oz) milk, lukewarm
175 g (6 oz) butter, softened,
 plus extra for greasing
250 g (9 oz) plain flour
3 eggs
1 teaspoon salt
30 g (1¼ oz) caster sugar

Dissolve the yeast in the milk. Grease a 20-cm (8-inch) brioche mould or deep cake tin with butter. Place the flour in a bowl, make a well in the centre and pour in the yeast and milk mixture, 2 eggs, the salt, butter and sugar. Mix by hand for 10 minutes or by machine set on slow speed for 5 minutes, until the dough is glossy and elastic.

Place in the tin, cover loosely with oiled clingfilm and allow to rise for 6 hours in a warm room. Beat the remaining egg and brush gently over the brioche to glaze, then bake for 30–40 minutes, until golden brown and the tin sounds hollow when tapped underneath.

POOR MAN'S BRIOCHE
brioche du pauvre

Preparation time: 10 minutes
Cooking time: 30–40 minutes
Serves 6

30 g (1¼ oz) butter, melted and cooled,
   plus extra for greasing
1 egg, separated
30 g (1¼ oz) caster sugar
1 teaspoon salt
200 g (7 oz) plain flour
150 ml (¼ pint) milk, plus extra to glaze
2 teaspoons baking powder

Preheat the oven to 180°C/350°F/Gas Mark 4 and grease an 18-cm (7-inch) brioche mould or deep cake tin with butter. Whisk the egg yolk with the sugar and salt until light and frothy. In a separate bowl, whisk the egg white until stiff and fold this into the egg yolk and sugar mixture. Stirring continuously, add the flour, butter, milk and the baking powder, mixing lightly but thoroughly. Place the dough in the tin. Take a floured wooden spoon handle and press this deep into the centre of the brioche, making a depression in the centre. Brush a little milk gently over the brioche to glaze, then bake for 30–40 minutes, until golden brown and the tin sounds hollow when tapped underneath.

LAST-MINUTE BRIOCHE
brioche à la minute

Preparation time: 15 minutes
Cooking time: 25–30 minutes
Serves 6

100 g (3½ oz) butter, melted,
   plus extra for greasing
Pinch of salt
1 tablespoon caster sugar
1 tablespoons orange flower water
1 tablespoon brandy
4 eggs
300 g (11 oz) plain flour
2 teaspoons baking powder
Milk or 1 egg, to glaze

Preheat the oven to 200°C/400°F/Gas Mark 6 and grease a 20-cm (8-inch) savarin mould with butter. Add a pinch of salt to the melted butter then add the sugar, orange flower water and brandy. Beat the eggs lightly and add to the butter mixture. Stir in the flour and the baking powder and beat until the mixture is smooth and glossy. Place the dough in the tin and brush with milk or beaten egg to glaze. Bake for 25–30 minutes, until golden brown and the tin sounds hollow when tapped underneath.

Note: The dough can also be shaped into a ring and baked on a greased baking tray.

NORWEGIAN-STYLE BRIOCHE
brioche norvégienne

Preparation time: 20 minutes,
  plus 1 hour rising time
Cooking time: 30–40 minutes
Serves 6

50 g (1¾ oz) butter, softened,
  plus extra for greasing
250 g (9 oz) plain flour
40 g (1½ oz) caster sugar
25 g (1 oz) fresh yeast, or 1 sachet
  of dried yeast
150 ml (¼ pint) milk, lukewarm
30 g (1¼ oz) raisins
30 g (1¼ oz) candied orange peel, chopped
1 egg, beaten

Dissolve the yeast in the milk. Place the flour in a bowl with half the butter and half the sugar. Mix to combine, then add the milk mixture. Allow the dough to rise for 20 minutes at room temperature. Add the remaining butter and sugar to the mixture and mix again to a soft dough. Allow to rise for 15 minutes at room temperature.

Knead in the raisins and candied orange peel. Place the dough in the tin. Allow to rise for 20 minutes in a warm room. Take a floured wooden spoon handle and press this deep into the centre of the brioche, making a depression in the centre.

Preheat the oven to 200°C/400°F/Gas Mark 6 and grease an 18-cm (7-inch) brioche mould or deep cake tin with butter. Brush gently with the beaten egg to glaze and bake for 30–40 minutes, until golden brown and the tin sounds hollow when tapped underneath.

Note: The dough can also be shaped and placed on a greased baking tray instead of in a brioche tin.

RAPID BRIOCHE
brioche rapide

Preparation time: 10 minutes
Cooking time: 45 minutes
Serves 6

Butter, for greasing
175 g (6 oz) plain flour
3 teaspoons baking powder
175 ml (6 fl oz) crème fraîche
2 eggs, beaten
30 g (1¼ oz) caster sugar
1 teaspoon salt

Preheat the oven to 180°C/350°F/Gas Mark 4 and grease a 900-g (2-lb) brioche or loaf tin with butter. In a bowl, mix flour and baking powder, then add the crème fraîche. Add one beaten egg, the sugar and salt. Mix to a soft dough. Place in the prepared tin. Brush with the remaining beaten egg to glaze and bake for 45 minutes, or until golden brown.

Rapid Brioche

MILK LOAF
pain au lait

Preparation time: 30 minutes,
   plus 6–7 hours rising time
Cooking time: 40–50 minutes
Serves 6

300 ml (½ pint) milk
10 g (¼ oz) fresh yeast, or ½ sachet
   of dried yeast
300 g (11 oz) plain flour,
   plus extra for dusting
75 g (2½ oz) butter, plus extra for greasing
30 g (1¼ oz) caster sugar
½ teaspoon salt
4 eggs
60 g (2 oz) Muscatel raisins

Heat 50 ml (2 fl oz) milk in a pan until lukewarm, then add the yeast, stirring to dissolve. Combine this with 100 g (3½ oz) flour. Shape into a soft ball of dough, place in an oiled bowl, cover and allow to rise in warm place until doubled in size.

Heat the remaining milk in a saucepan, together with the butter, sugar and salt, stirring to dissolve. Remove from the heat and allow to cool to lukewarm. Place the remaining flour in a bowl, make a well in the centre and break 3 eggs into this. Using your hands or a wooden spoon, gradually incorporate the flour into the eggs. Gradually add the lukewarm milk mixture, a tablespoon at a time, kneading for about 5 minutes after each addition. This process can also be done in a mixer set on slowest speed. Transfer the dough to a floured work surface and knead until smooth, adding the raisins at the end. Finally, knead in the risen dough set aside earlier, making sure it is evenly blended.

Place the dough in an oiled bowl, cover and allow to rise in a warm place for 5–6 hours. Preheat the oven to 200°C/400°F/Gas Mark 6 and grease a 20-cm (8-inch) brioche mould or deep cake tin with butter. When the dough has doubled in volume, shape it into a round loaf and place in the tin. Beat the remaining egg and brush over the loaf to glaze. Bake for 40–50 minutes, until deep golden brown and the tin sounds hollow when tapped underneath.

Note: The dough can also be shaped as above and baked on a greased baking tray.

INSTANT PARISIAN BRIOCHE
brioche parisienne instantanée

Preparation time: 10 minutes
Cooking time: 30–40 minutes
Serves 6

125 g (4¼ oz) butter, softened,
   plus extra for greasing
200 g (7 oz) plain flour
2 teaspoons baking powder
½ teaspoon salt
2 teaspoons caster sugar
60 g (2 oz) crème fraîche
1 tablespoon rum
2 eggs

Preheat the oven to 180°C/350°F/Gas Mark 4 and grease a 20-cm (8-inch) savarin or ring mould with butter. Mix the flour and baking powder in a bowl. Make a well in the centre and into it put the salt, sugar, crème fraîche, rum and butter. Add the eggs and mix well until mixture is smooth and glossy. Place the mixture in the tin and bake for 30–40 minutes, until golden brown and the tin sounds hollow when tapped underneath.

TARTS
AND
PASTRIES

French pastries can seem daunting to make at home when in fact there are only a few basic recipes required to make them (Basics Recipes, p. 28). A basic choux dough recipe is the basis for dozens of cream-filled classics and a simple puff pastry is the foundation for a Napoleon, pithivier and palmier. To ensure the best results, use the finest ingredients available.

CHOUX PASTRIES

Choux pastry is the basis for some of the best French pastries. Be sure to preheat the oven properly as choux pastry must be baked in a hot oven. To prepare them in advance, the paste can be made the day before, left in a covered bowl and refrigerated overnight.

CREAM BUNS
choux à la creme pâtissière

Preparation time: 20 minutes, plus
  cooling time
Cooking time: 15 minutes
Serves 6

1 quantity Choux Buns (p. 32)
1 quantity Crème Pâtissière (p. 41)

Make some large choux buns, about 7.5 cm (3 inches) in diameter. When they have cooled, make a horizontal slit near the top. Fill generously with thick crème pâtissière, allowing a little to show through the slit.

CARAMELIZED CHOUX BUNS
choux caramelisés

Preparation time: 20 minutes, plus
    cooling time
Cooking time: 15 minutes
Serves 6

1 quantity Choux Buns (p. 32)
1 quantity Crème Pâtissière (p. 41)
450 g (1 lb) caster sugar

Make some large choux buns, about 7.5 cm (3 inches)
in diameter. When they have cooled, using a piping bag
fitted with a large plain nozzle, pierce each bun through
the base and fill generously with crème pâtissière.

To make a light caramel, pour the caster sugar into
a saucepan over medium heat until the sugar is slightly
melted around the edges, about 5 minutes. Using a
wooden spoon, gently stir until the sugar has completely
melted and is amber coloured, about 10 minutes.
Quickly dip the top of each choux bun in the caramel
and allow to dry on a rack, caramel side up.

SALAMBOS
salambos

Preparation time: 20 minutes, plus
    cooling time
Cooking time: 15 minutes
Serves 6

1 quantity Choux Buns (p. 32)
1 quantity Crème Pâtissière (p. 41)
450 g (1 lb) caster sugar
Slivered almonds

Make some large choux buns, about 7.5 cm (3 inches)
in diameter. When they have cooled, using a piping bag
fitted with a large plain nozzle. Use the nozzle to pierce
each bun through the base and fill generously with
crème pâtissière. Top with caramel (see above) and
sprinkle slivered almonds on top immediately.

Note: The choux buns can also be iced with a Kirsch
Icing (p. 37) instead of caramel.

POLKAS
polkas

Preparation time: 40 minutes, plus
    chilling time
Cooking time: 20–25 minutes
Serves 6

Butter, for greasing
1 quantity Shortcrust Pastry (p. 33)
Plain flour, for dusting
1 quantity Choux Pastry (p. 32)
2 eggs
1 quantity Crème Pâtissière (p. 41)
Icing sugar, to decorate

Preheat the oven to 200°C/ 400°F/Gas Mark 6 and grease
a baking tray with butter. Dust a work surface with flour
and roll the shortcrust pastry dough out to a thickness of
3 mm (⅛ inch) and cut it into 8-cm (3¼-inch) discs. Place
them on the prepared tray. Make the choux pastry and
place it in a piping bag fitted with a large plain nozzle. Pipe
a line of choux pastry around the edge of each pastry disc
to make 'crown' shapes. Beat the eggs and brush over
the choux pastry crowns to glaze. Bake for 20–25 minutes
until golden and the bases cooked through. When the
pastries are cool, pipe crème pâtissière into the centre of
each. Dredge generously with icing sugar and carefully
caramelize the sugar covering the pastries under the grill
or with a kitchen torch.

CHOUX BUNS WITH CREAM

choux à la Chantilly

Preparation time: 20 minutes, plus cooling time
Cooking time: 15 minutes
Serves 6

1 quantity Choux Buns (p. 32)
1 quantity Sweetened Whipped Cream (p. 38)
Slivered almonds
Icing sugar, for dusting

Make some large choux buns, about 7.5 cm (3 inches) in diameter. When they have cooled, make a horizontal slit near the top. Fill generously with the sweetened whipped cream. Sprinkle with slivered almonds and dust with icing sugar.

SAINT-HONORÉ

Saint-Honoré

Preparation time: 1 hour 15 minutes,
    plus chilling and cooling time
Cooking time: 30 minutes
Serves 6

1 quantity Shortcrust Pastry (p. 33)
1 quantity Choux Pastry, Method A (p. 32)
Butter, for greasing
Plain flour, for dusting
1 egg, beaten
1 quantity Crème Pâtissière (p. 41)
450 g (1 lb) caster sugar
1 quantity Saint-Honoré Cream (p. 44)

Shape the shortcrust pastry into a ball, cover with clingfilm and chill while you make the choux pastry. Place the choux pastry into a piping bag fitted with a large plain nozzle.

Preheat the oven to 200°C/400°F/Gas Mark 6 and grease two baking trays with butter. Dust a work surface with flour and roll the shortcrust pastry out to a thickness of 5 mm (¼ inch). Form a 23-cm (9-inch) circle and place on one baking tray. Prick all over with a fork and brush with the egg.

Starting 2.5 cm (1 inch) inside the edge of the pastry and using half of the choux pastry, pipe it in a spiral onto the shortcrust pastry base, finishing in the centre, leaving space between the lines to allow it to puff up in the oven. Use the remaining choux pastry to make small choux buns, piping them onto the other baking tray. Bake both for 15 minutes, then remove the choux buns and continue cooking the base for a further 5–10 minutes until golden and cooked through. Once cooled, fill the small choux buns with the crème pâtissière.

To make a light caramel, pour the caster sugar into a saucepan over medium heat until sugar is slightly melted around the edges, about 5 minutes. Using a wooden spoon, gently stir until the sugar has completely melted and is amber coloured, about 10 minutes. Dip the top of each bun in the caramel, then immediately stick them around the outer edge of the choux pastry base. Fill the centre of the cake with Saint-Honoré Cream, piping this in a decorative herringbone pattern if desired. The centre of the cake can also be filled with whipped cream or vanilla ice cream, or both.

Choux Buns with Cream

Pont-Neuf Pastries

PONT-NEUF PASTRIES
Pont-Neufs

Preparation time: 40 minutes, plus
    chilling and cooling time
Cooking time: 20–25 minutes
Serves 6

1 quantity Shortcrust Pastry (p. 33)
Butter, for greasing
Plain flour, for dusting
1 quantity Choux Pastry (p. 32)
1 quantity Crème Pâtissière (p. 41)
1 egg, beaten
Icing sugar, to decorate

Grease a baking tray with butter. Dust the work surface with flour and roll the shortcrust pastry out to a thickness of 3 mm (⅛ inch). Set aside a quarter of the pastry for decorating. Use a round pastry cutter to stamp out 8-cm (3-inch) discs from the remaining pastry. Place on the baking tray and prick each disc with a fork.

Preheat the oven to 180°C/350°F/Gas Mark 4. Mix together equal amounts of choux pastry and crème pâtissière and transfer to a piping bag fitted with a large plain nozzle. Pipe the mixture onto the pastry discs, leaving a small margin around the edge and doming the centre slightly. Place two strips of the reserved pastry in a cross shape on top of each pastry disc and brush with beaten egg to glaze. Bake for 20–25 minutes until golden and the bases are cooked through. Dredge with icing sugar to serve.

ÉCLAIRS
éclairs

Preparation time: 30 minutes, plus
    cooling time
Cooking time: 20 minutes
Serves 6

1 quantity Choux Pastry (p. 32)
Butter, for greasing

Preheat the oven to 200°C/400°F/Gas Mark 6 and grease a baking tray with butter. Pipe or spoon the choux pastry dough into fingers on the prepared tray. Bake for 20 minutes and allow to cool. When cooled, slit the éclairs along the side, fill and ice as desired (p. 153).

Chocolate Éclairs

CHOCOLATE ÉCLAIRS
éclairs au chocolat

Preparation time: 30 minutes, plus
  cooling time
Cooking time: 20 minutes
Serves 6

1 quantity Choux Pastry (p. 32)
1 quantity Chocolate Crème
  Pâtissière (p. 41)
1 quantity Chocolate Icing (p. 37)

Preheat the oven to 200°C/400°F/Gas Mark 6 and grease a baking tray with butter. Pipe or spoon the choux pastry dough into fingers on the prepared tray. Bake for 20 minutes and allow to cool. When cooled, slit the éclairs along the side, fill with chocolate crème pâtissière and top with chocolate icing.

ALMOND ÉCLAIRS
éclairs à la frangipane

Preparation time: 30 minutes, plus
  cooling time
Cooking time: 20 minutes
Serves 6

1 quantity Choux Pastry (p. 32)
1 quantity Almond Custard (p. 45)
1 quantity Kirsch Icing (p. 37)

Preheat the oven to 200°C/400°F/Gas Mark 6 and grease a baking tray with butter. Pipe or spoon the choux pastry dough into fingers on the prepared tray. Bake for 20 minutes and allow to cool. When cooled, slit the éclairs along the side, fill with almond custard and top with Kirsch-flavoured icing.

COFFEE ÉCLAIRS
éclairs au café

Preparation time: 30 minutes, plus
  cooling time
Cooking time: 20 minutes
Serves 6

1 quantity Choux Pastry (p. 32)
1 quantity Coffee Crème Pâtissière (p. 41)
1 quantity Coffee Fondant Icing (p. 36)

Preheat the oven to 200°C/400°F/Gas Mark 6 and grease a baking tray with butter. Pipe or spoon the choux pastry dough into fingers on the prepared tray. Bake for 20 minutes and allow to cool. When cooled, slit the éclairs along the side, fill with coffee crème pâtissière, and top with coffee fondant icing.

PARIS-BREST
Paris-Brest

Preparation time: 25 minutes, plus 24 hours
    chilling time and cooling time
Cooking time: 10 minutes
Serves 6

For the Choux Pastry:
40 g (1½ oz) semi-salted butter
65 g (2¼ oz) plain flour
2 whole eggs

For the Crème Pâtissière:
150 g (5 oz) caster sugar
5 egg yolks
100 g (3½ oz) plain flour
750 ml (1¼ pints) full-fat milk, hot

For the Praline Filling:
200 g (7 oz) butter, softened
200 g (6¾ oz) almond and hazelnut
    chocolate spread (see note)
400 g (14 oz) Crème Pâtissière (see above)

To finish:
Butter, for greasing
200 g (7 oz) shredded almonds, toasted
Icing sugar, for sprinkling

To make the choux pastry, bring 125 ml (4½ fl oz) water and the butter to the boil in a pan. Remove from the heat, pour in the flour and stir quickly with a wooden spoon to make a smooth paste. Put the pan back over a gentle heat and stir for 1 minute to dry out the batter. Remove from the heat, beat in the 2 whole eggs one at a time, and mix well. Allow to cool, then chill in the refrigerator overnight.

Next, make the crème pâtissière. Beat the sugar and egg yolks in a large bowl until the mixture turns thick and white. Add the flour and stir continuously, pouring in the milk a little at a time. Put the mixture back into the milk pan and cook for 5–6 minutes over a gentle heat. Transfer to a clean bowl, cool and chill in the refrigerator. Next, make the praline filling. Beat the butter and chocolate spread together. Mix in the well-chilled crème pâtissière and beat together. Store the praline filling in the refrigerator for 12 hours.

On the day it is to be served, preheat the oven to 250°C/500°F/Gas Mark 9. Grease a baking tray with butter. Pipe the choux paste onto the tray in a ring, 25 cm (10 inches) in diameter, like a bicycle wheel. Bake for 10–12 minutes, or until the pastry is well risen and golden brown. Turn the oven off and leave the pastry to dry for 3–4 minutes with the oven door open. Remove from the oven and allow to cool to room temperature. Put the chilled praline filling in a piping bag with a fluted nozzle.

Once the pastry is completely cold, carefully split it in half with a sharp knife and cover the base with praline filling, using the piping bag to make swirls. Sprinkle the praline filling with all but a few almonds. Cover with the choux pastry lid and sprinkle the Paris-Brest with the remaining almonds and icing sugar.

Note: To make 6 individual, pipe the choux pastry into 6 rings, 8 cm (3¼ inches) in diameter and then bake as instructed. Almond and hazelnut chocolate spreads are available at specialty shops. It may be substituted with Nutella though it will not taste the same.

Paris-Brest

PUFF PASTRIES

*Puff pastry is a light, flaky pastry made from layers
of pastry dough. Puff pastry must be kept cold while
working with it to prevent the butter from
melting prematurely.*

CREAM HORNS
cornets à la crème

Preparation time: 1 hour, plus chillling and
  cooling time
Cooking time: 30 minutes
Makes 12

Butter, for greasing
1 quantity Puff Pastry (p. 31)
1 egg yolk
1 quantity Crème Pâtissière (p. 41) or
  Sweetened Whipped Cream (p. 38)

Preheat the oven to 220°C/425°F/Gas Mark 7 and grease
a baking tray with butter. Roll the puff pastry out very
thinly. Cut into long strips 2–3 cm (¾–1¼ inches) wide.
Butter some cream horn moulds and wrap a pastry
strip in a spiral round the outside of each mould, sealing
the edges with a little water as you go. Glaze with the
egg yolk mixed with 1 teaspoon warm water. Place on
the prepared tray and bake for 30 minutes, or until
golden brown. Lift the horns off the moulds, taking care
not to break them. Allow to cool. Use a piping bag to fill
with the crème pâtissière or cream.

ICED MATCHSTICKS
allumettes glacées

Preparation time: 2 hours 20 minutes, plus
  chilling time
Cooking time: 10–15 minutes
Serves 6

1 quantity Puff Pastry (p. 31)
1 quantity Royal Icing (p. 36)

Preheat the oven to 180°C/350°F/Gas Mark 4 and line
a baking tray with greaseproof paper. Complete the
final turn of the puff pastry and roll out strips 10 cm
(4 inches) wide and 30 cm (12 inches) long. The pastry
should be 5 mm (¼ inch) thick. Cover the pastry strips
with royal icing and carefully cut out batons 3–4 cm
(1¼–1½ inches) wide. Bake for 10–15 minutes until the
icing is no darker than cream coloured.

Note: Ideally, the oven should be hot at the bottom and
cooler at the top, to avoid caramelizing the icing, which
should be a pale cream colour.

Cream Horns

Apple Turnovers

APPLE TURNOVERS

chaussons aux pommes

Preparation time: 1 hour, plus chilling time
Cooking time: 30 minutes
Serves 6

Butter, for greasing
1 quantity Puff Pastry (p. 31)
Plain flour, for dusting
250 g (6 oz) Apple Purée (p. 276)
1 egg yolk
60 g (2 oz) caster sugar

Preheat the oven to 220°C/425°F/Gas Mark 7 and grease a baking tray with butter. Roll the puff pastry out very thinly on a floured work surface. Using a bowl or pastry cutter, cut out even circles 12 cm (5 inches) in diameter. Place 1–2 tablespoons of apple purée on each one. Moisten the edges with a little water, fold in half and press down to seal, forming a crescent shape. Place on the prepared tray. Brush with the egg yolk to glaze and sprinkle with the sugar. Bake for 30 minutes.

Note: For jam turnovers, replace the apple purée with the jam of your choice.

APPLE TURNOVERS WITH CINAMMON

chaussons aux pommes

Preparation time: 1 hour, plus chilling time
Cooking time: 30 minutes
Serves 6

3 apples
60 g (2 oz) caster sugar
½ teaspoon ground cinnamon
Butter, for greasing
1 quantity Puff Pastry (p. 31)
Plain flour, for dusting
1 egg yolk

Peel, core and cut the apples into 1-cm (½-inch) dice and place in a bowl with 3 tablespoons of the sugar and cinnamon. Stir to coat the apples in the spiced sugar.

Preheat the oven to 220°C/425°F/Gas Mark 7 and grease a baking tray with butter. Roll the puff pastry out very thinly on a floured work surface. Using a bowl or pastry cutter, cut out even circles 12 cm (5 inches) in diameter. Place a good tablespoon of apples on each one. Moisten the edges with a little water, fold in half and press down to seal, forming a crescent shape. Place on the prepared tray. Brush with the egg yolk to glaze and sprinkle with the remaining sugar. Bake for 30 minutes.

DARTOIS

dartois

Preparation time: 1 hour, plus chilling time
Cooking time: 25 minutes
Serves 6

For the almond paste:
125 g (4¼ oz) ground almonds
60 g (2 oz) butter, softened
2 eggs
100 g (3½ oz) caster sugar
1 teaspoon vanilla extract

Butter, for greasing
250 g (9 oz) Puff Pastry (p. 31)

Prepare the almond paste by mixing the almonds, butter, eggs, sugar and vanilla together and set aside, covered, at room temperature. Preheat the oven to 220°C/425°F/Gas Mark 7 and grease a baking tray with butter. Roll the puff pastry out to a 22 × 30-cm (8 × 12-inches) rectangle, 5 mm (¼ inch) thick. Cut the pastry lengthwise into 2 strips, one 10 cm (4 inches) wide, the other 12 cm (5 inches) wide.

Prepare 2 strips, one 8–10 cm (3–4 inches) wide, the other 2 cm (¾ inch) wider. Place the larger one on the prepared tray. Spoon the almond paste, which should be quite soft, onto this strip and fold in 1 cm (½ inch) of the edges over the almond paste all round. Put on the second piece of pastry like a lid, seal the edges with water and flute the edges so that they stand upright. Mark with a knife every 4–5 cm (1½–2 inches) to show the individual portions of dartois. Bake for 25 minutes, or until deep golden brown. Immediately after baking, gently cut the dartois in slices at the marked portions.

PALMIERS

palmiers

Preparation time: 1 hour, plus chilling time
Cooking time: 15–20 minutes
Serves 6

200 g (7 oz) plain flour
100 g (3½ oz) butter
1 teaspoon salt
125 g (4¼ oz) caster sugar
Butter, for greasing

Follow the instructions for the puff pastry (p. 31) with the flour, butter, salt and 2 tablespoons of water. Preheat the oven to 220°C/425°F/Gas Mark 7 and grease a baking tray with butter. Sprinkle a work surface with some of the sugar and roll out the pastry to 5 mm (¼ inch) thick, in a strip 10–20 cm (4–8 inches) wide.

Fold the short ends of the pastry in so that the 2 edges meet in the middle, then fold again in the same way. Cut the pastry into slices 1 cm (½ inch) thick. Open the slices out slightly to form heart shapes. Sprinkle the baking tray with the remaining sugar and put the heart shapes flat on the tray. Bake the palmiers for 15–20 minutes, turning them over once during cooking.

Palmiers

APRICOT, PLUM OR CHERRY TART
tarte aux abricots, prunes, cerises

Preparation time: 10 minutes
Cooking time: 45 minutes
Serves 6

Butter, for greasing
1 quantity Shortcrust Pastry (p. 33) or
   Rough Puff Pastry (p. 31)
500 g (1 lb 2 oz) fruit, such as apricots,
   plums or cherries
Caster sugar, to taste

Preheat the oven to 180°C/350°F/Gas Mark 4 and grease a 23-cm (9-inch) tart tin with butter. Make the pastry and use it to line the tart tin. Stone the fruits, and cut in half if using apricots or plums. Arrange inside the pastry case inside the pastry case, in concentric circles if a round tart tin is used, working from the outside to the centre, cut sides down. If you want to bake the tart in a square or rectangular tin, arrange the fruits in parallel rows. Sprinkle with caster sugar to taste and bake for 45 minutes.

TWELFTH NIGHT CAKE
galette des rois

Preparation time: 2 hours 10 minutes, plus
   chilling time
Cooking time: 25–30 minutes
Serves 6

1 quantity Puff Pastry (p. 31)
1 egg yolk
1 quantity Water Icing (p. 37)

Preheat the oven to 180°C/350°F/Gas Mark 4 . After all the turns, placing an uncooked haricot bean or charm in the final turn, roll out the puff pastry on the work surface into an even square 2 cm (1 inch) thick. Trim off the corners of the square to obtain a round shape. Roll out with a rolling pin until 1.5 cm (¾ inch) thick. Using a knife, trace a pattern of parallel lines obliquely across the surface. Repeat in the opposite direction, resulting in a diamond-shaped lattice pattern. Mix the egg yolk with 1 teaspoon of water and brush over the pastry to glaze. Place on a dampened baking tray and bake for 30 minutes until crisp and golden. Brush the surface with water icing 5 minutes before the end of the cooking time.

Variation: Make a Shortcrust Pastry (p. 33) or a Sweet Pastry dough (p. 33). Line a 23-cm (9-inch) buttered cake tin with the pastry. Spread Almond Cream (p. 44) into the base. Sprinkle with slivered almonds and bake for 25 minutes.

Cherry Tart

PITHIVIERS

pithiviers

Preparation time: 1 hour, plus chilling time
Cooking time: 30 minutes
Serves 6

350 g (12 oz) blanched almonds
175 g (6 oz) caster sugar
1 teaspoon almond extract
1 teaspoon grated lemon zest
3 eggs
175 g (6 oz) butter, softened
250 g (9 oz) Puff Pastry (p. 31)
1 egg yolk, for glazing

Preheat the oven to 190°C/375°F/Gas Mark 5. Pound the almonds in a mortar, or process in a blender, with the sugar, almond extract and lemon zest. Add the three eggs, one by one, and the butter. Knead the mixture. Line a pie dish or tart tin with half the puff pastry. Fill with the almond mixture. Cover with another pastry circle, moisten the edges with a little water and press to seal. Brush with the egg yolk to glaze. With a sharp knife, starting in the centre, score patterns on the pastry out to the edges, like the spokes of a wheel. Bake for 30 minutes, or until golden brown.

ARLÉSIENNE OU SACRISTAINS

Arlésiennes ou Sacristains

Preparation time: 2 hours 10 minutes, plus
   chilling time
Cooking time: 15–20 minutes

Butter, for greasing
1 quantity Puff Pastry (p. 31)
1 egg, beaten
Icing sugar or caster sugar, for dredging
Ground almonds (optional)

Recipe photograph p. 166

Preheat the oven to 180/350°F/Gas Mark 4 and line a baking tray with buttered greaseproof paper. Roll the puff pastry out into a sheet 4 to 5 mm (⅛ to ¼ inch) thick. Cut into strips 1.5 cm (½ inch) wide and 10 cm (4 inches) long. Brush with the egg to glaze and dredge generously with icing or caster sugar.

If desired, sprinkle with ground almonds. Twist the dough, ensuring that the ends of each twist are slightly moistened and pressed on the baking tray to adhere, so they will keep their shape as they bake. Transfer to the baking tray and bake for 15–20 minutes.

Pithiviers

Arlésienne ou Sacristains

Jalousies

Butterflies

JALOUSIES
Jalousies

Preparation time: 2 hours 20 minutes,
  plus chilling time
Cooking time: 25–30 minutes
Serves 6

1 quantity Puff Pastry (p. 31)
150 g (5 oz) redcurrant jelly
50 g (1¾ oz) almonds, chopped
1 egg, beaten

Recipe photograph p.167

Preheat the oven to 180°C/350°F/Gas Mark 4. Roll the puff pastry out into a strip 40–50 cm (16–20 inches) long, about 12 cm (4½ inches) wide and 3–4 mm (⅛–¼ inch) thick. Cut the pastry strip so that you have two 25-cm (10-inch) pieces. Spread a layer of redcurrant jelly on one piece of puff pastry and cover with the other piece. Using a sharp knife, cut slits in the top layer of pastry 5 mm (¼ inch) apart, stopping short of the edges. Brush the tart with beaten egg to glaze.

Place on a slightly damp baking tray lined with greaseproof paper and bake for 25–30 minutes until crisp and golden brown. Warm the remaining redcurrant jelly with 2 tablespoons of water in a small pan, stirring until smooth. Take the tart out of the oven and brush with redcurrant jelly. Sprinkle with the almonds.

Note: The redcurrant jelly can be replaced by warmed, sieved apricot jam, and the almonds by nibbed sugar or Almond Cream (p. 44).

BUTTERFLIES
papillons

Preparation time: 2 hours 10 minutes,
  plus chilling time
Cooking time: 15–20 minutes
Serves 6

Butter, for greasing
1 quantity Puff Pastry (p. 31)
1 egg, beaten
Icing sugar or caster sugar, for dredging

Preheat the oven to 180°C/350°F/Gas Mark 4 and line a baking tray with buttered greaseproof paper. Roll the puff pastry out into a sheet 7 mm (⅞ inch) thick. Cut this into rectangles, approximately 5 × 2 cm (2 × ¾ inch). Twist both ends through 180 degree in opposite directions, taking care not to tear the pastry, then brush egg on both sides to glaze and generously dredge with icing sugar or caster sugar. Place the pastries on the baking tray and bake for 15–20 minutes.

NAPOLEON

mille-feuilles

Preparation time: 2 hours 30 minutes,
  plus chilling and cooling time
Cooking time: 20 minutes
Serves 6

Butter, for greasing
1 quantity Puff Pastry (p. 31)
1 egg, beaten
1 quantity Crème Pâtissière (p. 41)
Icing sugar or caster sugar, for dredging

Make the puff pastry. Preheat the oven to 180°C/350°F/
Gas Mark 4. Roll the dough out into a 36 × 36 cm
(14 × 14 inch) square. Prick all over with a fork and place
on a slightly damp but ungreased baking tray. Bake the
pastry for 15–20 minutes until it is dry and crisp.

Using a serrated knife, cut the square into 3 equal
12 × 36 cm (4½ × 14 inch) rectangles, and each of these
rectangles into 6 small 12 × 6 cm (4½ × 2½ inch) rectangles.

Cut the cooked pastry lengthways into 3 equal-sized
strips. Once cooled, spread some crème pâtissière over
one of these and cover with a second pastry strip.
Spread this layer with more crème pâtissière and finish
by placing the third pastry strip on top. Dredge very
generously with icing sugar. The icing sugar can be
branded in a diamond pattern with a red-hot skewer
if desired.

Napoleon

TARTS

Fruit tarts are an ideal way to show off seasonal produce. When working the dough, the work surface should be dusted very lightly with flour. Too much of it can toughen the pastry dough.

APPLE TART
tarte aux pommes

Preparation time: 20 minutes, plus
   chilling time
Cooking time: 30–40 minutes
Serves 6

Butter, for greasing
Plain flour, for dusting
1 quantity Puff Pastry (p. 31)
1 egg, beaten
1 quantity Apple Purée (p. 276)
4–5 apples
Granulated sugar, to taste

Preheat the oven to 180°C/350°F/Gas Mark 4 and grease a baking tray with butter. Dust the work surface with flour and roll out the puff pastry to a thickness of 1 cm (½ inch). Cut the sheet into a square, reserving four strips of pastry to form a border all round the square. Dampen the surface round the edges of the square and stick the strips in place. Transfer to the baking tray and flute the edges with a pastry crimper or back of a knife. Brush the border strips with the lightly beaten egg to glaze. Prick the pastry base all over with a fork to prevent the centre of the tart from rising too much.

Spread the apple purée to cover the pastry square, excluding the borders. Peel, core and thinly slice the apples. Arrange them, overlapping, so that they completely cover the purée. Sprinkle the apple slices liberally with granulated sugar. Bake for 30–40 minutes until the tart is cooked through and the sugar forms a very shiny glaze.

ALMOND AND RUM TARTLETS
tartelettes au rhum et pâte d'amandes

Preparation time: 20 minutes, plus
   chilling time
Cooking time: 20 minutes
Serves 6

30 g (1¼ oz) butter, softened,
   plus extra for greasing
1 quantity Shortcrust Pastry (p. 33)
100 g (3½ oz) ground almonds
100 g (3½ oz) caster sugar
3 eggs
2 tablespoons rum
150 g (5 oz) apricot jam, to glaze
Almonds, toasted and chopped,
   to decorate (optional)

Preheat the oven to 160°C/325°F/Gas Mark 3. Grease twelve 6-cm (2½ inch) tartlet tins with butter. Roll out the shortcrust pastry to a thickness of about 3 mm (⅛ inch) and use it to line the tins.

Place the ground almonds, sugar and eggs in a bowl and mix to combine. Add the butter and rum and stir until smooth. Fill the tartlet moulds with this mixture and bake for 20 minutes. Warm the apricot jam with 3 tablespoons of water and sieve it to make a smooth purée. Once the tartlets are cooked, brush apricot jam on top to glaze and, if wished, sprinkle over the almonds.

JAM TART

tarte aux fruits, à la confiture

Preparation time: 20 minutes,
    plus chilling time
Cooking time: 25 minutes
Serves 6

1 quantity Shortcrust Pastry (p. 33)
250 g (9 oz) fruit jam or compote
    of your choice

Roll out the shortcrust pastry case and line a 25-cm (10-inch) tart pan. Blind bake for 15 minutes, or until golden brown. Fill with cooked fruit or jam of your choice.

TARTLETS WITH CRÈME PÂTISSIÈRE AND PINEAPPLE

tartelettes à la crème et à l'ananas

Preparation time: 20 minutes,
    plus chilling time
Cooking time: 10–15 minutes
Serves 6

Butter, for greasing
1 quantity Rich Sweet Pastry (p. 35)
1 quantity Crème Pâtissière (p. 41)
2 tablespoons of Kirsch
3 slices of pineapple

Preheat the oven to 160°C/325°F/Gas Mark 3 and grease six 9-cm (3½-inch) tart tins with butter. Roll out the pastry to a thickness of about 3 mm (⅛ inch) and use it to line the tins. Place greaseproof paper and baking beans in each tartlet and bake blind for 10–15 minutes. Remove the paper and baking beans and allow the tartlets to cool.

Flavour the crème pâtissière with the Kirsch and spread a little of this on the base of each tartlet case. Cut each pineapple slice in half and trim into diamond shapes, using one half-pineapple slice to top each tart.

Jam Tart

Jam-Filled Pastry

JAM-FILLED PASTRY

galette grillée à la confiture

Preparation time: 30 minutes,
  plus chilling time
Cooking time: 35–45 minutes
Serves 6

Butter, for greasing
Plain flour, for dusting
½ quantity Puff Pastry (p. 31)
1 egg yolk, to glaze
200 g (7 oz) redcurrant jelly or
  raspberry jam

Preheat the oven to 180°C/350°F/Gas Mark 4. Grease a baking tray with butter. Dust the work surface with flour and roll out to 20 × 30 cm (8 × 12 inches). Trim the edges with a sharp knife, just enough to make them even and to give a cut edge all the way round, which aids raising. Lay the pastry on to the baking tray and flute or pinch up the edges to form a raised border. Fill with jam. Cut the remaining pastry into 1-cm (½-inch) strips and arrange these in a lattice pattern over the entire surface of the jam. Brush the pastry surfaces with egg yolk to glaze and bake for 35–45 minutes, until golden brown and the base is cooked through.

COGNAC AND ALMOND TARTLETS

petits gâteaux en moules

Preparation time: 15 minutes,
  plus 30 minutes chilling time
Cooking time: 20–30 minutes
Serves 6

300 g (11 oz) butter, softened,
  plus extra for greasing
300 g (11 oz) plain flour, plus extra
  for dusting
50 ml (2 fl oz) brandy
1 egg
A red fruit jam (optional)

For the almond filling:
250 g (9 oz) ground almonds
250 g (13 oz) caster sugar
8 egg whites

Preheat the oven to 180°C/350°F/Gas Mark 4. Grease 6 individual tart tins, which should be at least 3 cm (1¼ inches) deep, or 12 smaller tartlet tins, with butter. Place the flour, brandy and egg in a bowl and add 3 tablespoons of cold water. Mix to combine and then add the butter and knead to make a smooth dough. Cover and chill for 30 minutes. Dust the work surface with flour, roll out the dough to a scant 5 mm (¼ inch) and line the tins with it. If desired, spread a little fruit jam into the tart.

Make the almond filling by lightly whisking the egg whites and mixing in the ground almonds and sugar. Pour the filling into each pastry lined mould. Bake the tartlets for 20–30 minutes until golden brown (exact timing will depend upon the chosen size of the tartlets).

Note: The ground almonds in the filling can be replaced with other ground nuts, such as pecans, walnuts or hazelnuts, or a combination.

Linzertorte

LINZERTORTE
linzertorte

Preparation time: 30 minutes
Cooking time: 25–30 minutes
Serves 6

125 g (4¼ oz) butter, plus extra for greasing
200 g (7 oz) plain flour, plus extra for
dusting 125 g (4¼ oz) caster sugar
1 egg yolk
125 g (4¼ oz) ground almonds
1 teaspoon ground cinnamon,
    or more to taste
3 teaspoons cocoa powder,
    or more to taste
250 g (9 oz) raspberry jam with whole fruits

Ensure your hands are cool when preparing this dough. Preheat the oven to 190°C/375°F/Gas Mark 5 and grease a 23-cm (9-inch) tart tin with butter. Mix the flour, butter, sugar, egg yolk and ground almonds together. Add the cinnamon and cocoa powder and knead to a smooth dough. The pastry should have a good colour. Dust the work surface with flour and roll out the dough to a scant 5 mm (¼ inch). Line the tin with the pastry, reserving the offcuts.

Line the pastry case with greaseproof paper and fill with baking beans or uncooked rice. Bake for 10 minutes, then gently remove the greaseproof paper and baking beans or rice and spread raspberry jam over the base. Gather the pastry offcuts into a ball, roll out and cut into narrow strips using a pastry wheel. Lay these strips in a lattice pattern over the jam and put the tart back in the oven to finish cooking for 15–20 minutes.

PINEAPPLE TART
tarte à l'ananas

Preparation time: 20 minutes,
    plus chilling and cooling time
Cooking time: 40–45 minutes
Serves 8

1 quantity Rich Sweet Pastry (p. 35)
1 egg, lightly beaten

For the filling:
2 sliced pineapple
1 egg
150 g (5 oz) caster sugar
1 tablespoon Kirsch
100 g (3½ oz) butter, melted

Preheat the oven to 180°C/350°F/Gas Mark 4. Line a 23-cm (9-inch) loose-based tart tin or 6–8 individual tartlet tins with the pastry, reserving a little of the dough. Bake blind for 10–15 minutes and then brush the pastry base with the egg and return to the oven for 2 minutes. Remove and leave to cool.

Dice one of the pineapple slices and crush the other. For the filling, beat together the egg, sugar, sliced and crushed pineapple, kirsch and the butter in a bowl. Pour this mixture onto the cooked pastry. Decorate the tart or tartlets with strips of pastry 5 mm (¼ inch) wide, and brush them with a little more egg. Bake for 30–35 minutes, or until golden and risen slightly.

RICE PUDDING TART
tarte au riz

Preparation time: 20 minutes, plus
  chilling time
Cooking time: 25 minutes
Serves 6

Butter, for greasing
1 quantity Shortcrust Pastry (p. 33)
1 quantity Rice Milk Pudding (p. 265)
Vanilla extract or grated lemon zest

Preheat the oven to 180°C/350°F/Gas Mark 4 and grease
a 23-cm (9-inch) tart tin with butter. Line the tart tin
with the pastry. Line the pastry case with greaseproof
paper and fill with baking beans or uncooked rice. Bake
for 15 minutes. Remove the paper and beans or rice.

Flavour the rice pudding with vanilla extract or grated
lemon zest and pour into the pastry case. Bake for
a further 10 minutes.

WALNUT TART
tarte aux noix

Preparation time: 35 minutes, plus
  chilling and cooling time
Cooking time: 45 minutes
Serves 6

Butter, for greasing
1 quantity Rich Sweet Pastry (p. 35)
1 egg
250 g (9 oz) thick crème fraîche
100 g (3½ oz) caster sugar
100 g (3½ oz) ground walnuts
1 teaspoon ground cinnamon
Icing sugar
10 walnut halves

Preheat the oven to 180°C/350°F/Gas Mark 4 and grease
a 23-cm (9-inch) tart tin with butter. Make the pastry
and line the tart tin with it, pressing it out by hand to
a thickness of 3–4 mm (⅛–¼ inch). Prepare the filling by
mixing the egg, crème fraîche, sugar, ground walnuts
and cinnamon together. Spread the filling over the base
of the tart and bake for 45 minutes.

Once cool, sprinkle the tart with icing sugar and
decorate with the walnuts. This tart should be eaten cold.
If refrigerated it will keep for 3–4 days.

PEAR TART
tarte aux poires

Preparation time: 20 minutes, plus
  chilling and cooling time
Cooking time: 10–15 minutes
Serves 6

Butter, for greasing
1 quantity Rich Sweet Pastry (p. 35)
1 quantity Crème Pâtissière (p. 41)
2 tablespoons of Kirsch
3 pears, thinly sliced
Sieved apricot jam or Royal Icing (p. 36)

Recipe photograph p.182

Preheat the oven to 160°C/325°F/Gas Mark 3. Grease six
9-cm (3½-inch) tart tins with butter. Roll out the pastry
to a thickness of about 3 mm (⅛ inch) and use it to line
the tins. Place greaseproof paper and baking beans in
each tartlet and bake blind for 10–15 minutes. Remove
the paper and baking beans and allow the tartlets to
cool. Flavour the crème pâtissière with the Kirsch and
spread a little of this on the base of each tartlet case.
Cut each pear slice in half and trim into diamond
shapes, using one sliced half-pear to top each tart.
Glaze with sieved apricot jam or royal icing.

Walnut Tart

Pear Tart

Alsace Tart

ALSACE TART

tarte à l'alsacienne

Preparation time: 20 minutes, plus
    chilling time
Cooking time: 30–40 minutes
Serves 6

1 quantity Shortcrust Pastry (p. 33)
500 g (1 lb 2 oz) apricots or apples,
    peeled, cored and sliced
50 g (1¾ oz) plain flour
2 eggs
100 g (3½ oz) caster sugar
100 ml (3½ fl oz) crème fraîche

Recipe photograph p. 183

Preheat the oven to 180°C/350°F/Gas Mark 4. Grease a 20-cm (8-inch) tar tin. Roll out the pastry to a thickness of about 3 mm (⅛ inch) and use it to line the tart tin. Prepare an uncooked shortcrust pastry case. Arrange the fruit on the pastry. In a bowl, beat the flour, eggs, sugar and crème fraîche until just smooth. Pour over the fruit and bake for 30–40 minutes.

Note: To make a Rhubarb Tart, replace the apricots or apples with 500 g (1 lb 2 oz) rhubarb cut into 3-cm (1¼-inch) slices. Coat with the custard mixture and bake. Sprinkle with extra sugar to taste.

STRAWBERRY OR RASPBERRY TARTLETS

tartelettes aux fraises ou framboises

Preparation time: 15 minutes, plus
    chilling and cooling time
Cooking time: 10–15 minutes
Serves 6

Butter, for greasing
1 quantity Shortcrust Pastry (p. 33)
    or Rich Sweet Pastry (p. 35)
500 g (1 lb 2 oz) soft fruit, such as
    strawberries or raspberries
200 g (7 oz) redcurrant jelly
1 quantity Sweetened Whipped
    Cream (p. 38) or Crème Pâtissière
    (p. 41) (optional)

Preheat the oven to 160°C/325°F/Gas Mark 3. Grease six 10-cm (4-inch) tart tins or twelve 6-cm (2½-inch) tartlet tins with butter. Roll out the pastry to a thickness of about 3 mm (⅛ inch) and use it to line the moulds. Place greaseproof paper and baking beans in each tartlet and bake blind for 10–15 minutes. Remove the paper and baking beans and allow the tartlets to cool.

Shortly before serving, if desired, spread with whipped cream or crème pâtissière before arranging the fruit inside the tartlet cases. Make a redcurrant syrup by placing the redcurrant jelly in a small pan with 3 tablespoons of water. Heat gently until a syrupy liquid is obtained. Dip a pastry brush into this syrup and glaze the fruits with it.

Note: For currant tartlets, replace the fruit with 700 g (1 lb 8½ oz) of currants. Remove the currants from their stalks before placing in the tarts.

Strawberry Tartlets

PUMPKIN TART

tarte au potiron

Preparation time: 30 minutes, plus
   chilling time
Cooking time: 55 minutes
Serves 6

Butter, for greasing
1 quantity Sweet Pastry (p. 32)
1 kg (2¼ lb) pumpkin flesh, diced
3 eggs
150 g (5 oz) caster sugar
80 g (2¾ oz) plain flour
Pinch of salt
Grated zest of 1 unwaxed lemon
180 g (6¼ oz) crème fraîche

Preheat the oven to 180°C/350°F/Gas Mark 4 and grease a deep 23-cm (9-inch) tart tin with butter. Line the tart tin with the pastry. Line the pastry case with greaseproof paper and fill with baking beans or uncooked rice and bake for 15 minutes. Remove the paper and beans or rice. Meanwhile, place the pumpkin flesh in a covered saucepan and gently cook with no added water until tender. Purée the cooked pumpkin until very smooth. In a bowl, beat the eggs, sugar and flour. Add about 500 g (1 lb 2 oz) pumpkin purée. Add the salt, lemon zest and crème fraîche. Pour this filling into the pastry case and cook for 40 minutes.

MIRLITONS

mirlitons

Preparation time: 25 minutes, plus
   chilling time
Cooking time: 20 minutes
Serves 6

Butter, for greasing
1 quantity Shortcrust Pastry (p. 33)
4 eggs
1 teaspoon vanilla extract
125 g (4¼ oz) caster sugar
60 g (2 oz) ground almonds
60 g (2 oz) slivered almonds
Icing sugar, to decorate

Preheat the oven to 160°C/325°F/Gas Mark 3. Grease 12 barquette moulds with butter. Roll out the pastry to a thickness of about 3 mm (⅛ inch) and use it to line the moulds. Place the eggs, vanilla, sugar and ground almonds into a bowl and stir until thoroughly combined. Fill each tartlet with a little of the mixture. Scatter the almonds on top, sprinkle with icing sugar and bake for 20 minutes.

Pumpkin Tart

Grape Tartlets

GRAPE TARTLETS

tartelettes au raisin

Preparation time: 25 minutes, plus
  chilling time
Cooking time: 20 minutes
Serves 6

Butter, for greasing
1 quantity Sweet Pastry (p. 32)
225 g (8 oz) ripe seedless grapes
250 ml (8 fl oz) Sugar Syrup, cooked
  to soft-ball stage (p. 17)
250 g (5 oz) plum or apricot jam

Preheat the oven to 180°C/350°F/Gas Mark 4. Grease 12 tartlet tins with butter. Roll out the pastry to a thickness of about 3 mm (⅛ inch) and use it to line the tins. Place greaseproof paper and baking beans in the pastry-lined tins and bake blind for 15 minutes.

While the pastry is cooking, poach the grapes in a soft-ball syrup for 1 minute. The grapes should be totally coated in syrup, without losing their shape. Once the tartlets are cooked, discard the paper and baking beans and allow them to cool. Arrange the grapes in the tartlet cases. Warm the plum or apricot jam with 6 tablespoons of the syrup used to poach the grapes. Sieve to make a smooth glaze and brush the grapes with this glaze. Return to the oven for 5 minutes.

CONVERSATIONS

conversations

Preparation time: 35 minutes, plus
  chilling time
Cooking time: 15–20 minutes
Serves 4

Butter, for greasing
1 quantity Shortcrust Pastry (p. 33)
1 quantity Crème Pâtissière (p. 41)
1 teaspoon vanilla extract
1 quantity Royal Icing (p. 36)

Preheat the oven to 180°C/350°F/Gas Mark 4. Grease 6 individual tart tins or 12 smaller tartlet tins with butter. Reserve one-quarter of the shortcrust pastry to cover and decorate the tartlets. Roll out the remaining pastry to a thickness of 3 mm (⅛ inch) and use it to line the tartlet tins. Prick the bottom of each one with a fork.

Make the crème pâtissière and flavour it with vanilla. Fill the pastry-lined tarts with the crème pâtissière. Roll out three-quarters of the remaining pastry and cover each tartlet with it. Brush the lids generously with royal icing and decorate with the remaining pastry, cut into thin strips and arranged in a lattice pattern. Bake for 15–20 minutes.

CHESTNUT TARTLETS
tartelettes aux marrons

Preparation time: 40 minutes, plus
    chilling time
Cooking time: 10–15 minutes
Serves 6

Butter, for greasing
1 quantity Sweet Pastry (p. 32)
1 × 450 g (1 lb) tin unsweetened
    chestnut purée
3 tablespoons Kirsch
75 g (2½ oz) caster sugar
1 quantity Chocolate Icing (p. 37)

Preheat the oven to 180°C/350°F/Gas Mark 4. Grease twelve 10-cm (4-inch) barquette moulds with butter. Roll out the pastry to a thickness of about 3 mm (⅛ inch) and use it to line the moulds. Place greaseproof paper and baking beans in the pastry-lined moulds and bake blind for 10–15 minutes. Discard the paper and baking beans. Place the chestnut purée in a bowl and beat with the Kirsch and sugar to make a smooth purée, then fill each tartlet with chestnut purée and coat with chocolate icing.

BOURDALOUE APPLES
pommes à la bourdaloue

Preparation time: 40 minutes, plus
    chilling time
Cooking time: 35–40 minutes
Serves 6

200 g (7 oz) caster sugar
5 apples
1 quantity Rich Sweet Pastry (p. 35)
1 quantity Almond Cream (p. 44)

Make a syrup with 500 ml (18 fl oz) water and 150 g (5 oz) of the sugar, by heating until the sugar dissolves. Peel, core and quarter the apples and poach in the syrup at a very gentle simmer for 5 minutes

Preheat the oven to 200°C/400°F/Gas Mark 6. Use the pastry to line a fairly deep 23–25-cm (9–10-inch) tart tin or ovenproof dish. Line the pastry case with greaseproof paper and fill with baking beans or uncooked rice. Bake for 10 minutes. Remove the paper and beans or rice.

Spread half of the almond cream in the pastry case. Drain the apple quarters well and place them on the almond cream. Spread the rest of the almond cream over the top and return to the oven for a further 25–30 minutes, until golden.

To make a light caramel, pour the remaining sugar into a saucepan and warm over medium heat until sugar is slightly melted around the edges, about 5 minutes. Using a wooden spoon, gently stir until the sugar has completely melted and is amber coloured, about 10 minutes. Pour over the tart immediately.

Chestnut Tartlets

Rhubarb Tart

RHUBARB TART

tarte à la rhubarbe

Preparation time: 20 minutes, plus
    chilling time
Cooking time: 30–40 minutes
Serves 6

1 quantity Shortcrust Pastry (p. 33)

For the filling:
50 g (1¾ oz) plain flour
2 eggs
100 g (3½ oz) caster sugar
100 ml (3½ fl oz) crème fraîche
500 g (1 lb 2 oz) rhubarb , cut into 3-cm
    (1¼-inch) slices

Preheat the oven to 180°C/350°F/Gas Mark 4. Line
a 23–25-cm (9–10-inch) tart tin with the pastry. In a bowl,
beat the flour, eggs, sugar and crème fraîche until just
smooth. Coat the rhubarb in the mixture and pour into
the pastry case. Bake for 30–40 minutes.

GRAPE TART

flan aux raisins

Preparation time: 20 minutes, plus
    chilling time
Cooking time: 45 minutes
Serves 6

150 g (5 oz) plain flour
85 g (3 oz) butter, plus extra for greasing
200 g (7 oz) seedless white grapes
60 g (2 oz) ground almonds
100 ml (3½ fl oz) milk
1 egg
100 g (3½ oz) caster sugar

Preheat the oven to 160°C/325°F/Gas Mark 3. Make
a shortcrust pastry (p. 33) with the flour and butter.
Grease a shallow 23-cm (9-inch) tart tin with butter.
Roll out the pastry and use it to line the tart tin. Fill
the pastry with the grapes. In a bowl, mix together the
almonds, milk, egg and 50 g (1¾ oz) of the sugar. Pour
over the grapes. Sprinkle with the remaining sugar
and bake for 45 minutes.

Tarte Tatin

TARTE TATIN

tarte tatin

Preparation time: 25 minutes, plus
   chilling and cooling time
Cooking time: 30 minutes
Serves 6

125 g (4¼ oz) caster sugar
500 g (1 lb 2 oz) apples
1 quantity Shortcrust Pastry (p. 33)
40 g (1½ oz) butter

Preheat the oven to 200°C/400°F/Gas Mark 6. Take a metal flameproof 20-cm (8-inch) pie dish with a solid base and place in it 100 g (3½ oz) of the sugar and 1–2 tablespoons water. Place the dish over a medium heat until the sugar is slightly melted around the edges, about 5 minutes. Using a wooden spoon, gently stir until the sugar has completely melted and is a dark amber colour, about 12–13 minutes. Ensure the base of the dish is coated in caramel and allow to cool.

For the filling, peel, core and thinly slice the apples. Arrange close together in a ring on the caramel in the dish and sprinkle with the remaining sugar. Dot with the butter. Roll out the pastry to a thickness of 5 mm (¼ inch) and place over the apples, tucking the pastry into the tin all round so that the fruit is completely covered. Bake for 30 minutes, then turn out immediately onto a serving dish so that the caramelized apples are on top.

PUMPKIN FLAN

flan au potiron

Preparation time: 30 minutes, plus
   chilling time
Cooking time: 1 hour 20 minutes
Serves 8–10

500 g (1 lb 2 oz) pumpkin flesh, diced
70 g (2½ oz) plain flour
150 g (5 oz) caster sugar
Grated zest of 1 unwaxed lemon
Pinch of salt
3 eggs
250 ml (9 fl oz) milk
1 quantity Shortcrust Pastry (p. 33)

Place the pumpkin flesh with 2–3 tablespoons of water in a pan and cook over low heat for 45–60 minutes until very tender. In a blender or food processor, process to a smooth purée. Place the flour in a pan and add the sugar, lemon zest, salt and eggs. Mix until smooth and then whisk in the milk and pumpkin purée. Place the pan over medium heat and bring briefly to simmering point, whisking constantly to make a smooth sauce.

Preheat the oven to 200°C/400°F/Gas Mark 6 and grease a deep 23–25-cm (9–10-inch) tart tin with butter. Dust the work surface with flour and roll out the pastry dough to a thickness of 3 mm (⅛ inch). Use it to line the tart tin. Pour in the pumpkin filling and bake for 30 minutes. Reduce the oven temperature to 160°C/325°F/Gas Mark 3 and bake for another 20 minutes, or until set in the centre.

Note: Tinned pumpkin purée can be used as an alternative to preparing it as above. Use the same quantity.

PRUNE TART

tarte aux pruneaux

Preparation time: 15 minutes, plus chilling time
Cooking time: 30–35 minutes
Serves 6

1 quantity Shortcrust Pastry (p. 33)
20 Agen prunes, stoned and cooked in advance
1 quantity Crème Anglaise (p. 49)

Preheat the oven to 180°C/350°F/Gas Mark 4 and grease a 23-cm (9-inch) tin with butter. Line the tart tin with the pastry and bake blind for 10–15 minutes. Arrange the prunes in the pastry base and cover with crème anglaise. Return the tart to the oven and bake for a further 20 minutes.

ORANGE TART

tarte à l'orange

Preparation time: 20 minutes, plus
  chilling and cooling time
Cooking time: 30–35 minutes
Serves 6–8

1 quantity Rich Sweet Pastry (p. 35)
1 egg, lightly beaten

For the filling:
1 egg
150 g (5 oz) caster sugar
Grated zest and juice of 1 orange
85 g (3 oz) butter, melted

Preheat the oven to 180°C/350°F/Gas Mark 4. Line a 23-cm (9-inch) loose-based tart tin or 6–8 individual tartlet tins with the pastry, reserving a little of the dough. Bake blind and then brush the pastry base with the egg and return to the oven for 2 minutes. Remove and leave to cool.

For the filling, beat together the egg, sugar, orange zest and juice and the butter in a bowl. Pour this mixture onto the cooked pastry. Decorate the tart or tartlets with strips of pastry 5 mm (¼ inch) wide, and brush them with a little more egg. Bake for 30–35 minutes, or until golden and risen slightly.

Variation: To make lemon tartlets, replace the orange with one lemon. The filling will be less sweet.

Lemon Tartlets

BISCUITS

French biscuits are quick and easy to make with readily available ingredients that are always on hand, such as milk, eggs, sugar and vanilla. They can be crisp and buttery, soft and chewy, or sandwiched with a rich filling. To make biscuits successfully, make sure ingredients are all measured accurately and they are at the specified temperature. Most biscuits will keep well for a couple of days in an airtight container.

CLASSIC BISCUITS

These recipes are delicious and easy to make, and can be served as an accompaniment to a dessert or on their own. Recipes such as Langues de Chat and Tuiles require the use of a piping bag to lay out the batter – always leave plenty of space between each biscuit and pipe them evenly to ensure they do not spread during baking.

HAZELNUT TUILES
tuiles aux noisettes

Preparation time: 10 minutes
Cooking time: 8–10 minutes
Serves 6

Butter, for greasing
2 egg whites plus 1 egg yolk
95 g (3¼ oz) caster sugar
60 g (2 oz) plain flour
½ teaspoon vanilla extract
60 g (2 oz) ground hazelnuts

Preheat the oven to 200°C/400°F/Gas Mark 6. Grease two baking trays with butter. Use a spatula to mix the egg whites with the sugar in a mixing bowl. Stir in the flour, egg yolk and vanilla extract. Mix well. Spoon half-tablespoons of the mixture, well spaced out on the prepared trays and sprinkle each with a pinch of the ground hazelnuts.

Bake for 8–10 minutes. The tuiles should be golden brown round their edges. Remove one by one with a fish slice or spatula and shape them while they are still hot by bending them very briefly round the neck of a wine bottle or draping them over a rolling pin to cool.

SWEET SLICES
tranches sucrées

Preparation time: 10 minutes
Cooking time: 20–25 minutes
Serves 6

100 g (3½ oz) butter, chilled and
   diced, plus extra for greasing
200 g (7 oz) plain flour,
   plus extra for dusting
150 g (5 oz) caster sugar
2 eggs
½ teaspoon bicarbonate of soda
Nibbed sugar, to decorate

Preheat the oven to 200°C/400°F/Gas Mark 6 and grease a baking tray with butter. Place the chilled butter and flour in a mixing bowl and rub together until the mixture resembles breadcrumbs. Stir in the sugar, 1 egg and the bicarbonate of soda. Do not add water, as the dough should be firm. Dust the work surface with flour and roll out the dough to a thickness of 5 mm (¼ inch). Beat the remaining egg and brush over the dough to glaze. Cut into rectangles, approximately 6 × 3 cm (2½ × 1¼ inches). Sprinkle generously with the nibbed sugar then place on the prepared tray and bake for 20–25 minutes.

Hazelnut Tuiles

Cigarettes

CIGARETTES

cigarettes

Preparation time: 10 minutes
Cooking time: 7–10 minutes
Serves 6

75 g (2½ oz) butter, softened,
   plus extra for greasing
4 large egg whites
150 g (5 oz) caster sugar
100 g (3½ oz) plain flour
Pinch of salt
1 teaspoon vanilla extract
50 g (1¾ oz) ground almonds

Preheat the oven to 200°C/400°F/Gas Mark 6 and grease a baking tray with butter. In a bowl, whisk the egg whites for 1 minute. Add the sugar, flour, salt, vanilla extract and the ground almonds and stir with a wooden spoon until smooth. Add the softened butter and continue to stir until well combined.

Transfer the mixture to a piping bag fitted with a 1-cm (½-inch) round nozzle. Pipe it out into discs, 2 cm (1 inch) in diameter, on to the prepared tray, leaving space between them. Bake for 7–10 minutes until pale golden brown. Carefully detach the biscuits using a fish slice or spatula, one at a time, from the tray and curl them while still hot around a pencil-sized cylindrical object.

BIARRITZ

biarritz

Preparation time: 20 minutes
Cooking time: 20–25 minutes
Serves 6

40 g (1½ oz) butter, melted and cooled,
   plus extra for greasing
4 egg whites
40 g (1½ oz) ground almonds
40 g (1½ oz) ground hazelnuts
40 g (1½ oz) plain flour
160 g (5½ oz) caster sugar
2 drops orange extract or orange oil
100 g (3½ oz) dark chocolate, chopped

Preheat the oven to 180°C/350°F/Gas Mark 4 and grease a baking tray with butter. Whisk the egg whites until stiff. Sprinkle in the ground almonds and hazelnuts, folding in gently, followed by the flour, sugar, melted butter and orange extract or orange oil. Incorporate each ingredient gently but thoroughly.

Using a piping bag or two teaspoons, arrange small, well-spaced mounds of the mixture on the prepared tray. Bake for 20–25 minutes. Melt the chocolate in a heatproof bowl set over a pan of barely simmering water. Once cooled, dip half of each biscuit in the melted chocolate and leave to set before serving.

CLOTTED CREAM BISCUITS

gâteaux à la crème cuite

Preparation time: 5 minutes
Cooking time: 10 minutes
Serves 6

Butter, for greasing
125 ml (4½ fl oz) clotted cream
125 g (4¼ oz) caster sugar
125 g (4¼ oz) plain flour
1 teaspoon vanilla extract

Preheat the oven to 180°C/350°F/Gas Mark 4 and grease a baking tray with butter. Mix the cream, sugar, flour and vanilla together. Put small piles of the dough on the prepared tray, well spaced out. Bake for 10 minutes, or until the edges of the biscuits brown. These biscuits keep very well.

HELENETTES

hélénettes

Preparation time: 5 minutes
Cooking time: 8–10 minutes
Serves 3

1 egg yolk
40 g (1½ oz) butter, softened,
   plus extra for greasing
50 g (1¾ oz) caster sugar
50 g (1¾ oz) plain flour
50 g (1¾ oz) ground almonds or hazelnuts

Preheat the oven to 200°C/400°F/Gas Mark 6 and grease a baking tray with butter. In a bowl, beat the egg yolk and sugar for 1 minute. Stir in the butter, followed by the flour and the ground almonds or hazelnuts. Arrange the mixture in small mounds on the prepared tray, well spaced apart. Bake for 8–10 minutes until golden.

Note: Double the recipe to make more biscuits, or multiply as required.

Clotted Cream Biscuits

MILANESE BISCUITS WITH LEMON

gâteaux de milan no. 1

Preparation time: 10 minutes,
    plus chilling time
Cooking time: 8–10 minutes
Serves 12

125 g (4¼ oz) butter, softened,
    plus extra for greasing
Pinch of salt
500 g (1 lb 2 oz) caster sugar
Grated zest of 1 unwaxed lemon
6 egg yolks
500 g (1 lb 2 oz) plain flour

Preheat the oven to 200°C/400°F/Gas Mark 6 and grease a baking tray with butter. In a bowl, beat the butter until pale and creamy. Beat in the salt, sugar, lemon zest and 5 of the egg yolks. Stir in the flour and knead the dough briefly until it is smooth. Chill the dough until firm.

Dust the work surface with flour and roll out the dough to a thickness of approximately 5 mm (¼ inch). Use a pastry cutter to cut out your chosen shapes. Transfer the biscuits to the baking tray and brush with the remaining egg yolk to glaze. Bake for 8–10 minutes.

MILANESE BISCUITS WITH VANILLA

gâteaux de milan no. 2

Preparation time: 10 minutes,
    plus chilling time
Cooking time: 8–10 minutes
Serves 12

250 g (9 oz) butter, softened,
    plus extra for greasing
500 g (1 lb 2 oz) caster sugar
1 teaspoon vanilla extract, or
    other flavouring
Pinch of salt
6 egg yolks
550 g (1 lb 4 oz) plain flour,
    plus extra for dusting

Preheat the oven to 200°C/400°F/Gas Mark 6 and grease two baking trays with butter. Beat the butter, sugar, vanilla and salt until pale and creamy. Beat in 5 of the egg yolks and then the flour, adding a few drops of cold water if necessary to form a smooth dough. Chill the dough until firm.

Dust a work surface with flour and roll out the dough to 5 mm (¼ inch) thick. Use a pastry cutter to cut out your chosen shapes, place on the prepared trays and brush with the remaining egg yolk. Bake for 8–10 minutes, or until golden.

MILANESE BISCUITS WITH CINNAMON
gâteaux de milan no. 3

Preparation time: 10 minutes,
    plus chilling time
Cooking time: 8–10 minutes
Serves 12

300 g (11 oz) butter, plus extra for greasing
Pinch of salt
250 g (9 oz) caster sugar
½ teaspoon ground cinnamon
6 egg yolks
500 g (1 lb 2 oz) plain flour, plus extra
    for dusting

Preheat the oven to 200°C/400°F/Gas Mark 6 and grease a baking tray with butter. In a bowl, beat the butter until pale and creamy. Beat in the salt, sugar, cinnamon and 5 of the egg yolks. Stir in the flour and knead the dough briefly until it is smooth. Chill the dough until firm.

Dust the work surface with flour and roll out the dough to a thickness of approximately 5 mm (¼ inch). Use a pastry cutter to cut out your chosen shapes. Transfer the biscuits to the prepared tray and brush with the remaining egg yolk to glaze. Bake for 8–10 minutes.

BERLIN RINGS
couronnes de berlin

Preparation time: 20 minutes
Cooking time: 20–30 minutes
Serves 6

250 g (9 oz) butter, softened,
    plus extra for greasing
4 eggs
100 g (3½ oz) caster sugar
250 g (9 oz) plain flour
Nibbed sugar, to decorate

Preheat the oven to 180°C/350°F/Gas Mark 4 and grease a baking tray with butter. Hard-boil 2 of the eggs. Remove their yolks and mix these thoroughly with the yolks of the 2 remaining raw eggs. Discard the cooked egg white. Stir in the sugar and then, adding a little at a time, the flour and the butter. Knead the dough until it is smooth.

Break off large, walnut-sized pieces and roll these out, using the palms of your hands, to form cylinders. Join their ends to form rings and place on the prepared tray. Whisk the remaining raw egg whites until they form soft peaks and brush over the biscuits to glaze. Sprinkle with the nibbed sugar and bake for 20–30 minutes.

SOFT MACAROONS
macarons à la crème

Preparation time: 10 minutes,
    plus cooling time
Cooking time: 20 minutes
Serves 8

250 g (9 oz) ground almonds
250 g (9 oz) caster sugar
60 g (2 oz) crème fraîche
1 egg white
1 teaspoon vanilla extract

Preheat the oven to 160°C/325°F/Gas Mark 3 and line a baking tray with greaseproof paper. In a bowl, combine the almonds and sugar. Add the crème frâiche, egg white and vanilla and stir gently until thoroughly mixed.

Form walnut-sized balls of the mixture and place onto the baking tray, well spaced apart. Bake for 20 minutes until the macaroons are pale golden and still slightly soft in the centre. Turn the baking tray halfway through cooking, if necessary, to ensure even browning. Leave the macaroons to cool completely on the tray before removing from the paper.

MINI MACAROONS
petits macarons

Preparation time: 10 minutes
Cooking time: 10–15 minutes
Serves 6

100 g (3½ oz) ground almonds
100 g (3½ oz) caster sugar
4 egg whites

Preheat the oven to 190°C/375°F/Gas Mark 5 and line a baking tray with greaseproof paper. Using a wooden spoon, mix all of the ingredients together in a bowl until thoroughly combined. Place teaspoon-sized mounds of the mixture on the baking tray and bake for 10–15 minutes until pale golden in colour.

Soft Macaroons

Little Almond 'Rocks'

LITTLE ALMOND 'ROCKS'
rochers aux amandes

Preparation time: 20 minutes
Cooking time: 15 minutes
Serves 6

Butter, for greasing
3 egg whites
250 g (9 oz) caster sugar
250 g (9 oz) ground almonds

Preheat the oven to 120°C/250°F/Gas Mark 1 and grease a baking tray with butter. Stir the egg whites and sugar together in a pan set over low heat until the mixture thickens, about 15 minutes. Stir in the ground almonds. Beat briefly to prevent the mixture sticking to the base of the pan. Arrange in little mounds on the prepared tray, evenly spaced. Bake for 15 minutes.

SPOON BISCUITS
biscuits à la cuillère

Preparation time: 25 minutes
Cooking time: 10–15 minutes
Serves 6

Butter, for greasing
85 g (3 oz) caster sugar
3 eggs, separated
A few drops of orange-flower water
85 g (3 oz) plain flour
Icing sugar, for sprinkling

Preheat the oven to 160°C/325°F/Gas Mark 3 and grease a baking tray with butter. Place the sugar and egg yolks in a large bowl and, using an electric whisk, whisk for 5 minutes until pale and tripled in volume, adding the orange-flower water.

Whisk the egg whites to stiff peaks in a separate bowl. Fold the egg and sugar mixture and the egg whites together, along with the flour. Spoon or pipe into fingers on the baking tray. Sprinkle with icing sugar and bake for 10–15 minutes, without allowing the biscuits to colour.

WIESBADEN BISCUITS
pains de wiesbaden

Preparation time: 20 minutes,
    plus 30 minutes resting time
Cooking time: 20–25 minutes
Serves 6

250 g (9 oz) plain flour
Scant ½ teaspoon baking powder
125 g (4¼ oz) caster sugar
125 g (4¼ oz) butter, softened,
    plus extra for greasing
2 eggs plus 1 egg yolk
½ teaspoon ground cinnamon or grated
    zest of 1 unwaxed lemon

In a bowl, combine the flour and baking powder. In a separate bowl, mix together the sugar, butter, 1 whole egg and 1 egg yolk, then add the cinnamon or lemon. Add to the dry mixture and mix well, then work the dough by hand and shape it into a log. Allow to rest for 30 minutes at room temperature.

Preheat the oven to 180°C/350°F/Gas Mark 4 and grease a baking tray with butter. Cut the dough into 12-mm (½-inch) slices. Shape each slice into a small log, and pinch the ends as you flatten the top slightly, to form a boat shape. Beat the remaining egg lightly and brush over the biscuits to glaze. Bake for 20–25 minutes.

DOLLAR BISCUITS
dollars

Preparation time: 10 minutes
Cooking time: 15–20 minutes
Serves 6

100 g (3½ oz) butter, softened,
    plus extra for greasing
1 egg
1½ tablespoons rum
125 g (4¼ oz) caster sugar
150 g (5 oz) plain flour

Preheat the oven to 180°C/350°F/Gas Mark 4 and grease a baking tray with butter. Whisk the egg and rum together. Mix in the sugar, butter and flour. Put small piles of the dough on the prepared tray, well spaced apart, and bake for 15–20 minutes, or until golden brown.

Wiesbaden Biscuits

Petit Beurre Biscuits

PETIT BEURRE BISCUITS

petits beurres

Preparation time: 15 minutes,
  plus 1 hour resting time
Cooking time: 25–30 minutes
Serves 6

100 g (3½ oz) butter, chilled and diced,
  plus extra for greasing
250 g (9 oz) plain flour, plus extra for
dusting
50 g (1¾ oz) caster sugar
Pinch of salt
100 ml (3½ fl oz) double cream

Preheat the oven to 180°C/350°F/Gas Mark 4 and grease a baking tray with butter. In a bowl, rub the chilled butter into the flour until the mixture resembles breadcrumbs, then make a well in the centre. Place the sugar, salt and cream in the well. Combine these by hand with the butter and flour mixture, working it just long enough to shape into a smooth ball of dough. Cover the bowl and allow the dough to rest for 1 hour at room temperature.

Dust the work surface with flour and roll out the dough to a thickness of 5 mm (¼ inch). Cut out rectangles approximately 5 cm × 10 cm (2 inches × 4 inches), either using a sharp knife and a ruler, or a rectangular pastry cutter. Prick the biscuits evenly with a fork and place on the baking tray. Bake for 25–30 minutes until pale golden brown.

LITTLE ALMOND BALLS

petits pains soufflés aux amandes

Preparation time: 15 minutes
Cooking time: 10 minutes
Serves 6

175 g (6 oz) butter, plus extra for greasing
175 g (6 oz) caster sugar
Grated zest of 1 unwaxed lemon
4 eggs
250 g (9 oz) plain flour
1 teaspoon baking powder
100 g (3½ oz) almonds, chopped

Preheat the oven to 200°C/400°F/Gas Mark 6 and grease a baking tray with butter. Beat the butter, sugar and lemon zest until pale and creamy. Beat in 3 of the eggs, one at a time. Mix the flour and baking powder in a separate bowl before adding them to the butter and sugar mixture. Beat for another minute to incorporate more air.

Shape the mixture into walnut sized balls and roll them in the chopped almonds. Place on the prepared tray. Brush with the remaining egg, lightly beaten. Bake for 10 minutes.

Snowballs

SNOWBALLS
boules de neige

Preparation time: 15 minutes,
  plus cooling time
Cooking time: 20–25 minutes
Serves 6

100 g (3½ oz) butter, softened,
  plus extra for greasing
125 g (4¼ oz) caster sugar
1 egg, beaten with 1 tablespoon milk
1 teaspoon vanilla extract
250 g (9 oz) plain flour
2 teaspoons baking powder
4 tablespoons apricot jam, warmed and
  sieved (see note)
100 g (3½ oz) desiccated coconut

Preheat the oven to 180°C/350°F/Gas Mark 4 and grease a baking tray with butter. Beat the butter and sugar in a bowl until pale and creamy. Stir in the egg and vanilla. Mix the flour and baking powder in a separate bowl, then stir them in. The mixture should be fairly thick. Knead briefly until smooth.

Break off walnut-sized pieces of dough, shape these into balls and place on the baking tray. Bake for 20–25 minutes, increasing the oven temperature to 200°C/400°F/Gas Mark 6 after 10 minutes. When the snowballs have cooled, roll them first in the apricot jam and then roll them in the desiccated coconut.

Note: For preference, use smooth apricot jam, which will not require sieving. If especially thick, mix the jam with 2 tablespoons of hot water when warming it.

ALMOND SLICES
pains d'amandes

Preparation time: 15 minutes,
  plus 4 hours chilling time
Cooking time: 15 minutes
Serves 6

2 eggs
60 g (2 oz) caster sugar
1 teaspoon vanilla extract
½ teaspoon salt
75 g (2½ oz) ground almonds
100 g (3½ oz) butter, melted,
  plus extra for greasing
1 teaspoon baking powder
250 g (9 oz) plain flour

Mix the eggs in a bowl with the sugar, vanilla, salt, almonds and melted butter. Mix the flour and baking powder in a separate bowl, then gradually add to the liquid mixture and blend to form a smooth, firm dough. Shape the dough into a log, wrap in clingfilm and leave to chill in the refrigerator for 4 hours.

Towards the end of this time, preheat the oven to 200°C/400°F/Gas Mark 6 and grease a baking tray with butter. Cut the ball of dough into slices 1 cm (½ inch) thick. Place these in a single layer on the prepared tray and bake in a hot oven for 15 minutes.

Note: You may need to use two baking trays.

MARZIPAN BISCUITS

massepains

Preparation time: 20 minutes
Cooking time: 30 minutes
Serves 6

15 g (½ oz) plain flour, plus extra for dusting
125 g (4¼ oz) blanched almonds
200 g (7 oz) caster sugar
2 egg whites
Grated zest of 1 unwaxed lemon
½ quantity Ganache (p. 38) (optional)

Preheat the oven to 180°C/350°F/Gas Mark 4 and dust a baking tray with flour. Process the almonds with the sugar and egg whites in a food processor, or by hand in a pestle and mortar, to form a semi-liquid paste. Add the flour and lemon zest. Arrange small piles of this mixture on the baking tray. Bake for 30 minutes, until golden. If desired, sandwich in pairs with ganache in the middle.

ALMOND STRAWS

allumettes

Preparation time: 2 hours 10 minutes,
    plus chilling time
Cooking time: 15–20 minutes
Serves 6

Butter, for greasing
1 quantity Puff Pastry (p. 31)
1 egg, beaten
50 g (1¾ oz) almonds, coarsely chopped

Preheat the oven to 200°C/400°F/Gas Mark 6 and line a baking tray with buttered greaseproof paper. Roll the puff pastry out into a sheet 4–5 mm (⅛–¼ inch) thick and glaze with the egg. Cut into strips 1.5 cm (½ inch) wide and 10 cm (4 inches) long and transfer to the baking tray. Sprinkle with the almonds and bake for 15–20 minutes.

HONEY SPICE BISCUITS

petits pains d'épice de ménage

Preparation time: 10 minutes,
    plus 15 minutes resting time
Cooking time: 15 minutes
Serves 6

Butter for greasing
500 g (1 lb 2 oz) plain flour
40 g (1½ oz) caster sugar
2 teaspoons ground aniseed
2 teaspoons baking powder
500 g (1 lb 2 oz) runny honey
1 egg yolk

Preheat the oven to 190°C/375°F/Gas Mark 5 and grease a baking tray with butter. In a bowl mix together the flour, sugar, aniseed and baking powder. Add the honey. When the dough is smooth, transfer it to a floured work surface and roll it out with a rolling pin to a thickness of 5 mm (¼ inch). Using pastry cutters, cut out various shapes from the dough. Place on the baking tray and brush with a little egg yolk to glaze. Allow to rest for 15 minutes, then bake for 15 minutes.

Marzipan Biscuits

Langues de Chat

LANGUES DE CHAT

langues de chat

Preparation time: 20 minutes
Cooking time: 20 minutes
Serves 6

80 g (2¾ oz) butter, plus extra for greasing
80 g (2¾ oz) caster sugar
2 eggs
85 g (3 oz) plain flour

Preheat the oven to 190°C/375°F/Gas Mark 5 and grease a baking tray with butter. Beat the butter until creamy. Beat in the sugar and then the eggs, one by one. Stir in the flour. Spoon or pipe fingers of the mixture onto the baking tray and bake for 20 minutes. The biscuits should be golden brown on the edges, but pale in the middle.

Note: This buttery crisp, known as 'Cats' Tongues', gains its name from its long, flat shape.

CREAM LANGUES DE CHAT

langues-de-chat à la crème

Preparation time: 15 minutes
Cooking time: 15 minutes
Serves 6

Butter, for greasing
200 g (7 oz) double cream
250 g (9 oz) caster sugar
250 g (9 oz) plain flour
Grated zest of 1 unwaxed lemon
4 egg whites

Preheat the oven to 190°C/375°F/Gas Mark 5 and grease a baking tray with butter. Mix the cream and the sugar. Add the flour and the grated lemon rind. Whisk the egg whites until stiff and fold into the mixture. Spoon or pipe fingers onto the baking tray and bake for 15 minutes.

ALMOND CRESCENTS
croissants aux amandes

Preparation time: 25 minutes,
    plus 30 minutes for chilling time
Cooking time: 20–25 minutes
Serves 6

200 g (7 oz) butter, plus extra for greasing
280 g (10 oz) plain flour
100 g (3½ oz) ground almonds
175 g (6 oz) caster sugar
flaked almonds (optional)

Mix together the butter, flour, almonds and 100 g (3½ oz) of the sugar. Knead the dough lightly into a ball. If it is difficult to handle, place in the refrigerator for 30 minutes to firm up. Preheat the oven to 180°C/350°F/Gas Mark 4 and grease a baking tray with butter. Shape into small crescents. Place on the prepared tray and bake for 20–25 minutes. Sprinkle the biscuits with the remaining sugar while still hot.

Note: Flaked almonds may be added on top of the crescents just before they go into the oven.

ALMOND BATONS
bâtons aux amandes

Preparation time: 20 minutes
Cooking time: 15 minutes
Serves 6

125 g (4¼ oz) butter, softened,
    plus extra for greasing
160 g (5½ oz) caster sugar
2 eggs
250 g (9 oz) plain flour, plus extra
    for dusting
125 g (4¼ oz) almonds, coarsely chopped

Preheat the oven to 190°C/375°F/Gas Mark 5 and grease a baking tray with butter. Beat the softened butter with 60 g (2 oz) of the sugar until pale and creamy. Stir in the eggs and the flour, then the almonds.

Dust the work surface with flour and briefly knead the dough until smooth. Roll into long cylinders, approximately 1½ cm (¾ inch) in diameter, then cut into 6 cm (2½ inch) lengths. Roll these in the remaining sugar and place on the baking tray. Bake for 15 minutes.

Almond Crescents

SOUVAROFFS

souvaroffs

Preparation time: 10 minutes,
  plus 30 minutes chilling and cooling time
Cooking time: 10–12 minutes
Serves 6

200 g (7 oz) butter, softened,
  plus extra for greasing
100 g (3½ oz) caster sugar
250 g (9 oz) plain flour, plus extra for
dusting
½ teaspoon salt
1 teaspoon vanilla extract
Redcurrant or raspberry jelly,
  to sandwich the biscuits
Icing sugar, for sprinkling

Mix together the butter, sugar, flour, salt and vanilla to make a soft dough. If the dough is difficult to handle, chill it in the refrigerator for 30 minutes.

Preheat the oven to 180°C/350°F/Gas Mark 4 and grease a baking tray with butter. Roll out on a lightly floured work surface to a thickness of 2.5 mm (⅛ inch). Cut into 5-cm (2-inch) circles. Place on the prepared tray and bake for 10–12 minutes. Allow to cool, then sandwich the biscuits together in pairs using redcurrant or raspberry jelly. Sprinkle with icing sugar.

BLITZKUCHEN

blitzkuchen

Preparation time: 15 minutes
Cooking time: 15 minutes
Serves 6

125 g (4¼ oz) butter, plus extra for greasing
125 g (4¼ oz) caster sugar, plus
  extra for sprinkling
Grated zest of 1 unwaxed lemon
2 eggs
125 g (4¼ oz) plain flour
65 g (2¼ oz) slivered almonds

Preheat the oven to 200°C/400°F/Gas Mark 6 and thoroughly grease a baking sheet with butter. Beat the butter, sugar, and lemon zest until pale and creamy, then beat in the eggs. Stir in the flour. Place the dough on the prepared tray and roll it out until it is fairly thin. Sprinkle with the almonds and with sugar to taste. Bake for 15 minutes and cut into squares or diamonds while still hot.

Souvaroffs

SABLÉS

*Sablés, also known as French shortbread, French
butter cookie or Breton biscuit, originate from
Normandy in northern France. The dough should
be handled gently and not overmixed so the
biscuits are light and crumbly.*

SABLÉS
sablés

Preparation time: 20 minutes
Cooking time: 12 minutes
Serves 6

125 g (4¼ oz) cold butter, diced,
    plus extra for greasing
125 g (4¼ oz) caster sugar
250 g (9 oz) plain flour, plus
    extra for dusting
Pinch of salt
1 egg, lightly beaten
Grated lemon zest, vanilla extract
    or ground cinnamon, to taste

Preheat the oven to 180°C/350°F/Gas Mark 4 and grease
a baking tray with butter. Put the sugar, flour and salt
into a bowl and rub the butter in with your fingertips
until the mixture resembles fine breadcrumbs. Add the
egg and the chosen flavouring and turn out onto
a floured work surface. Knead lightly to form a dough.
Roll out to 5 mm (¼ inch) thick and use biscuit cutters
to cut into desired shapes. Place the biscuits on the
prepared tray and bake for 12 minutes until pale golden
and crisp.

ALMOND SABLÉS
sablés aux amandes

Preparation time: 15 minutes
Cooking time: 15 minutes
Serves 6

150 g (5 oz) butter, softened, plus extra
    for greasing
250 g (9 oz) plain flour, plus extra for dusting
90 g (3¼ oz) caster sugar
Pinch of salt
1 large egg
2 tablespoons rum
Grated zest of 1 unwaxed lemon
75 g (2½ oz) ground almonds
Milk, to glaze

Preheat the oven to 180°C/350°F/Gas Mark 4 and grease
a baking tray with butter. Place the flour in a mixing
bowl, or heap it up on a pastry slab, and make a well in
the centre. Add the butter, sugar, salt, egg, rum, lemon
zest and ground almonds. Work these into the flour to
form a smooth dough. Dust the work surface with flour
and roll out the dough to 7 mm (⅜ inch) thick. Cut this
sheet into diamond shapes and place the biscuits on the
baking tray. Brush their surfaces with a little milk and
bake for 15 minutes.

VANILLA SABLÉS
sablés à la vanille

Preparation time: 10 minutes,
  plus 1–2 hours chilling time
Cooking time: 8–10 minutes
Serves 6

60 g (2 oz) caster sugar
Pinch of salt
160 g (5½ oz) butter, softened,
  plus extra for greasing
2 egg yolks, plus 1 whole egg
1 teaspoon vanilla extract
200 g (7 oz) plain flour, plus
  extra for dusting

In a bowl, combine the sugar, salt, butter, egg yolks and vanilla. Add the flour and bring together to form a rough dough. Place on the work surface and 'smear' a section of the dough forward with the heel of your hand. Repeat until all the dough has been worked in this manner, keeping it in one piece throughout. Cover with clingfilm and chill for 1–2 hours.

Towards the end of this time, preheat the oven to 200°C/400°F/Gas Mark 6 and grease a baking tray with butter. Dust a clean, dry work surface with flour and roll the dough into a sheet 5 mm (¼ inch) thick. Using a pastry cutter, cut out into 10-cm (4-inch) circles. Cut each circle in half. Place on the prepared tray. Beat the remaining whole egg and brush onto the biscuits to glaze. Bake for 8–10 minutes.

CITRON SABLÉS
sablés au cédrat

Preparation time: 15 minutes
Cooking time: 10 minutes
Serves 6

150 g (5 oz) butter, softened,
  plus extra for greasing
125 g (4¼ oz) candied citron peel,
  finely chopped
250 g (9 oz) plain flour, plus
  extra for dusting
100 g (3½ oz) caster sugar
2 eggs
Pinch of salt
Grated zest of 1 unwaxed lemon

Preheat the oven to 200°C/400°F/Gas Mark 6 and grease a baking tray with butter. Place the candied peel and flour in a large bowl and make a well in the centre. Add the butter, sugar, 1 egg, salt and lemon zest to the well and bring together to form a soft, smooth dough.

Dust the work surface with flour and roll the dough out to a thickness of 1 cm (½ inch). Cut out the biscuits with a pastry cutter and place them on the pepared tray. Beat the remaining egg and brush over the biscuits to glaze. Bake for 10 minutes.

ORANGE SABLÉS
sablés à l'orange

Preparation time: 15 minutes,
    plus 1 hour chilling time
Cooking time: 10 minutes
Serves 6

250 g (9 oz) plain flour, plus
    extra for dusting
125 g (4¼ oz) butter, diced, plus extra
    for greasing
100 g (3½ oz) caster sugar
Pinch of salt
Grated zest of 1 unwaxed orange
Juice of ½ orange
1 egg yolk
1 × 40-g (1½-oz) piece candied orange peel

In a bowl mix the flour, butter, sugar, salt, orange zest and juice, and knead until smooth. Cover with clingfilm and chill for approximately 1 hour in the refrigerator.

Preheat the oven to 200°C/400°F/Gas Mark 6 and grease a baking tray with butter. Dust a work surface with flour and roll the dough into 5 mm (¼ inch) thick. Use a small round pastry cutter to cut out circles. Place on the baking tray and brush with egg yolk to glaze. Cut the candied orange peel into small, thin circles or diamond shapes and place one in the centre of each biscuit. Bake for 10 minutes until golden.

CRISP SABLÉS
sablés sec

Preparation time: 10 minutes,
    plus 1 hour chilling
Cooking time: 10–15 minutes
Serves 6

200 g (7 oz) plain flour, plus
    extra for dusting
100 g (3½ oz) caster sugar
Pinch of salt
125 g (4¼ oz) butter, diced,
    plus extra for greasing
2 eggs, beaten
1 teaspoon vanilla extract or
    grated zest of 1 unwaxed lemon

Mix the flour, sugar and salt in a mixing bowl. Make a well in the centre and add the butter, 1 egg and the vanilla or lemon zest. Work these ingredients together until combined and then shape the dough into a ball. Cover with clingfilm and chill for approximately 1 hour in the refrigerator.

Preheat the oven to 200°C/400°F/Gas Mark 6 and grease a baking tray with butter. Dust a work surface with flour and roll the dough into 5 mm (¼ inch) thick. Use a small round pastry cutter to cut out circles. Place on the baking tray and brush with the remaining egg to glaze. Bake for 10–15 minutes until golden.

Orange Sablés

NORMANDY SABLÉS

sablés normands

Preparation time: 10 minutes
Cooking time: 15 minutes
Serves 6

150 g (5 oz) butter, softened,
　plus extra for greasing
250 g (9 oz) plain flour, plus extra
　for dusting
65 g (2¼ oz) caster sugar
1 egg yolk
1 egg, lightly beaten

Preheat the oven to 180°C/350°F/Gas Mark 4 and grease a baking tray with butter. Mix the butter, flour, sugar and egg yolk in a bowl until combined, then turn out onto a lightly floured work surface and briefly knead to make a smooth dough. Roll out to 1 cm (½ inch) thick and cut into triangles or other shapes using a biscuit cutter. Brush with the beaten egg to glaze. Place the biscuits on the prepared tray and bake for 15 minutes, or until golden brown.

NANTES SABLÉS

sablés nantais

Preparation time: 10 minutes, plus
　20 minutes chilling time
Cooking time: 15 minutes
Serves 6

2 egg yolks, plus 1 whole egg
100 g (3½ oz) caster sugar
Pinch of salt
1 teaspoon vanilla extract
200 g (7 oz) plain flour, plus
　extra for dusting
100 g (3½ oz) butter, softened,
　plus extra for greasing

Beat the egg yolks and sugar in a mixing bowl for 1 minute. Stir in the salt, vanilla and flour. Work in the butter until a smooth, homogenous dough is formed. If the dough is difficult to handle, chill it in the refrigerator for 20 minutes.

Preheat the oven to 200°C/400°F/Gas Mark 6 and grease a baking tray with butter. Dust the work surface with flour and roll the dough out to 5 mm (¼ inch) thick. Cut into circles using a pastry cutter and place on the prepared tray. Beat the remaining whole egg and brush over the biscuits to glaze. Bake for 15 minutes or until golden brown.

NIORT SABLÉ

sablés niortais

Preparation time: 10 minutes
Cooking time: 15 minutes
Serves 8

175 g (6 oz) butter, diced,
　plus extra for greasing
1 egg
175 g (6 oz) caster sugar
Pinch of salt
2 teaspoons rum
250 g (9 oz) plain flour

Preheat the oven to 150°C/300°F/Gas Mark 2 and grease a 23-cm (9-inch) shallow fluted cake or flan tin with butter, preferably one with a loose base. Mix the egg in a bowl with the sugar, salt and rum. Add the flour, and the butter. Work together lightly until the mixture forms a crumbly dough. Place the dough in the tin, spreading it out and pressing it lightly into an even layer. Bake for 15 minutes, until golden.

Normandy Sablés

GALETTES AND CROQUANTES

Galettes and croquantes are crunchy biscuits that can be served any time of the day, but are ideal with tea or coffee. A few basic ingredients and minimal baking time are all that's needed.

CRUNCHY CROQUANTES
croquantes

Preparation time: 10 minutes
Cooking time: 10 minutes
Makes 36 biscuits

Butter, for greasing
240 g (8½ oz) caster sugar
3 eggs
Pinch of salt
125 g (4¼ oz) plain flour

Preheat the oven to 200°C/400°F/Gas Mark 6 and grease two baking trays with butter. Place the sugar in a bowl then add the eggs and salt. Stir well. Add the flour and combine until the mixture is smooth.

Drop spoonfuls of the mixture on the prepared trays, making sure they are well-spaced apart. Bake for 10 minutes until pale golden brown. Remove the hot biscuits from the baking trays using a palette knife. You will have enough mixture to cook two batches of biscuits.

ANISEED BISCUITS
croquets à l'anis

Preparation time: 10 minutes
Cooking: 20–25 minutes
Serves 8

85 g (3 oz) butter, softened,
   plus extra for greasing
250 g (9 oz) plain flour, plus
   extra for dusting
2 small whole eggs, plus 1 egg yolk
Pinch of salt
200 g (7 oz) caster sugar
1 teaspoon ground aniseed

Preheat the oven to 180°C/350°F/Gas Mark 4 and grease a baking tray with butter. In a mixing bowl, combine the flour with the two whole eggs and a pinch of salt. Add the butter, sugar and aniseed. Work the dough by hand until it forms a smooth ball. Dust the work surface with flour and roll out the dough to a thickness of 5 mm (¼ inch). Cut out into a variety of shapes, as desired. Brush with the remaining egg yolk to glaze and place on the prepared tray. Bake for 20–25 minutes.

CROQUETS FROM ALSACE
croquets alsaciens

Preparation time: 15 minutes
Cooking time: 15 minutes
Serves 6

Butter, for greasing
250 g (9 oz) plain flour, plus
   extra for dusting
250 g (9 oz) ground almonds
250 g (9 oz) caster sugar
3 eggs

Preheat the oven to 200°C/400°F/Gas Mark 6. Grease a baking tray with butter and dust with flour. Mix the flour, almonds and sugar with 2 of the eggs to make a smooth dough. Dust the work surface with flour and roll out the dough to a 1½-cm (¾-inch) thick rectangle. Transfer the dough to the prepared tray, trimming the edges if necessary. Beat the remaining egg and brush over the dough to glaze. Bake for 15 minutes or until golden. While hot, cut into vertical strips, then crosswise to form pointed edges.

WHITE WINE GALETTES
galettes au vin blanc

Preparation time: 10 minutes
Cooking time: 20 minutes
Serves 6

100 g (3½ oz) butter, softened,
   plus extra for greasing
200 g (7 oz) plain flour, plus
   extra for dusting
3 tablespoons dry white wine
100 g (3½ oz) caster sugar
Pinch of salt
1 egg yolk

Preheat the oven to 200°C/400°F/Gas Mark 6 and grease a baking tray with butter. Place the flour in a large bowl and make a well in the centre. Pour in the wine, then add the butter, sugar and salt. Mix together by hand to form a dough. Dust the work surface with flour and roll out the dough to a thickness of 5 mm (¼ inch). Cut into circles using a round pastry cutter. Transfer to the prepared tray and brush with egg yolk to glaze. Bake for 20 minutes.

CROQUETS FROM CARCASSONNE

croquets de carcassonne

Preparation time: 20 minutes
Cooking time: 25–30 minutes
Serves 6

80 g (2¾ oz) butter, softened,
　plus extra for greasing
250 g (9 oz) plain flour, plus
　extra for dusting
4 small eggs
100 g (3½ oz) caster sugar
Grated zest of 1 unwaxed lemon
125 g (4¼ oz) whole almonds,
　roughly chopped

Preheat the oven to 160°C/325°F/Gas Mark 3 and grease a baking tray with butter. Heap the flour in a mound on the work surface and make a well in the centre. Beat 3 of the eggs in a small bowl. Place the sugar, beaten eggs and lemon zest in the flour well and stir with your hand held like a paddle, gradually incorporating a little of the flour. Stir in the softened butter and almonds and finally incorporate the rest of the flour. Work the dough briefly. The process described above can also be done with an electric mixer at lowest speed.

Turn the dough onto a floured work surface and use a large, heavy kitchen knife to roughly 'chop' it until you have broken up the almonds it contains. Knead the dough until it is homogenous, divide in half and shape it into two thick cylinders. Place them on the prepared tray and flatten slightly. Beat the remaining egg and use to glaze the dough.

Bake for 15 minutes, then raise the oven temperature to 200°C/400°F/Gas Mark 6. Bake for a further 10 minutes or until lightly browned. Using a sharp, serrated knife, immediately cut both 'loaves' into 1-cm (½-inch) thick slices. Carefully lay the slices flat on the baking tray and return to the oven for a few more minutes, turning them once so that they brown on both sides.

CREAM-FILLED CROQUANTES

croquantes fourrées

Preparation time: 40 minutes,
　plus cooling time
Cooking time: 20 minutes
Serves 6

½ quantity Crunchy Croquante
　Batter (p. 232)
125 g (4¼ oz) plain chocolate, chopped
60 g (2 oz) crème fraîche
125 g (4¼ oz) chocolate sprinkles

Make the croquantes. Roll them up while still hot and set aside to cool. To make the filling, place the chocolate in a small heatproof bowl set over a pan of barely simmering water. Heat, stirring occasionally until smooth. Take it off the heat and add the crème fraîche, stirring well. Allow the filling to cool slightly and place into a piping bag fitted with a large plain nozzle. Pipe the filling as far as possible into both ends of all the biscuits and then coat the rims of each biscuit on the outside with the chocolate mixture. Dip the ends of each biscuit into a bowl of the chocolate sprinkles: as the filling cools, they will adhere firmly.

Cream-Filled Croquantes

MANDARIN GALETTES
galettes à la mandarine

Preparation time: 35 minutes
Cooking time: 20 minutes
Serves 6

Butter, for greasing
2 unwaxed mandarins or tangerines
160 g (5½ oz) whole almonds, skinned
   and finely chopped
70 g (2½ oz) plain flour
100 g (3½ oz) caster sugar
2 eggs, one of them separated

Preheat the oven to 200°C/400°F/Gas Mark 6 and grease a baking tray with butter. Rinse and dry the mandarins and pare off their zests using a sharp vegetable peeler, taking care not to draw any of the white pith. Finely chop the zest. In a bowl, mix the chopped zest and almonds with the flour, sugar, 1 whole egg and 1 egg yolk. Whisk the egg white until stiff and fold into the biscuit mixture. Place small mounds of the dough, well spaced apart, on the prepared tray. Bake for 20 minutes.

GALETTES FROM NANTES
galettes nantaises

Preparation time: 25 minutes
Cooking time: 15–20 minutes
Serves 6

60 g (2 oz) butter, softened,
   plus extra for greasing
125 g (4¼ oz) plain flour, plus extra for dusting
40 g (1½ oz) ground almonds
1 teaspoon salt
60 g (2 oz) caster sugar
2 egg yolks
50 g (1¾ oz) whole blanched almonds, halved

Preheat the oven to 180°C/350°F/Gas Mark 4 and lightly grease a baking tray with butter. Knead together the flour, almonds, butter, salt and sugar. Roll out the dough thinly on a lightly floured work surface and cut into 8-cm (3-inch) circles. Put on the baking tray. Mark the tops with lines using a knife or the tines of a fork. Brush with beaten egg yolk. Decorate each biscuit with an almond half. Bake for 15–20 minutes, or until golden.

CHOCOLATE GALETTES
galettes au chocolat

Preparation time: 25 minutes
Cooking time: 10–12 minutes
Serves 6

Butter, for greasing
125 g (4¼ oz) ground almonds
125 g (4¼ oz) chocolate, grated
125 g (4¼ oz) caster sugar
1 egg
Icing sugar, for dusting

Preheat the oven to 180°C/350°F/Gas Mark 4 and lightly grease a baking tray with butter. Stir together the almonds, chocolate, sugar and egg in a bowl, then bring together and knead lightly with your hands to form a smooth dough.

Dust your hands with icing sugar and shape the dough into small walnut-sized balls, keeping the dough as cool as possible. Place on the prepared tray, press lightly on each one and bake for 10–12 minutes, until crisp.

Mandarin Galettes

NORWEGIAN CROQUETS

croquets norvégiens

Preparation time: 15 minutes
Cooking time: 15–20 minutes
Serves 6

75 g (2½ oz) butter,
  plus extra for greasing
250 g (9 oz) plain flour, plus
  extra for dusting
1 teaspoon baking powder
75 g (2½ oz) caster sugar
3 eggs

Preheat the oven to 200°C/400°F/Gas Mark 6. Grease a baking tray with butter and dust with flour. Mix the baking powder, flour and sugar. Add the butter and 2 of the eggs, and mix to make a smooth dough.

Dust a work surface with flour and roll out the dough to a thickness of 1½ cm (¾ inch). Cut into two equal-sized squares measuring 15 cm (6 inches) and place on the baking sheet. Beat the remaining egg and brush over the dough to glaze. Bake for 15 minutes or until golden.

Cut the squares in half, then into ½-cm (¼-inch) strips while still hot. Turn the biscuits over carefully and return to the oven for a few minutes to dry out and brown lightly on the undersides.

SAVOURY BISCUITS

*Plainer than sweet biscuits, savoury biscuits can be
served along with hors d'œuvres, or with cheese after
a meal. These snacks are quick and easy and great
for parties and picnics.*

SAVOURY BATONS
batons salés

Preparation time: 15 minutes,
    plus 1 hour resting time
Cooking time: 10 minutes
Serves 8

200 ml (7 fl oz) milk
75 g (2½ oz) butter, plus
    extra for greasing
250 g (9 oz) plain flour, sieved,
    plus extra for dusting
2 teaspoons fine sea salt

Gently heat the milk and butter until it is lukewarm and
the butter has melted. Remove from the heat and add
the flour and 1 teaspoon of salt, all at once. Stir vigorously
for 2 minutes or until the dough is very smooth and
supple. Allow to rest for 1 hour at room temperature.

Preheat the oven to 200°C/400°F/Gas Mark 6 and
grease a baking tray with butter. Mix the remaining salt
with 3 tablespoons of water and set aside. Dust the work
surface with flour and roll out the dough until 5 mm
(¼ inch) thick. Cut into 1.5-cm × 10-cm (½-inch × 4-inch)
strips. Place these on the baking tray. Brush the surfaces
with the salty water and bake for 10 minutes until
golden brown.

SAVOURY GALETTES
galettes salées

Preparation time: 15 minutes
Cooking time: 15–20 minutes
Serves 6

60 g (2 oz) butter, plus extra for greasing
250 g (9 oz) plain flour, plus extra for
dusting
1 teaspoon baking powder
50 ml (2 fl oz) milk
1½ teaspoons salt

Preheat the oven to 200°C/400°F/Gas Mark 6 and
lightly grease a baking tray with butter. Rub the butter
into the flour until it resembles breadcrumbs. Make
a well and place in it the baking powder, milk and salt.
Mix, then knead to a smooth dough. Roll out to
a thickness of 5 mm (¼ inch) on a lightly floured work
surface and cut into circles. Place on the prepared tray
and bake for 15–20 minutes, or until golden brown.

Gruyère Matchsticks

GRUYÈRE MATCHSTICKS
allumettes au gruyère

Preparation time: 10 minutes
Cooking time: 20 minutes
Serves 6

150 g (5 oz) butter, plus extra for greasing
150 g (5 oz) plain flour
150 g (5 oz) Gruyère cheese, grated
Salt and pepper, to taste
Pinch of cayenne pepper

Preheat the oven to 200°C/400°F/Gas Mark 6 and grease a baking tray with butter. Place the flour and butter in a bowl and rub together with your fingertips until the mixture resembles breadcrumbs. Add the cheese and season with salt, pepper and cayenne. Knead the dough until it is smooth. Dust the work surface with flour and roll the dough out to a sheet 3–4 mm (⅛–¼ inch) thick. Cut this into strips ½ cm (¼ inch) wide. Place these strips on the prepared tray and bake for 20 minutes.

PARMESAN BISCUITS
fondants au parmesan

Preparation time: 10 minutes
Cooking time: 20 minutes
Serves 6

150 g butter, softened,
    plus extra for greasing
150 g plain flour, plus
    extra for dusting
150 g Parmesan cheese, finely grated
1 egg yolk

Preheat the oven to 200°C/400°F/Gas Mark 6 and grease a baking tray with butter. In a bowl, combine the flour, butter and cheese until a rough dough is formed. Do not add any salt. Dust the work surface with flour and briefly knead the dough until smooth. Roll out the dough to a thickness of 1 cm (½ inch) and use a pastry cutter to cut out small biscuits, approximately 5 cm (2 inches) in diameter. With a knife, draw a few parallel lines on each biscuit. Transfer the biscuits to the prepared tray and brush with egg yolk to glaze. Bake for 20 minutes.

LITTLE SAVOURY BATONS
bâtonnets salés

Preparation time: 15 minutes
Cooking time: 20–25 minutes
Serves 8

200 g (7 oz) butter, melted and cooled,
    plus extra for greasing
250 g (9 oz) plain flour, plus
    extra for dusting
500 ml (18 fl oz) milk
Pinch of fine sea salt
2 egg yolks
1 teaspoon sea salt flakes or crystals

Preheat the oven to 150°C/300°F/Gas Mark 2 and grease a baking tray with butter. Place the flour in a mixing bowl. Make a well in the centre and pour in the butter, milk and pinch of salt. Mix thoroughly, then place on a floured work surface and knead until the dough is smooth, elastic and no longer sticky. Break off walnut-sized pieces and roll them into cylinders approximately 1 cm × 7.5 cm (½ inch × 3 inches). Place on the prepared tray and brush with egg yolk to glaze. Sprinkle with salt flakes or crystals. Bake for 20–25 minutes until crisp and light golden brown.

CHEESE STRAWS

pailles au fromage

Preparation time: 10 minutes
Cooking time: 10 minutes
Serves 6

125 g (4¼ oz) butter, diced,
    plus extra for greasing
125 g (4¼ oz) plain flour, plus
    extra for dusting
300 g (11 oz) Cheddar cheese, grated
1 teaspoon salt
2 egg yolks plus 1 whole egg
Pinch of cayenne pepper

Preheat the oven to 200°C/400°F/Gas Mark 6 and grease a baking tray with butter. In a bowl, combine the flour, 200 g (7 oz) of the cheese, salt, butter and egg yolks until the mixture forms a dough. Dust a work surface with flour and roll out the dough to a rectangle of 1 cm (½ inch) thick. Cut into long, narrow strips. Place these on the prepared tray. Beat the remaining whole egg and brush over the cheese straws to glaze. Sprinkle with the remaining grated cheese and cayenne pepper. Bake for 10 minutes.

THIN SAVOURY BISCUITS

palets salés

Preparation time: 10 minutes,
    plus 2 hours chilling time
Cooking time: 10 minutes
Serves 8

500 g (1 lb 2 oz) plain flour
60 g butter, softened,
    plus extra for greasing
100 ml (3½ fl oz) milk
100 ml (3½ fl oz) water
20 g (¾ oz) fine sea salt

Combine all the ingredients together in a bowl to form a rough dough. Place on the work surface and 'smear' a section of the dough forward with the heel of your hand. Repeat until all the dough has been worked in this manner, keeping it in one piece throughout. Cover with clingfilm and chill in the refrigerator for approximately 2 hours.

Preheat the oven to 200°C/400°F/Gas Mark 6 and grease a baking tray with butter. Dust the work surface with flour and roll out the dough into a sheet ½ cm (¼ inch) thick. Use a pastry cutter to cut out small biscuits, approximately 5 cm (2 inches) in diameter. Prick the biscuits evenly with a fork. Place on the prepared tray and bake for 10 minutes until golden brown. Spread these biscuits with butter when serving.

PUFFY CHEESE STRAWS
allumettes au fromage

Preparation time: 35 minutes
Cooking time: 20 minutes

125 g (4¼ oz) butter, diced,
    plus extra for greasing
125 g (4¼ oz) plain flour, plus
    extra for dusting
Pinch of salt
125 g (4¼ oz) Gruyère cheese, finely grated
2–3 tablespoons milk

Line a baking tray with buttered greaseproof paper. In a mixing bowl, combine the flour, butter, salt and 100 g (3½ oz) of the Gruyère cheese until it resembles coarse breadcrumbs. Stir in just enough milk to make a fairly firm dough.

Dust the work surface with flour and roll the dough out to a long rectangle. Fold the strip of dough as for puff pastry (p. 31). Repeat this rolling, folding and turning operation 4 times without leaving the dough to rest between 'turns'. Repeat the operation twice more but sprinkle the strip of pastry with half the remaining Gruyère cheese before each folding.

Roll out the dough into a sheet 1 cm (½ inch) thick. Cut the sheet into rectangles measuring 2 × 8 cm (1 × 3¼ inches). Preheat the oven to 200°C/400°F/ Gas Mark 6. Place the cheese straws on to the baking tray and bake for 15–20 minutes.

CHEESE GALETTES
galettes au fromage

Preparation time: 10 minutes
Cooking time: 15–20 minutes
Serves 10

300 g (11 oz) butter, softened,
    plus extra for greasing
250 g (9 oz) plain flour, plus
    extra for dusting
200 g (7 oz) Gruyère cheese,
    finely grated
Pinch of salt
1 egg yolk

Preheat the oven to 180°C/350°F/Gas Mark 4 and line a baking tray with buttered greaseproof paper. Combine the flour, butter, Gruyère cheese and salt in a mixing bowl. Mix and then knead until the mixture forms a soft dough. Dust the work surface with flour and roll out the dough into a sheet 1 cm (½ inch) thick. Cut out 5-cm (2-inch) discs with a pastry cutter and transfer to the prepared tray. Use a knife to make a pattern of intersecting lines on the surface of each biscuit. Brush with egg yolk to glaze. Bake for 15–20 minutes.

MILK and EGG PUDDINGS

Milk and egg puddings, known as entremets in France, are delicious and simple desserts to serve at the end of a meal. From soufflés to baked egg custards, and crème brûlées to meringues, their presentation is extremely varied and the way to make them changes according to the end result you want to achieve. Most require careful attention to the oven temperature and timings.

CUSTARDS

A basic egg custard or flan is both simple and delicious. For a thicker custard, cook the mixture longer until it coats the back of a spoon, but do not allow it to boil.

EGG CUSTARD
œufs au lait

Preparation time: 15 minutes
Cooking time: 45 minutes
Serves 6

500 ml (18 fl oz) milk
125 g (4¼ oz) caster sugar
Vanilla extract, coffee essence, liqueur
   or other flavouring, to taste
4 eggs, lightly beaten

Preheat the oven to 150°C/300°F/Gas Mark 2. Place the milk, sugar and the chosen flavouring in a pan. Bring to the boil over a low heat. Remove from the heat and add the eggs, stirring constantly. Pour the custard into a 1-litre (1¾-pint) dish and place in a roasting tin half-filled with hot water, then bake in the oven for 45 minutes.

FRUIT CUSTARD

flan aux fruits

Preparation time: 25 minutes
Cooking time: 50–60 minutes
Serves 6

500 g (1 lb 2 oz) strawberries
   or apricots
150 g (5 oz) caster sugar
750 ml (1¼ pints) milk
5 eggs, beaten
1 teaspoon vanilla extract
Grated zest of 1 unwaxed lemon
Butter, for greasing
200 g (7 oz) sponge fingers
Icing sugar, to decorate

Hull or stone the fruit and cut them into small pieces. Place them in a pan with 100 g (3½ oz) of the sugar and cook over low heat to a jam-like consistency. In a separate pan, bring the milk to the boil. Break the eggs into a bowl and whisk while carefully adding the boiling milk. Stir in the vanilla, lemon zest and rest of the sugar.

Preheat the oven to 160°C/325°F/Gas Mark 3 and grease a deep ovenproof dish with butter. Arrange a layer of sponge fingers in the bottom of the dish, cover with the thick fruit purée and top with another layer of sponge fingers. Pour the milk and egg mixture evenly all over the top layer of sponge fingers. Bake for 50–60 minutes. Dredge with icing sugar before serving.

COUNTRY-STYLE APPLE FLAN

flan campagnard

Preparation time: 15 minutes
Cooking time: 40 minutes
Serves 6

800 ml (scant 1½ pints) milk
4 eggs
60 g (2 oz) plain flour
125 g (4¼ oz) caster sugar
Pinch of salt
Orange flower water, to taste
500 g (1 lb 2 oz) apples

Place the milk in a pan and heat to boiling point. Break the eggs into a bowl and beat them as you add the flour, sugar and salt. Continue beating as you gradually and carefully add the boiling hot milk. When the batter is smooth, flavour with orange flower water.

Preheat the oven to 140°C/275°F/Gas Mark 1 and grease a fairly wide, shallow ovenproof dish with butter. Peel and core the apples, cut them into thin rings and arrange these in the dish. Pour the egg and milk mixture all over them. Bake for 40 minutes and dredge generously with sugar before serving.

Strawberry Frangipane

STRAWBERRY FRANGIPANE
frangipane aux fraises

Preparation time: 20 minutes
Cooking time: 15–20 minutes
Serves 6

Butter, for greasing
5 egg yolks
150 g (5 oz) ground almonds
200 g (7 oz) caster sugar
500 g (1 lb 2 oz) small strawberries

Preheat the oven to 190°C/375°F/Gas Mark 5 and grease an ovenproof dish that will hold the strawberries in a single layer. Place the egg yolks and sugar in a heatproof bowl set over a pan of barely simmering water. Whisk until pale, tripled in volume and slightly warm. Fold in the almonds. Hull the strawberries and place them in the dish. Cover with the almond frangipane and bake for 15–20 minutes. Serve hot or cold.

RICE CUSTARD
flan de riz

Preparation time: 25 minutes
Cooking time: 10 minutes
Serves 6

150 g (5 oz) short-grain rice
Milk (see method)
210 g (7¼ oz) caster sugar
2 teaspoons vanilla extract
25 g (1 oz) butter, plus extra for greasing
4 eggs, separated
500 g (1 lb 2 oz) apples, peeled, cored and quartered

Place the rice in a receptacle which holds it snugly, or in a measuring jug. Measure out 2½ times its volume in milk. Rinse the rice thoroughly, drain and place in a pan with the measured milk and simmer very gently for 15 minutes. Sweeten with 80 g (2¾ oz) of the sugar and flavour with 1 teaspoon of the vanilla extract. When the rice is cooked, remove from the heat and stir in the butter and the egg yolks.

Preheat the oven to 200°C/400°F/Gas Mark 6 and grease a fairly wide, shallow ovenproof dish with butter. Place the apples straight into a pan containing 500 ml (18 fl oz) of water, the remaining vanilla extract and 80 g (2¾ oz) sugar. Quickly bring to the boil and simmer for 10 minutes. When the apples are tender, spread the rice out in the dish and arrange the drained apple quarters on top.

Whisk the egg whites until they form stiff peaks, adding the remaining sugar towards the end. Cover the apples with this meringue and bake for 10 minutes. Serve immediately.

PINEAPPLE CUSTARD
flan à l'ananas

Preparation time: 25 minutes,
    plus chilling time
Cooking time: 1 hour
Serves 6

185 g (6½ oz) caster sugar
1 x 1 kg (2¼-lb) tin pineapple chunks,
    fruit and juice separated
6 eggs
40 g (1½ oz) plain flour
Juice of 1 lemon
2 tablespoons Kirsch

Prepare the day before. To make a light caramel, pour 85 g (3 oz) of the sugar and 2 tablespoons water into a saucepan and heat over medium heat until the sugar is slightly melted around the edges, about 5 minutes. Using a wooden spoon, gently stir until the sugar has completely melted and is amber coloured. Carefully pour it into a 20-cm (8-inch) charlotte mould to coat the insides.

Preheat the oven to 180°C/350°F/Gas Mark 4. Crush three-quarters of the pineapple and place with the juice from the tin and the remaining sugar in a non-reactive pan. Bring to the boil and boil for 5 minutes. Dice the remaining pineapple and add to the pan. Cook for a further 5 minutes. Break the eggs into a large bowl and whisk in the flour, lemon juice and Kirsch. Add the pineapple.

Pour the mixture into the prepared mould, place in a roasting tin half-filled with hot water and bake for 1 hour. Cool and store in the refrigerator. Turn out and serve the next day.

SPONGE FINGER CUSTARD
flan aux biscuits

Preparation time: 40 minutes,
    plus chilling time
Cooking time: 45 minutes

100 g (3½ oz) sponge fingers
100 ml (3½ fl oz) rum
1 quantity Egg Custard (p. 246)
50 g (1¾ oz) caster sugar

Preheat the oven to 150°C/300°F/Gas Mark 2. Cut the sponge fingers into short lengths and dip them in the rum. Make the egg custard.

To make a light caramel, pour the sugar into a saucepan and heat over medium heat until sugar is slightly melted around the edges, about 5 minutes. Using a wooden spoon, gently stir until the sugar has completely melted and is amber coloured. Carefully pour it into 20-cm (8-inch) mould or ovenproof dish to coat the insides.

Once set and cooled, pour in the custard, adding the sponge finger pieces as you go and pushing them down into the custard. Place the mould in a roasting tin half-filled with hot water. Bake for 45 minutes. Allow the dessert to cool, then chill. Dip the mould in boiling water for 30 seconds and turn out the baked custard just before serving. Serve very cold.

Pineapple Custard

SMALL CUSTARD POTS

crème prise en pots

Preparation time: 15 minutes
Cooking time: 45 minutes
Serves 6

500 ml (18 fl oz) milk
125 g (4¼ oz) caster sugar
Vanilla extract, coffee essence,
    liqueur or other flavouring,
    to taste
4 eggs, lightly beaten

Preheat the oven to 150°C/300°F/Gas Mark 2. Place the milk, sugar and the chosen flavouring in a pan. Bring to the boil over a low heat. Remove from the heat and add the eggs, stirring constantly until the mixture thickens. Pour the custard into 6 individual ramekins. Place the dishes in a roasting tin half-filled with hot water and bake in the oven for 25 minutes. Take care that the water does not boil.

CRÈME CARAMEL

crème renversée

Preparation time: 20 minutes,
    plus chilling time
Cooking time: 45 minutes
Serves 6

1 litre (1¾ pints) milk
160 g (5¼ oz) caster sugar
Flavouring of your choice, such as
    rum or vanilla extract, to taste
6 large eggs, beaten

Preheat the oven to 150°C/300°F/Gas Mark 2. Place the milk and 100 g (3½ oz) of the sugar with your choice of flavouring in a pan and bring to the boil over low heat. Remove from the heat and add the eggs, stirring constantly.

To make a light caramel, pour the remaining sugar into a saucepan and heat over medium heat until the sugar is slightly melted around the edges, about 5 minutes. Using a wooden spoon, gently stir until the sugar has completely melted and is amber coloured. Carefully pour it into an ovenproof dish to coat the insides.

When the caramel has set, fill the dish with the custard and place in a roasting tin half-filled with hot water. Bake for 45 minutes. Allow the dessert to cool, then chill. Dip the mould in boiling water for 30 seconds and turn out the baked custard just before serving. Serve very cold.

Small Custard Pots

Parisian Custard

PARISIAN CUSTARD

flan à la parisienne

Preparation time: 10 minutes,
    plus cooling time
Cooking time: 45 minutes
Serves 6

30 g (1¼ oz) butter, melted,
    plus extra for greasing
200 g (7 oz) plain flour
100 g (3½ oz) caster sugar
4 eggs
Vanilla sugar, to taste
1 litre (1¾ pints) milk

Preheat the oven to 180°C/350°F/Gas Mark 4 and grease a 20-cm (8-inch) charlotte mould with butter. Put the flour in a bowl. Make a well and put the sugar, eggs and butter into it, then beat to combine. Stir the vanilla sugar into the milk and add to the flour and egg mixture. Beat the batter until completely smooth. Pour into the prepared mould, place in a roasting tin half-filled with hot water and bake for 45 minutes. Turn out and serve cold.

ORANGE CUSTARD

flan à l'orange

Preparation time: 10 minutes,
    plus chilling time
Cooking time: 20 minutes
Serves 6

2 eggs
2 egg yolks
60 g (2 oz) caster sugar
450 ml (16 fl oz) orange juice

Prepare 2–3 hours in advance. Preheat the oven to 150°C/300°F/Gas Mark 2. Beat the eggs with the sugar. Warm the orange juice and add it a little at a time to the egg mixture. Pour into 6 individual ramekins and place in a roasting tin half-filled with hot water. Bake in the oven for 15–20 minutes, or until set. Cool and refrigerate for 2–3 hours.

VANILLA CRÈME BRÛLÉE
crème brûlée à la vanille

Preparation time: 20 minutes,
   plus 4 hours chilling time
Cooking time: 30–35 minutes
Serves 6

500 ml (18 fl oz) milk
500 ml (18 fl oz) whipping cream
4 vanilla pods, split lengthways
100 g (3½ oz) caster sugar
10 egg yolks
100 g (3½ oz) brown sugar

Prepare in advance. Preheat the oven to 150°C/300°F/ Gas Mark 2. Mix together the milk, cream, vanilla pods and 50 g (1¾ oz) of caster sugar. Bring just to the boil over low heat then remove from the heat and cool. Scrape the seeds out of the vanilla pods into the milk and rinse the empty pods for another use. Meanwhile, beat the egg yolks in a bowl with the remaining caster sugar until pale and foamy. Pour the vanilla-flavoured milk over the eggs and mix well.

Pour into a 1.75-litre (3-pint) ovenproof dish or 6 individual ramekins. Place the dish or ramekins in a roasting tin half-filled with hot water. Bake for 30–35 minutes, or until just set (the water must not boil). Cool to room temperature, then refrigerate for 3–4 hours.

Shortly before serving, sprinkle the custard with the brown sugar and put the dish under a very hot grill for just long enough to caramelize. The sugar will form small balls on the surface. Alternatively, use a kitchen torch to carefully caramelize the sugar.

'BEAUTIFUL AND GOOD' CRÈME CARAMEL
crème belle et bonne

Preparation time: 1½ hours,
   plus cooling time
Cooking time: 1¼ hours
Serves 6

250 g (9 oz) caster sugar
500 ml (18 fl oz) milk
6 eggs
1 teaspoon vanilla extract
400 ml (14 fl oz) red wine
4 small pears, diced
6 medium pears, peeled,
   cored and halved
200 ml (7 fl oz) double cream

Make a crème caramel (p. 252) with 200 g (7 oz) of the sugar, the milk, eggs and vanilla in a bowl. Pour it into a 20-cm (8-inch) ring mould.

Bring the wine and remaining sugar to the boil in a large pan. Add the diced pears and simmer in the wine for 10 minutes. Remove with a slotted spoon and set aside. Simmer the halved pears in the wine syrup for 20 minutes, or until tender.

When the crème caramel has cooked, allow it to cool and turn it out on to a dish. Arrange the halved pears around the ring and the diced pears in the centre. Whisk the cream to soft peaks and use it to decorate the crème caramel.

Vanilla Crème Brûlée

FRUIT PUDDINGS

Stewed fruit not only enhances the appearance of a pudding but will also improve the flavour. It is worth buying the freshest seasonal fruit to ensure the tastiest dessert.

ALMOND AND CURRANT PUDDING
pudding aux amandes et aux raisins

Preparation time: 20 minutes,
  plus cooling time
Cooking time: 55 minutes
Serves 6

200 g (7 oz) butter, softened, plus
  extra for greasing
6 eggs
100 g (3½ oz) caster sugar
375 g (13 oz) ground almonds
250 g (9 oz) currants
125 g (4¼ oz) sultanas
1 quantity Rum Sauce (p. 46)

Preheat the oven to 160°C/325°F/Gas Mark 3 and grease a 20-cm (8-inch) charlotte mould or ovenproof dish with butter. Place the eggs and sugar in a heatproof bowl set over a pan of barely simmering water and whisk for 10 minutes until pale and foamy. Fold in the softened butter, ground almonds, currants and sultanas. Transfer this mixture to the dish and bake for 55 minutes. Turn out when cold and serve with rum sauce poured over and around the pudding.

BAKED PEARS
poires tapées au four

Preparation time: 5 minutes
Cooking time: 20 minutes
Serves 6

6 pears, washed
caster sugar, for sprinkling

Preheat the oven to 200°C/400°F/Gas Mark 6. Place the pears upright in an ovenproof dish, trimming a little off the base if necessary to make them stand upright. Bake until they are tender and pale golden brown, approximately 20 minutes. Sprinkle with sugar while still very hot and serve.

FLAMING PEARS
poires flambantes

Preparation time: 15 minutes
Cooking time: 25 minutes
Serves 6

500 g (1 lb 2 oz) pears, peeled
125 g (4¼ oz) caster sugar
1 teaspoon vanilla extract
100 ml (3½ fl oz) rum

Preheat the oven to 200°C/400°F/Gas Mark 6. Place the pears in a deep saucepan just wide enough to accommodate them standing upright. Add 300 ml (10 fl oz) water, 100 g (3½ oz) of the sugar and the vanilla and cook over very low heat for 10–15 minutes to half cook them. Transfer the pears to an ovenproof dish. Pour the cooking syrup over them and sprinkle with the remaining sugar. Bake for 10 minutes. Warm the rum, pour over the pears and set it alight. Serve immediately.

APPLES WITH MERINGUE
pommes meringuées

Preparation time: 30 minutes
Cooking time: 25 minutes
Serves 6

6 Reinette apples (see note), peeled,
    cored and halved
150 g (5 oz) caster sugar
1 teaspoon vanilla extract
Butter, for greasing
3 egg whites
2 tablespoons raspberry jelly

Preheat the oven to 200°C/400°F/Gas Mark 6 and grease an ovenproof dish with butter. Make a sugar syrup with 250 ml (8 fl oz) water, 100 g (3½ oz) sugar and the vanilla. Poach the apples in the syrup until tender, approximately 10 minutes.

When the apples are cooked, drain off the sugar syrup and arrange them in the dish. Whisk the egg whites until they form stiff peaks. Fold in the remaining sugar and the raspberry jelly, mixing gently but thoroughly. Cover the apples with this topping and bake for 15 minutes.

Note: Reinette apples can be replaced with any medium-sized, aromatic eating apples that remain intact when cooked.

APPLES STUFFED WITH CANDIED FRUIT
pommes farcies au fruits confits

Preparation time: 20 minutes
Cooking time: 35 minutes

60 g (2 oz) butter, plus
    extra for greasing
6 apples
100 g (3 ½ oz) assorted candied
    fruit, chopped
60 g (2 oz) raisins
5 tablespoons rum
60 g (2 oz) caster sugar

Preheat the oven to 200°C /400°F /Gas Mark 6 and grease a baking sheet. Peel the apples, remove the stem and core them to within 1 cm (½ inch) from the bottom. Remove the core leaving a cavity of 2 cm (¾ inch). Reserve the pulp. In a bowl, mix together the candied fruit, raisins and rum. Fill in each apple with the mixture, sprinkle with sugar and top with a dab of butter. Place the apples on the baking sheet and bake for 35 minutes, basting occasionally with a little water. Serve hot.

APPLE TIMBALE
timbale de pommes

Preparation time: 15 minutes
Cooking time: 1 hour
Serves 6

120 g (4 oz) butter, plus extra for greasing
200 g (7 oz) slightly stale bread,
    very thinly sliced
500 g (1 lb 2 oz) apples, peeled, cored
    and sliced
100 g (3½ oz) caster sugar
Crème Anglaise (p. 49), to serve (optional)

Preheat the oven to 160°C/325°F/Gas Mark 3. Grease a 20-cm (8-inch) charlotte mould with butter. Line the base with a layer of bread, then a layer of apples. Sprinkle with some of the sugar, dot with butter and continue in this manner, layering the bread, apples, sugar and butter, until the mould is full. Pour over 100 ml (3½ fl oz) water. Bake for 1 hour. Carefully turn out. Serve on its own or with crème anglaise.

BAKED APPLES
pommes tapées

Preparation time: 5 minutes
Cooking time: 20 minutes
Serves 6

6 eating apples, washed
Caster sugar, to taste

Preheat the oven to 190°C/375°F/Gas Mark 5. Place the apples in an ovenproof dish. Bake them until their skins are lightly wrinkled and golden, approximately 20 minutes. They must be cooked through to the core. Sprinkle with sugar and serve hot.

PIEDMONT APPLES

pommes à la piémontaise

Preparation time: 35 minutes,
    plus cooling time
Cooking time: 1 hour
Serves 6

9 apples
90 g (3¼ oz) butter, plus extra for greasing
180 g (6¼ oz) caster sugar
150 ml (1¼ pint) milk
125 g (4¼ oz) cornflour
100 g (3½ oz) dried figs, diced
60 g (2 oz) walnuts, coarsely chopped
3 tablespoons rum
6 Amaretti biscuits, crushed
1 quantity Kirsch-flavoured Syrup
    for Babas (p. 48)

Preheat the oven to 200°C/400°F/Gas Mark 6. Wash 6 of the apples and place in an ovenproof dish with 50 g (1¾ oz) butter and 60 g (2 oz) sugar. Bake, turning them once in the butter and sugar, for 20 minutes or until cooked through.

Stir a few tablespoons of the milk into the cornflour until smooth. Heat the remaining milk to boiling point, then stir in 60 g (2 oz) of the sugar and the cornflour mixture, stirring continuously over low heat until the mixture is very thick. Grease a 20-cm (8-inch) savarin mould with butter and pour in the thickened milk. Allow to cool. Grease an ovenproof serving dish or platter, large enough to take the mould, with butter.

Make a syrup with 100 ml (3½ fl oz) water, the remaining 60 g (2 oz) of the sugar and the rum. Peel, core and thickly slice the remaining 3 apples and add to the syrup with the diced figs. Cook gently for 15–20 minutes until the apples are tender and the figs are softened. Remove from the heat and add the walnuts.

Turn the set milk and cornflour ring out onto the greased serving dish. Melt the remaining 40 g (1½ oz) of butter and brush it over the surface of the milk ring. Fill the centre of the mould with the cooked, sliced apple. Cut the baked apples in half and arrange them, together with the figs and walnuts, on top of the sliced apples. Sprinkle with the crushed Amaretti. Place in the oven for 10–15 minutes until hot and lightly browned and serve accompanied by Kirsch-flavoured syrup.

CHERRY GÂTEAU

gâteau de cerises

Preparation time: 15 minutes,
    plus 10 minutes cooling
Cooking time: 45–50 minutes
Serves 6

1 piece of brioche, 140–150 g (4¾–5 oz)
100 ml (3½ fl oz) milk
125 g (4¼ oz) butter, plus extra for greasing
125 g (4¼ oz) caster sugar
125 g (4¼ oz) ground almonds
4 eggs
600 g (1 lb 5 oz) black cherries, washed,
    stoned and stalks removed
2 tablespoons Kirsch, to serve

Cut the brioche into cubes and place in a bowl. Pour over the milk and set aside. Preheat the oven to 160°C/325°F/Gas Mark 3 and generously grease an 18-cm (7-inch) charlotte mould with butter.

Place the butter in a heatproof bowl set over a pan of barely simmering water and allow it to melt. Beat in the sugar and almonds and remove from the heat. Mash the brioche and milk together to form a smooth paste, then add it to the almond mixture. Beat in the eggs one by one, then stir in the cherries.

Pour the mixture into the prepared charlotte mould and bake for 45–50 minutes. Leave to cool for 10 minutes before turning out on to a serving plate. Serve warm or cold, sprinkled with the Kirsch.

PUMPKIN CUSTARD

flan au potiron

Preparation time: 20 minutes
Cooking time: 1 hour 35 minutes
Serves 6

300 g (11 oz) pumpkin flesh, diced
Butter, for greasing
50 g (1¾ oz) plain flour
3 eggs
150 g (5 oz) caster sugar
500 ml (18 fl oz) milk
Pinch of salt
Grated zest of 1 unwaxed lemon

Place the pumpkin flesh with 3–4 tablespoons of water in a pan and cook over low heat for 45–60 minutes until very tender. Process to a smooth purée. Preheat the oven to 200°C/400°F/Gas Mark 6 and grease a 20-cm (8-inch) charlotte mould or ovenproof dish with butter. Place the flour in a mixing bowl and beat in the eggs, one at a time, followed by the sugar, milk and salt. Add the lemon zest and the pumpkin purée. Whisk until very smooth. Pour the mixture into the mould and bake for 35 minutes. Serve hot or cold.

Cherry Gâteau

PLUM CHARLOTTE
charlotte aux quetsches

Preparation time: 40 minutes
Cooking time: 1 hour 40 minutes
Serves 6

200 g (7 oz) caster sugar
1 kg (2¼ lb) quetsche plums (small, tender-
   skinned red plums) or Victoria plums,
   stoned and chopped
1 x 500 g (1 lb 2 oz) white loaf,
   crusts removed
125 g (4¼ oz) butter, melted, plus
   extra for greasing

Make a syrup by combining 250 ml (8 fl oz) water and the sugar in a pan. Bring slowly to the boil while you prepare the fruit. Place the plums in the syrup. Boil until they have reduced to a thick compôte, approximately 60 minutes. Stir frequently towards the end so they do not stick to the bottom of the pan.

Cut the white loaf into fairly thin slices and brush both sides of the slices with melted butter. Grease an 18–20-cm (7–8-inch) charlotte mould with butter. Use the bread to neatly line the bottom and sides of the charlotte mould. Preheat the oven to 200°C/400°F/Gas Mark 6. Spoon half of the compôte into the bread-lined mould and cover with a layer of buttered bread. Add the remaining compôte and another layer of bread. Press the dessert down gently with your hand to remove any air pockets. Bake for 30–40 minutes until crisp and golden. Turn out carefully and serve hot or cold.

FROSTED GRAPES
raisins givrés

Preparation time: 10 minutes
Cooking time: 10 minutes
Serves 6

500 g (1 lb 2 oz) grapes, rinsed and dried
2 egg whites
300 g (11 oz) caster sugar

Preheat the oven to 100°C/200°F/Gas Mark ½ and line a baking tray with greaseproof paper. Cut off stems containing equal numbers of grapes from a bunch.

Whisk the egg whites until they form soft peaks. One by one, dip the grapes into the egg whites, then dust them lightly in the sugar, repeating with two thin applications of sugar if necessary to make an even coating. Place the grapes on the prepared tray and dry in a very low oven for 10 minutes.

VIENNESE APRICOTS
abricots viennoise

Preparation time: 25 minutes, plus
    overnight soaking and chilling
Cooking time: 1 hour 20 minutes
Serves 6

250 g (9 oz) dried apricots
260 g (9¼ oz) caster sugar
1 litre (1¾ pints) milk
6 eggs
2 teaspoons vanilla extract
1 quantity vanilla-flavoured
    Crème Caramel (p. 252)

Soak the apricots overnight in just enough water to cover. Next day, place the apricots in a pan with 100 g (3½ oz) sugar and cook them in their soaking liquid over low heat for 30–40 minutes until very tender. Drain them, allow to cool and then chill.

Make the crème caramel and bake in a 23-cm (9-inch) savarin mould coated with caramel and place in a roasting tin half-filled with hot water.

Bake for 45 minutes. Allow the custard to cool and then chill. Dip the mould in boiling water for 30 seconds and turn out the baked custard just before serving, decorated with the cold, cooked apricots.

APRICOT WITH MERINGUE
abricots meringués

Preparation time: 15 minutes
Cooking time: 1 hour
Serves 6

For the rice milk pudding:
500 ml (18 fl oz) milk
50 g (1¾ oz) caster sugar
1 teaspoon vanilla extract
Pinch of salt
100 g (3½ oz) short-grain rice

For the layered toppings:
200 g (8 oz) caster sugar
500 g (1 lb 2 oz) fresh apricots,
    halved and stoned
Butter, for greasing
3 tablespoons Kirsch
3 eggs, separated

In a medium saucepan, bring the milk, sugar, vanilla and salt to a boil. Rinse the rice and add it to the pan, reduce to a simmer and cook for 45–60 minutes. Set aside.

Make a syrup with 500 ml (18 fl oz) water with 120 g (4 oz) caster sugar (p. 17). Add the apricots and poach them in the syrup.

Preheat the oven to 200°C/400°F/Gas Mark 6 and grease an ovenproof dish with butter. Drain half the cooked apricots and dice them. Stir these into the cooked, hot rice pudding along with the Kirsch and 3 egg yolks. Pour this mixture into the dish and top with the remaining apricot halves. Whisk the egg whites until they form stiff peaks, gradually adding the sugar to make a glossy meringue. Spread the meringue gently over the apricot halves and bake for 5–10 minutes to lightly brown the meringue. Serve hot.

Far Breton

FAR BRETON
far breton

Preparation: 20 minutes,
   plus overnight soaking
Cooking: 40 minutes

Butter for greasing
125 g (4¼ oz) plain flour
Generous pinch of salt
4 eggs
100 g (3½ oz) caster sugar
1 litre (1¾ pints) milk
200 ml (7 fl oz) rum
250 g (9 oz) prunes,
   soaked overnight

Preheat the oven to 180°C/350°F/Gas Mark 4. Grease an ovenproof dish with butter. In a large bowl, mix together the flour and salt. Add the eggs one by one, mixing thoroughly to create a smooth batter. Whisk the batter to introduce air into it. Add the sugar, then the milk. Stir in the rum.

Drain the prunes, add them to the mixture and pour into the dish. Bake for 40 minutes. Serve hot or cold.

SEMOLINA AND HONEYED APRICOTS
abricots au miel

Preparation time: 15 minutes
Cooking time: 40 minutes
Serves 6

80 g (2¾ oz) butter, plus extra for greasing
500 g (1 lb 2 oz) fresh apricots, halved
   and stoned
150 g (5 oz) runny honey
500 ml (18 fl oz) milk
Pinch of salt
Grated zest of 1 unwaxed lemon
125 g (4¼ oz) semolina
50 g (1¾ oz) sponge fingers
100 ml (3½ fl oz) Kirsch

Preheat the oven to 200°C/400°F/Gas Mark 6 and grease two ovenproof dishes with butter, one of them a round serving dish. Place the apricot halves in the other dish and drizzle 75 g (2½ oz) of the honey all over them. Bake for 20 minutes.

Meanwhile, place the milk in a pan with the salt and remaining honey. Bring to the boil, then stir in the lemon zest and sprinkle in the semolina, stirring continuously. Cook over low heat until the semolina has cooked and is very thick, approximately 15 minutes. Remove the pan from the heat, stir in 30 g (1¼ oz) of the butter and pour the semolina mixture into the round serving dish, arranging it in a ring with a well in the centre. Place the cooked apricots in the centre of the semolina ring and crumble the sponge fingers over them. Sprinkle the crumbs with Kirsch. Melt the remaining butter and sprinkle this over the dessert. Return to the oven for 5–6 minutes and serve.

APRICOT COLBERT

abricots colbert

Preparation time: 15 minutes
Cooking time: 30 minutes
Serves 6

30 g (1¼ oz) butter, plus extra for greasing
650 ml (22 fl oz) milk
100 g (3½ oz) caster sugar
Pinch of salt
125 g (4¼ oz) semolina
Grated zest of 1 unwaxed lemon
2 eggs, separated
100 g (3½ oz) honey
400 g (14 oz) fresh apricots, stoned
300 g (11 oz) fresh cherries, stoned

Preheat the oven to 200°C/400°F/Gas Mark 6 and grease a 20-cm (8-inch) savarin mould with butter. Place the milk in a pan with 60 g (2 oz) of the sugar and the salt. Bring to the boil, then sprinkle in the semolina, stirring continuously, and simmer until cooked and thickened, 10–15 minutes. Remove from the heat and stir in the butter, followed by the lemon and egg yolks. Whisk the egg whites until they form stiff peaks and fold them into the semolina mixture.

Spoon this mixture into a prepared mould and place it in a roasting tin half-filled with hot water. Bake for 30 minutes. Meanwhile, place the honey in a pan with the remaining sugar and 500 ml (18 fl oz) water and cook to a syrup (p. 17). Poach the apricots in this until tender. Turn out the dessert when cold. Remove the apricots from their syrup and arrange around and on the semolina ring. Fill the central well with cherries and sprinkle with the apricot syrup.

BAKED BANANAS

bananes au four

Preparation time: 5 minutes
Cooking time: 20–25 minutes
Serves 6

Butter, for greasing
6 bananas
60 g (2 oz) seedless raspberry jam
80 g (2¾ oz) caster sugar

Preheat the oven to 180°C/350°F/Gas Mark 4 and grease a shallow ovenproof dish with butter. Peel the bananas. Cut them lengthways into strips (3 strips from each banana). Place half of the bananas in a single layer in the dish. Heat the jam briefly to soften it and brush some of this over the bananas in the dish. Cover with the remaining banana strips and sprinkle liberally with sugar. Sprinkle the remaining jam on top. Bake for 20–25 minutes. Serve hot.

Apricot Colbert

CLAFOUTIS
clafoutis

Preparation time: 30 minutes
Cooking time: 35 minutes
Serves 6

Butter for greasing
Sugar for dusting
6 eggs
40 g (1½ oz) plain flour
Pinch of salt
265 ml (9 fl oz) milk or 125 ml (4½ fl oz) milk
and 125 ml (4½ fl oz) crème fraîche
750 g (1 lb 10½ oz) black cherries,
washed and stoned
2 tablespoons Kirsch

Preheat the oven to 200°C/400°F/Gas Mark 6. Generously grease a shallow ovenproof dish with butter and generously dust with sugar. Place the eggs, flour and salt in a bowl. Stir in a little milk and mix until smooth. Start whisking to introduce air into the batter and gradually add the rest of the milk and the crème fraîche if using. The batter should be of the same consistency as pancake batter. Stir in the cherries and the Kirsch. Pour the cherry batter mixture into the dish, distributing the cherries evenly. Bake for 35 minutes. Sprinkle with sugar. Serve warm or cold.

BREAD PUDDING WITH CHERRIES
gâteau de pain aux cerises

Preparation time: 25 minutes,
plus cooling time
Cooking time: 1 hour 10 minutes
Serves 6

1 litre (1¾ pints) milk
500 g (1 lb 2 oz) fine, stale breadcrumbs
180 g (6¼ oz) caster sugar
3 eggs, beaten
300 g (11 oz) fresh cherries, washed
and stoned
100 ml (3½ fl oz) rum
500 ml (18 fl oz) Vanilla Crème
Anglaise (p. 49)
60 g (2oz) glacé cherries

Place the milk in a pan and bring to the boil. Remove from the heat and immediately add the breadcrumbs. Add 100 g (3½ oz) of the sugar. Allow to stand for a few minutes then beat the mixture with a wooden spoon until smooth and thick. Add the lightly beaten eggs, the fresh cherries and the rum.

Preheat the oven to 200°C/400°F/Gas Mark 6. To make a light caramel, pour the remaining sugar into a saucepan and heat over medium heat until the sugar is slightly melted around the edges, about 5 minutes. Using a wooden spoon, gently stir until the sugar has completely melted and is amber coloured. Carefully pour it into a 1.3-litre (2½-pint) pudding basin with caramel to coat the insides. Spoon the milk mixture into it and bake for 1 hour.

Turn out the dessert when cold, pour the crème anglaise over it and decorate with the glacé cherries.

Clafoutis

CHERRY CROÛTES

croûtes aux cerises

Preparation time: 20 minutes
Cooking time: 15–20 minutes
Serves 6

6 slices white bread
100 g (3½ oz) butter
450 g (1 lb) black cherries,
   washed and stoned
100 g (3½ oz) caster sugar

Preheat the oven to 190°C/375°F/Gas Mark 5. Heat 75 g (2½ oz) of the butter in a frying pan and fry the bread slices until golden brown on both sides. Arrange them in a single layer in a wide ovenproof dish. Place the cherries on the slices of toast. Melt the remaining butter, sprinkle this over the cherries and dredge with caster sugar. Bake for 15–20 minutes and serve immediately.

BAKED QUINCES

coings au four

Preparation time: 10 minutes
Cooking time: 45 minutes
Serves 6

1 kg (2¼ lb) quinces,
   peeled, cored and quartered
1 teaspoon vanilla extract
150 g (5 oz) caster sugar
50 g (1¾ oz) butter

Preheat the oven to 160°C/375°F/Gas Mark 3. Spread the quinces out in an ovenproof dish and pour over 300 ml (½ pint) cold water mixed with the vanilla extract. Sprinkle the sugar over the fruit, then dot with flakes of butter. Bake for 45 minutes. Spoon the cooking juices over the fruit from time to time to keep it moist. When the quinces are cooked, drain them and arrange them in a serving bowl. Reduce the cooking liquid if necessary by boiling it in a pan before pouring it all over the fruit.

APRICOT AND CHESTNUT CHARLOTTE

pain de marrons à l'abricot

Preparation time: 40 minutes
Cooking time: 40–45 minutes
Serves 6

60 g (2 oz) butter, plus
   extra for greasing
300 g (11 oz) tinned chestnut purée
125 g (4¼ oz) caster sugar
250 ml (8 fl oz) milk, hot
Pinch of salt
3 eggs, beaten
1 quantity Apricot Sauce (p. 48)

Preheat the oven to 190°C/375°F/Gas Mark 5 and grease a 20-cm (8-inch) charlotte mould with butter. Transfer the chestnut purée to a fairly large pan and stir in the sugar, butter, hot milk and a very small pinch of salt. Cook, stirring continuously over low heat, for 5 minutes. Remove the pan from the heat and stir in the eggs. Pour this mixture into the mould and bake for 40–45 minutes. When the dessert is cold, turn it out and serve covered with the apricot sauce.

RASPBERRY LOAF

pain de framboises

Preparation time: 30 minutes,
    plus cooling time
Cooking time: 30 minutes
Serves 6

Butter, for greasing
250 ml (8 fl oz) white wine
130 g (4½ oz) caster sugar
Juice of 1 lemon
1 teaspoon vanilla extract
250 g (9 oz) semolina

For the coulis:
250 g (9 oz) raspberries
100 g (3½ oz) icing sugar
Juice of ½ lemon

Preheat the oven to 150°C/300°F/Gas Mark 2, and grease one 20-cm (8-inch), or six individual charlotte moulds. Put 250 ml (8 fl oz) water and the wine, sugar, lemon juice and vanilla in a large pan. Boil for 5 minutes and then add the semolina all at once. Simmer for 15 minutes, stirring frequently. Pour the semolina mixture into the prepared moulds. Place in a roasting tin half-filled with hot water and bake for 30 minutes. Allow to cool, then turn out onto a serving dish.

To prepare the raspberry coulis, purée the raspberries in a blender or food processor, and add the sugar and lemon juice. Blend again for 2 minutes. Mash through a fine-mesh strainer with a wooden spoon to remove the seeds and refrigerate in a sealed container before serving. Spoon over the semolina before serving.

ITALIAN-STYLE PEARS

poires à l'italienne

Preparation time: 25 minutes,
    plus cooling time
Cooking time: 30 minutes
Serves 6

750 ml (1¼ pints) milk
Pinch of salt
250 g (9 oz) caster sugar, plus
    extra for sprinkling
Grated zest of 1 unwaxed lemon
125 g (4¼ oz) cornflour
80 g (2¾ oz) butter
6 pears, peeled, cored and halved
½ quantity Kirsch Sauce (p. 46)

Place all but 2 tablespoons of the milk in a saucepan with the salt, 100 g (3½ oz) of the sugar and the lemon. Heat to boiling point, stirring continuously. Mix the reserved milk with the cornflour and stir this into the hot milk, continuing to stir until the mixture has thickened. Add 40 g (1½ oz) of the butter and mix well. Pour into a fairly wide, shallow ovenproof dish, dot the surface with the remaining butter and set aside to cool.

Preheat the oven to 200°C/400°F/Gas Mark 6. Once cooled, evenly sprinkle the custard with 50 g (1¾ oz) of the sugar and bake for 10 minutes to brown the surface lightly.

Meanwhile, make a sugar syrup (p. 17) with the remaining 100 g (3½ oz) sugar and 250 ml (9 fl oz) water. Poach the pears in the syrup until tender, approximately 10 minutes. Drain the pears and arrange them on top of the baked custard. Sprinkle with Kirsch sauce. Return to the oven for 5 minutes, sprinkle with a little extra sugar and serve very hot.

Bread Pudding with Strawberries

BREAD PUDDING WITH STRAWBERRIES

gâteau de pain aux fraises

Preparation time: 20 minutes, plus
 soaking time
Cooking time: 50–60 minutes
Serves 6

60 g (2 oz) butter, plus extra for greasing
500 ml (18 fl oz) milk
350 g (12 oz) slices stale white bread, diced
180 g (6¼ oz) caster sugar
3 eggs, separated
200 g (7 oz) strawberry jam
500 ml (18 fl oz) Crème Anglaise (p. 49)
250 g (9 oz) small strawberries, hulled

Preheat the oven to 180°C/350°F/Gas Mark 4 and
grease a 20-cm (8-inch) charlotte mould with butter.
Bring the milk to the boil in a large saucepan. Remove
from the heat and add the bread. Leave to soak for an
hour, then stir well to make a thick, smooth paste. Beat
in the sugar, butter, strawberry jam and egg yolks.
Whisk the egg whites until they form stiff peaks and
fold into the bread mixture.

Place in the mould and bake for 50–60 minutes,
covering with foil towards the end if necessary. Once
cold, turn out the pudding and serve accompanied by
the crème anglaise and the strawberries.

PEACH CROÛTES

croûtes aux pêches

Preparation time: 25 minutes
Cooking time: 25–30 minutes
Serves 6

60 g (2 oz) butter, softened, plus
 extra for greasing
6 slices white bread
6 peaches, peeled, halved and stoned
100 g (3½ oz) caster sugar
5 tablespoons Kirsch or rum

Preheat the oven to 160°C/325°F/Gas Mark 3 and
grease a large, fairly shallow ovenproof dish with
butter. Use half of the butter to spread over the bread
slices and place these in a single layer in the dish. Place
a little sugar and a small piece of butter in each peach
hollow where the stones were. Place 2 peach halves
on each bread slice. Sprinkle with the remaining sugar.
Mix 100 ml (3½ fl oz) water with the Kirsch or rum and
sprinkle over the peaches. Bake for 25–30 minutes.
Serve immediately.

PEACHES WITH MERINGUE
pêches meringuées

Preparation time: 25 minutes
Cooking time: 55 minutes–1 hour 10 minutes
Serves 6

100 g (3½ oz) short-grain rice
400 ml (14 fl oz) milk
Pinch of salt
200 g (7 oz) caster sugar
3 egg yolks
500 g (1 lb 2 oz) peaches
1 quantity Italian Meringue (p. 286)
Butter, for greasing

Rinse the rice and place it in a medium saucepan with the milk and salt. Bring to a boil, then reduce to a simmer and cook for 45–60 minutes. When the rice is cooked, remove from the heat and stir in 100 g (3½ oz) of the sugar and the egg yolks.

In a saucepan, bring 750 ml (25 fl oz) water to a boil, then add the peaches and leave them to boil for 3–4 minutes. Drain and immediately place in a bowl of ice water. Peel them, cut them in half and remove their stones. Make the Italian meringue.

Preheat the oven to 200°C/400°F/Gas Mark 6 and grease a fairly shallow, round or oval ovenproof dish with butter. Arrange the rice in a dome shape in the dish and arrange the peach halves all round its base. Cover the dessert with half of the Italian meringue and place the rest in a piping bag fitted with a fluted nozzle. Pipe the remaining meringue decoratively on the dessert and sprinkle with the remaining sugar. Bake for 10 minutes to lightly brown the meringue.

APPLE COMPÔTE WITH MERINGUE
compôte de pommes meringuée

Preparation time: 20 minutes
Cooking time: 30–35 minutes
Serves 6

For the apple purée:
500 g apples
100 g caster sugar
zest of 1 unwaxed lemon

For the meringue:
3 egg whites
125 g (4¼ oz) caster sugar

To make the apple purée, wash and quarter the apples but do not peel or scoop them out. In a medium saucepan, bring the apples and 250 ml of water to a boil, then simmer for 15–20 minutes. Transfer the mixture to a blender and purée. Allow to cool.

Preheat the oven to 140°C/275°F/Gas Mark 1. Spread the apple purée out in a 20-cm (8-inch) ovenproof dish. Whisk the egg whites, sprinkling in the sugar, until they form stiff peaks. Cover the apple purée with the egg whites and sprinkle sugar evenly all over the surface. Bake for 30–35 minutes to lightly cook and brown the meringue.

Peaches with Meringue

APPLE HEDGEHOGS
pommes hérissons

Preparation time: 20 minutes
Cooking time: 10 minutes
Serves 6

6 apples
Juice of 1 lemon
150 g (5 oz) caster sugar
1 teaspoon vanilla extract
50 g (1¾ oz) slivered almonds

Peel, halve and core the apples, placing them in water with the lemon juice added. Make a sugar syrup (p. 17) with 250 ml (9 fl oz) water, the sugar and vanilla. Poach the apple halves in the syrup until tender, approximately 10 minutes.

Toast the almonds lightly for 2–4 minutes in a hot oven. Stick the almonds into the apple halves, making them look like hedgehog bristles. Serve cold.

APPLE CANDLE DESSERT
pommes en bougies

Preparation time: 10 minutes
Serves 6

4 very large apples
Approximately 16 walnut halves
Juice of ½ a lemon
1 round, flat milk pudding or round cake

Use an apple corer to cut cylinders of apple flesh out of the apples, avoiding the core area and trimming the cylinders to equal length if necessary. Place them in water acidulated with the lemon juice if they are not to be used immediately. Place a walnut half on top of each apple cylinder and decorate the dessert or cake with them, pushing the candles in securely. Set light to the walnuts when serving. Walnuts burn well.

NORMANDY APPLES IN PASTRY
bourdelots normands

Preparation time: 30 minutes
Cooking time: 35–45 minutes
Serves 6

Butter, for greasing
6 small Reinette apples
400 g (14 oz) Puff Pastry (p. 31)
6 tablespoons redcurrant jelly
1 egg, beaten

Preheat the oven to 180°C/350°F/Gas Mark 4 and grease a baking tray with butter. Peel the apples but keep them whole, removing nearly all of their cores, but stopping short to keep the base of the apple intact. Place 1 tablespoon of redcurrant jelly in each core cavity.

Roll out the puff pastry into a sheet 3 mm (⅛ inch) thick. Cut it into 6 equal pieces and wrap the apples in these, moistening the edges with water to achieve a good seal if necessary. Brush with the egg to glaze. Bake for 35–45 minutes, depending on the size of the apples. Serve hot or cold.

Note: Reinette apples can be replaced with any medium-sized, aromatic eating apples that remain intact when cooked.

Apple Hedgehogs

APRICOT CHARLOTTE
charlotte aux abricots

Preparation time: 30 minutes, plus 8 hours
 soaking and chilling time
Cooking time: 20–30 minutes
Serves 6

250 g (9 oz) dried apricots
500 ml (18 fl oz) dry white wine
4 leaves gelatine
250 g (9 oz) caster sugar
1 teaspoon vanilla extract
200 g (7 oz) sponge fingers
80 g (2¾ oz) almonds, skinned and chopped

Place the apricots in a non-reactive bowl with the wine
and set aside in a cool place for 6–8 hours. Transfer to
a saucepan, bring slowly to the boil and simmer gently
until the apricots are tender, 20–30 minutes. Soak the
gelatine in cold water for 5 minutes. When the wine has
almost completely evaporated from the apricots,
remove the pan from the heat and stir in the sugar,
vanilla and the drained gelatine leaves. When the
gelatine has completely dissolved, purée the mixture in
a blender.

Grease an 18–20-cm (7–8-inch) charlotte mould with
butter and then line the base and sides with sponge
fingers. Stir the almonds into the apricot purée. Pour
this mixture into the mould. Chill the charlotte
thoroughly. Unmould the charlotte by dipping the
mould in hot water first then turning out onto a serving
plate. Serve cold.

PEACH PUDDING
pudding maïzena aux pêches

Preparation time: 10 minutes,
 plus cooling time
Cooking time: 35 minutes
Serves 6

Butter, for greasing
1 litre (1¾ pints) milk
120 g (4 oz) caster sugar
75 g (2½ oz) cornflour
3 eggs, separated
500 g (1 lb 2 oz) peaches, peeled,
 halved and stoned
1 quantity light Sugar Syrup (p. 17)

Preheat the oven to 180°C/350°F/Gas Mark 4 and
grease a 20-cm (8-inch) charlotte mould with butter.
In a pan, bring 750 ml (1¼ pints) of the milk and 60 g
(2 oz) of the sugar to the boil. Mix the cornflour with
the remaining milk until smooth. Whisk the egg whites
until they form stiff peaks. Stir the egg yolks into the
cornflour mixture, then fold in the egg whites. Pour this
mixture into the boiling milk and mix well. Remove
from the heat.

To make a light caramel, pour the remaining sugar and
1 tablespoon of water into a saucepan and heat over
a medium heat until the sugar is slightly melted around
the edges, about 5 minutes. Using a wooden spoon,
gently stir until the sugar has completed melted and is
amber coloured, about 10 minutes. Carefully pour it
into the mould to coat the insides. Once set, pour in
the cornflour mixture. Bake for 20 minutes then allow
to cool. Poach the peaches for 6 minutes in the sugar
syrup. Turn out the corn pudding and decorate with
the peaches.

Note: The peaches may be replaced with any kind of
fresh or tinned fruit.

Apricot Charlotte

MERINGUES

Consisting only of egg whites and sugar, a meringue is one of the simplest desserts to make. After baking they should be completely dry and stored in an airtight container.

SWISS MERINGUE
meringue Suisse

Preparation time: 30 minutes
Cooking time: 40–50 minutes
Serves 6

Butter, for greasing
4 egg whites
250 g (9 oz) icing sugar, plus
   extra for sprinkling
1 teaspoon vanilla extract

Preheat the oven to 100°C/200°F/Gas Mark ½ and line a baking sheet with buttered greaseproof paper. Put the egg whites in a heatproof bowl together with the icing sugar (you can also use very fine caster sugar) and the vanilla extract. Place the bowl over a pan of barely simmering water and whisk until the mixture is tripled in volume and holds its shape. Remove from the heat and continue whisking the meringue mixture until it is completely cold. Using a piping bag, pipe the meringues onto the baking tray, sprinkle with icing sugar and bake for 40–50 minutes, until completely dry, without allowing to colour.

PRINCESSES

princesses

Preparation time: 35 minutes
Cooking time: 25–30 minutes
Serves 6

Butter, for greasing
70 g (2½ oz) unsweetened cocoa powder
100 g (3½ oz) caster sugar
2 egg whites

Preheat the oven to 120°C/250°F/Gas Mark 1 and line a baking tray with buttered greaseproof paper. Mix the cocoa and sugar together in a bowl. In a separate bowl, whisk the egg whites until very stiff and combine with the cocoa and sugar mixture, folding in gently but thoroughly, trying not to crush the air out of the egg whites.

Spoon or pipe little mounds of the meringue mixture on to the baking tray. it. Bake for 25–30 minutes. When the meringues are cooked, turn off the oven and allow them to finish drying in the oven with the door ajar.

WHITE LADY

dame blanche

Preparation time: 15 minutes
Cooking time: 30 minutes
Serves 6

Butter, for greasing
6 eggs, separated
150 g (5 oz) caster sugar
Grated zest of 1 unwaxed lemon

Preheat the oven to 140°C/275°F/Gas Mark 1 and grease a deep 20-cm (8-inch) cake tin or charlotte mould with butter. Whisk the egg whites until they form stiff peaks. Fold in the sugar and the grated lemon zest, taking care not to knock air out of the egg whites. Fill the dish with this mixture and place in a roasting tin half-filled with hot water. Bake for 30 minutes.

Remove the roasting tin from the oven and allow the dessert to cool completely in the water bath. Turn out when cold. Serve with a thick vanilla-flavoured crème anglaise (p. 49), made with the egg yolks left over from the 6 separated eggs.

MERINGUES

meringues

Preparation time: 30 minutes
Cooking time: 35–40 minutes
Serves 6

Butter, for greasing
125 g (4¼ oz) caster sugar
1 egg white

Preheat the oven to 100°C/200°F/Gas Mark ½ and line a baking tray with buttered greaseproof paper. Whisk the egg whites, adding a quarter of the sugar after 2 minutes, then delicately fold in the remaining sugar once the whites are very stiff. Place small mounds of the meringue mixture on the baking tray, well spaced apart, and bake for 35–40 minutes, until completely dry, without allowing to colour.

Note: The quantities can be multiplied to suit your needs.

MERINGUES WITH VANILLA

meringues avec vanille

Preparation time: 20 minutes
Cooking time: 1 hour
Serves 6

Butter, for greasing
Plain flour, for dusting
4 egg whites
250 g (9 oz) caster sugar
1 teaspoon vanilla extract
Icing sugar

Preheat the oven to 100°C/200°F/Gas Mark ½ and grease a baking tray with butter. Dust this with flour. Beat the egg whites until very stiff. Gently fold in the sugar and vanilla extract without crushing the air out of the beaten egg whites. Using a spoon or piping bag, place small amounts of the meringue mixture on the prepared baking sheet. Sprinkle with icing sugar and bake for 1 hour, until completely dry, without allowing to colour.

Meringues

ITALIAN MERINGUE
meringue à l'italienne

Preparation: 25 minutes
Cooking time: 40 minutes
Makes 25

250 g (9 oz) caster sugar
4 egg whites
butter, for greasing

Use the sugar and 75 ml (3 fl oz) water to make a sugar syrup and cook to the soft ball stage (p. 17). Whisk the egg whites until they form soft peaks. Continue whisking as you pour a very thin stream of the sugar syrup onto the egg whites, making sure that the syrup trickles down the inside of the mixing bowl without touching the whisk. The meringue will become very stiff and glossy.

If the meringue is to be baked rather than used in another recipe, preheat the oven to 120°C/250°F/Gas Mark 1. Line a baking tray with buttered greaseproof paper. Pipe individual meringues on the tray. Bake for 40 minutes, until set but not coloured. A little icing sugar can be sieved over the piped meringue if a dry, crisp product is desired.

Variation: To make a coffee meringue, whisk in 1–2 teaspoons of coffee extract.

CHOCOLATE MERINGUE
meringue à l'italienne

Preparation: 25 minutes
Cooking time: 40 minutes
Makes 25

80 g (2¾ oz) plain chocolate, chopped
250 g (9 oz) caster sugar
4 egg whites

Place the chocolate in a heatproof bowl set over a pan of barely simmering water and melt the chocolate. Stir until smooth.

Use the sugar and 75 ml (3 fl oz) water to make a sugar syrup and cook to the soft ball stage (p. 17). Whisk the egg whites until they form soft peaks. Continue whisking as you pour a very thin stream of the sugar syrup onto the egg whites, making sure that the syrup trickles down the inside of the mixing bowl without touching the whisk. The meringue will become very stiff and glossy. Carefully fold the chocolate into the meringue.

If the meringue is to be baked rather than used in another recipe, preheat the oven to 120°C/250°F/Gas Mark 1. Place greaseproof paper on a baking tray and pipe individual meringues on the tray. Bake for 40 minutes, until set. A little icing sugar can be sieved over the piped meringue if a dry, crisp product is desired.

Coffee Meringue

ALMOND MERINGUES
Meringues aux amandes

Preparation: 25 minutes
Cooking time: 40 minutes
Makes 25

250 g (9 oz) caster sugar
4 egg whites
Red food colouring
60 g (2 oz) slivered almonds

Use the sugar and 75 ml (3 fl oz) water to make a sugar syrup and cook to the soft ball stage (p. 17). Whisk the egg whites until they form soft peaks and add 1–2 drops of food colouring. Continue whisking as you pour a very thin stream of the sugar syrup onto the egg whites, making sure that the syrup trickles down the inside of the mixing bowl without touching the whisk. The meringue will become very stiff and glossy. Fold in the almonds.

If the meringue is to be baked rather than used in another recipe, preheat the oven to 120°C/250°F/ Gas Mark 1. Place greaseproof paper on a baking tray and use a spoon to place small mounds of individual meringues on the tray. Bake for 40 minutes, until set. A little icing sugar can be sieved over the piped meringue if a dry, crisp product is desired.

BAKED CUSTARD WITH MERINGUE TOPPING
flan à la neige

Preparation time: 15 minutes
Cooking time: 40–50 minutes
Serves 6

750 ml (1¼ pints) milk
160 g (5¼ oz) caster sugar
2 teaspoons vanilla extract
6 eggs
2 eggs, separated
2 tablespoons redcurrant jelly

Preheat the oven to 150°C/300°F/Gas Mark 2. Place the milk, 80 g (2¾ oz) of the sugar and the vanilla in a pan and slowly bring to the boil, allowing the flavours to infuse. Beat 6 whole eggs and 2 egg yolks with a fork and gradually whisk into the vanilla-flavoured milk. Pour the mixture into an ovenproof dish, filling it no more than two-thirds full. Place the dish in a roasting tin half-filled with hot water and bake for 40 minutes.

Remove the egg custard from the oven. Raise the oven temperature to 200°C/400°F/Gas Mark 6. Five minutes before serving, whisk the 2 egg whites until they form stiff peaks and fold in the remaining sugar. Spoon over the custard. Stir the redcurrant jelly vigorously to soften it, then pipe this decoratively over the meringue. Return the dessert to the oven for 5–10 minutes to lightly brown the meringue.

Baked Custard with Meringue Topping

FLOATING ISLAND
île flottante

Preparation time: 30 minutes,
    plus cooling time
Cooking time: 30–35 minutes
Serves 6

6 eggs, separated
200 g (7 oz) caster sugar
2 tablespoons nut brittle, finely crushed
750 ml (1¼ pints) milk

Preheat the oven to 160°C/325°F/Gas Mark 3. Whisk the egg whites until they form stiff peaks and fold in 60 g (2 oz) of the caster sugar. Add a touch of caramel colour by folding in the crushed almond brittle (or a few pralines).

To make a light caramel, pour the remaining 80 g (2¾ oz) sugar into a saucepan and heat over a medium heat until the sugar is slightly melted around the edges, about 5 minutes. Using a wooden spoon, gently stir until the sugar has completely melted and is amber coloured, about 10 minutes. Coat the inside of a deep 20-cm (8-inch) cake tin or charlotte mould with the caramel.

Transfer the meringue mixture to the mould, put in a bain-marie, and bake for 30–35 minutes until the meringue has set; it is cooked when a knife blade inserted deep into the centre comes out totally clean.

Make a Crème Anglaise (p. 49) with the egg yolks, remaining 60 g (2 oz) sugar and the milk. When the meringue 'island' is cold, turn it out onto a wide, deep serving plate. Pour the crème anglaise around it.

SNOWY MACAROONS
macarons à la neige

Preparation time: 15 minutes
Cooking time: 10 minutes
Serves 6

Butter, for greasing
10 crisp macaroons
100 ml (3 fl oz) rum
6 egg whites
150 g (5 oz) caster sugar
3 tablespoons raspberry or
    redcurrant jam or jelly

Preheat the oven to 200°C/400°F/Gas Mark 6 and grease a 20-cm (8-inch) baking dish with butter. Dip the macaroons in a small bowl of rum. Whisk the egg whites until they form stiff peaks. Set 2 tablespoons of the sugar aside and fold the remainder into the whisked egg whites very gently. Place half of the meringue in the dish. Place the rum-soaked macaroons on top. Briefly stir the jam or jelly to soften it. Spread a thin layer over the macaroons. Cover this with the remaining meringue and another thin layer of jam or jelly. Sprinkle with the reserved sugar. Bake for 10 minutes. The sugar topping should be pale golden brown.

Floating Island

SOUFFLÉS

Soufflés are simply made by folding stiffly whipped egg whites into a flavoured base. After baking, a soufflé should be puffed up and light, and it should be served immediately.

CHOCOLATE SOUFFLÉ
soufflé au chocolat

Preparation time: 10 minutes,
    plus cooling time
Cooking time: 35–40 minutes
Serves 6

Butter, for greasing
30 g (1¼ oz) caster sugar, plus extra
    for sprinkling
400 ml (14 fl oz) milk
140 g (4¾ oz) chocolate, chopped
15 g (½ oz) plain flour
5 eggs, separated

Preheat the oven to 190°C/375°F/Gas Mark 5 and grease a 23-cm (9-inch) soufflé dish or 6 individual ramekins with butter and sprinkle with sugar. Bring all but 2 tablespoons of the milk to simmering point in a saucepan over a low heat. Remove from the heat and stir in the chocolate. Mix the remaining milk, flour and sugar to a smooth paste and set aside.

Beat the egg yolks in a large bowl and pour on the chocolate milk, stirring. Stir in the flour and sugar paste, and allow to cool. Whisk the egg whites to stiff peaks and fold gently into the chocolate mixture. Pour into the prepared dish and gently level the surface. Place in the oven for 10 minutes, then increase the temperature to 200°C/400°F/Gas Mark 6 and cook for a further 25–30 minutes. Serve immediately.

VERY LIGHT CHOCOLATE SOUFFLÉ
soufflé au chocolat très leger

Preparation time: 20 minutes,
    plus cooling time
Cooking time: 25–30 minutes
Serves 6

40 g (1½ oz) butter, plus extra for greasing
400 ml (14 fl oz) milk
140 g (4¾ oz) plain chocolate, chopped
20 g (¾ oz) plain flour
30 g (1¼ oz) caster sugar
6 eggs, separated

Preheat the oven to 190°C/375°F/Gas Mark 5 and grease a 20-cm (8-inch) soufflé dish with butter. Place a baking tray in the oven to heat up. Place the milk in a saucepan and bring to simmering point, then stir in the chocolate. In a small pan, melt the butter and mix it with the flour. Gradually whisk this into the hot chocolate-flavoured milk. Whisk in the sugar and egg yolks over very low heat to make a smooth chocolate custard. Do not boil. Remove from the heat and allow to cool.

Whisk the egg whites until they form stiff peaks. Stir a quarter into the chocolate custard, making sure it is thoroughly mixed, then fold in the remainder. Transfer to the mould and place in the oven on the preheated baking tray. Bake for 25–30 minutes. Serve immediately.

Chocolate Soufflé

Vanilla Soufflé

VANILLA SOUFFLÉ
soufflé à la vanille

Preparation time: 20 minutes
Cooking time: 25–30 minutes
Serves 6

100 g (3½ oz) caster sugar
100 g (3½ oz) butter, plus extra for greasing
400 ml (14 fl oz) milk
1 vanilla pod, split lengthways
50 g (1¾ oz) plain flour
5 eggs, separated

Preheat the oven to 190°C/375°F/Gas Mark 5 and grease a 20-cm (8-inch) soufflé dish with butter and sprinkle with sugar. Bring the sugar, all but 2 tablespoons of milk and the vanilla pod to boiling point in a saucepan. Remove the vanilla pod, scrape out the seeds and set aside.

In another saucepan, stir 2 tablespoons of the hot milk into the flour, then gradually add the rest of the hot milk, stirring over a low heat until thickened. Remove from the heat. Stir the butter and vanilla seeds into the milk mixture. Mix in the egg yolks, and allow to cool. Whisk the egg whites to stiff peaks and fold gently into the mixture. Pour into the prepared dish and gently level the surface. Bake for 25–30 minutes and serve immediately.

Note: For a lemon soufflé, replace the vanilla pod with the finely grated zest of 2 lemons.

CHESTNUT SOUFFLÉ
soufflé aux marrons

Preparation time: 30 minutes,
    plus cooling time
Cooking time: 25–30 minutes
Serves 6

500 g (1 lb 2 oz) chestnuts
30 g (1¼ oz) butter, plus extra for greasing
500 ml (18 fl oz) milk
1 teaspoon vanilla extract
125 g (4¼ oz) caster sugar
4 eggs, separated

Make a slit in the skin of each chestnut, cook in boiling water for 15 minutes and peel off the shells and outer skins while still warm. Drain and allow to cool slightly, then peel off the skins while still warm.

Preheat the oven to 190°C/375°F/Gas Mark 5 and grease an 18-cm (7-inch) charlotte mould with butter. Put the chestnuts and milk in a saucepan, and bring to the boil, then reduce the heat and simmer for 15 minutes. Stir in the vanilla and sugar. Allow to cool a little and then process the chestnut mixture in a blender until smooth. Return to the pan and add the egg yolks, stirring constantly. Allow to cool. Whisk the egg whites until stiff and fold gently into the mixture. Pour into the prepared dish and bake for 25–30 minutes, or until golden and risen.

CANDIED FRUIT SOUFFLÉ
soufflé aux fruits confits

Preparation time: 20 minutes,
    plus cooling time
Cooking time: 35–40 minutes
Serves 6

50 g (1¾ oz) butter, plus extra for greasing
60 g (2 oz) caster sugar, plus extra
    for sprinkling
125 g (4¼ oz) candied fruit, diced
50 ml (2 fl oz) Curaçao or Kirsch
300 ml (½ pint) milk
40 g (1½ oz) plain flour
4 egg yolks
6 egg whites

Preheat the oven to 190°C/375°F/Gas Mark 5. Grease a soufflé dish with butter and sprinkle with sugar. Put the candied fruit in a bowl, pour over the Curaçao and leave to macerate. Place all but 2 tablespoons of the milk and sugar in a saucepan and bring to a boil. In another saucepan, stir 2 tablespoons of the milk into the flour to form a smooth paste, then gradually add the rest of the hot milk, stirring over a low heat until thickened. Remove from the heat. Stir in the butter and macerated fruit. Mix in the egg yolks, and allow to cool.

Whisk the egg whites until they firm stiff peaks and fold gently into the mixture. Pour into the prepared dish and gently level the surface. Bake for 10 minutes, then raise the oven temperature to 220°C/425°F/Gas Mark 7 and bake for a further 25–30 minutes. Serve immediately.

COFFEE SOUFFLÉ
soufflé au café

Preparation time: 20 minutes,
    plus cooling time
Cooking time: 30 minutes
Serves 6

300 ml (½ pint) milk
4 teaspoons instant coffee or
    coffee essence, as preferred
6 eggs, separated
40 g (1½ oz) rice flour
Pinch of salt
150 g (5 oz) caster sugar
Icing sugar, to decorate

Preheat the oven to 190°C/375°F/Gas Mark 5 and grease a 20-cm (8-inch) charlotte mould or soufflé dish with butter. Place a baking tray in the oven to heat up. Place the milk and coffee flavouring in a saucepan and bring to the boil. Whisk 4 egg yolks in a mixing bowl with the rice flour, salt and sugar. Add the hot milk slowly while whisking continuously. Pour back into the pan and whisk over gentle heat until thickened to a smooth coffee custard. Remove from the heat and allow to cool until tepid.

Whisk all the egg whites until they form stiff peaks. Stir a quarter into the tepid coffee custard, making sure it is thoroughly mixed but without deflating the whites, then fold in the remainder. Transfer to the mould and place in the oven on the preheated baking tray. Bake for 30 minutes. Sprinkle the surface with icing sugar and serve immediately.

VERMICELLI SOUFFLÉ

soufflé au vermicelle

Preparation time: 25 minutes, plus
    cooling time
Cooking time: 50–60 minutes
Serves 6

butter, for greasing
750 ml (1¼ pints) milk
100 g (3½ oz) caster sugar
2 teaspoons vanilla extract
120 g (4 oz) vermicelli pasta
4 eggs, separated

Preheat the oven to 140°C/275°F/Gas Mark 1 and grease
a 20-cm (8-inch) charlotte mould or soufflé dish with
butter. Place the milk, sugar and vanilla in a large
saucepan and bring to boiling point. Break the vermicelli
into short pieces and sprinkle into the hot milk. Cover
and cook over low heat for 10–15 minutes until the
vermicelli is very tender. Remove the pan from the heat
and allow to cool until tepid.

Whisk the egg whites until they form stiff peaks. Beat
2 egg yolks into the vermicelli mixture and then gently
fold in the egg whites. Pour into the mould and bake for
50–60 minutes. Serve immediately.

BANANA SOUFFLÉ
soufflé de bananes

Preparation time: 20 minutes
Cooking time: 30 minutes
Serves 6

20 g (¾ oz) butter, plus extra for greasing
25 g (1 oz) plain flour
250 ml (8 fl oz) hot milk
6 bananas, peeled
3 eggs, separated
50 g (1¾ oz) caster sugar
1 teaspoon vanilla extract
Pinch of salt

To make a béchamel sauce, melt the butter in a saucepan, stir in the flour and cook for 2–3 minutes to form a paste. Gradually add the hot milk, stirring continuously to prevent lumps from forming. Simmer for 10 minutes.

Preheat the oven to 190°C/375°F/Gas Mark 5 and grease an 18–20-cm (7–8-inch) soufflé dish or 6 individual soufflé dishes with butter. Purée the banana in a blender or food processor. Beat the banana purée into the sauce followed by the egg yolks, sugar and vanilla. Whisk the egg whites with the salt until they form stiff peaks and fold into the banana purée. Pour this mixture into the dish, gently level the surface and bake for 30 minutes, until well risen and golden brown. Serve immediately.

Note: If the béchamel sauce is too thick, add more milk.

RICE SOUFFLÉ
soufflé au riz

Preparation time: 20 minutes
Cooking time: 20–25 minutes
Serves 6

180 g (6¼ oz) short-grain rice
450 ml (15 fl oz) milk
Salt
150 g (5 oz) caster sugar
30 g (1¼ oz) butter, plus
    extra for greasing
Orange flower water
Grated zest of 1 unwaxed lemon
6 eggs, separated

Rinse the rice thoroughly, drain and place in a saucepan with the milk. Add a pinch of salt, the sugar, butter, orange flower water to taste and the grated lemon zest. Simmer for about 15 minutes. When the rice is very tender, push all these ingredients through a sieve. Stir in 4 egg yolks.

Preheat the oven to 160°C/325°F/Gas Mark 3 and grease an 18–20-cm (7–8-inch) soufflé dish with butter. Whisk the egg whites to stiff peaks and fold them into the mixture. Transfer the mixture to the soufflé dish and cook in a medium oven for 20–25 min. Serve immediately.

Banana Soufflé

TAPIOCA SOUFFLÉ
soufflé au tapioca

Preparation time: 15 minutes,
    plus cooling time
Cooking time: 25 minutes
Serves 6

20 g (¾ oz) butter, plus extra for greasing
750 ml (1¼ pints) milk
125 g (4¼ oz) caster sugar
60 g (2 oz) plain chocolate, chopped
100 g (3½ oz) tapioca
4 eggs, separated

Preheat the oven to 180°C/350°F/Gas Mark 4 and grease a 20-cm (8-inch) charlotte mould or soufflé dish with butter. Place the milk, sugar and chocolate in a saucepan and bring gently to simmering point. Sprinkle in the tapioca, stirring continuously, and cook over low heat for 10 minutes, stirring frequently. Beat in the butter and 3 of the egg yolks. Allow the mixture to cool until tepid. Whisk all the egg whites until they form stiff peaks and fold them gently into the chocolate mixture. Transfer to the mould and bake for 25 minutes. Serve immediately.

KÜMMEL SOUFFLÉ
soufflé au kümmel

Preparation time: 15 minutes,
    plus cooling time
Cooking time: 25–30 minutes
Serves 6

60 g (2 oz) butter, plus extra for greasing
200 ml (7 fl oz) milk
60 g (2 oz) caster sugar
35 g (1¼ oz) potato flour
3 tablespoons Kümmel liqueur
6 eggs, separated

Preheat the oven to 190°C/375°F/Gas Mark 5 and grease a 20-cm (8-inch) charlotte mould or soufflé dish with butter. Place the milk and sugar in a saucepan and bring to boiling point. Remove from the heat and allow to cool. While the milk is cooling, melt the butter in a saucepan and stir in the potato flour. Gradually add the sweetened milk to the butter mixture, followed by the Kümmel, stirring continuously. Return to the heat and cook gently until the mixture thickens. Remove from the heat and whisk in 4 of the egg yolks. Allow to cool until tepid.

In a separate bowl, whisk the 6 egg whites until they form stiff peaks and fold them into the milk mixture. Transfer to the mould and bake for 25–30 minutes. Serve immediately.

Variation: Instead of Kümmel, Curaçao, cherry brandy or anisette liqueur can be used as a flavouring.

MACAROON SOUFFLÉ

soufflé aux macarons

Preparation time: 20 minutes
Cooking time: 30–35 minutes
Serves 6

Butter for greasing
10 crisp macaroons
6 tablespoons apricot jam
60 g (2 oz) caster sugar
5 eggs, separated

Preheat the oven to 160°C/325°F/Gas Mark 3 and grease a 20-cm (8-inch) charlotte mould with butter. Reduce the macaroons to a fine powder in a food processor or with a rolling pin. Mix this with the apricot jam, sugar and egg yolks. Whisk the egg whites until they form stiff peaks and fold into the macaroon mixture. Transfer to the mould and bake for 30–35 minutes. Serve immediately.

STARCH PUDDINGS

A pudding generally contains an ingredient which acquires a very thick consistency when cooked, such as bread, rice or semolina. Other ingredients are included for richness and flavour, such as eggs, milk, sugar, fruit and liqueurs or spirits.

RICE AND APPLE PUDDING
pudding de riz aux pommes

Preparation time: 45–50 minutes,
    plus chilling time
Cooking time: 30 minutes
Serves 6

200 g (7 oz) short-grain rice
1 litre (1¾ pints) milk
Pinch of salt
Pinch of ground cinnamon
150 g (5 oz) caster sugar,
    plus extra for sprinkling
50 g (1¾ oz) butter
375 g (13 oz) apples

Rinse and drain the rice thoroughly. Place the milk in a saucepan with the salt, cinnamon, 80 g (2¾ oz) of the sugar and the butter. Bring slowly to boiling point, then add the rice and simmer gently for 25–30 minutes until tender. Stir frequently towards the end of the cooking time.

To make a light caramel, pour the remaining 70 g (2½ oz) sugar into a saucepan and heat over a medium heat until the sugar is slightly melted around the edges, about 5 minutes. Using a wooden spoon, gently stir until the sugar has completely melted and is amber coloured, about 10 minutes. Coat the inside of a 20-cm (8-inch) charlotte mould with caramel.

Preheat the oven to 190°C/375°F/Gas Mark 5. Peel and core the apples and slice them very thinly. Spoon an even layer of rice into the base of the mould, cover with a layer of apple slices and sprinkle with a little sugar, if needed, to sweeten the apples. Repeat this layering until all ingredients have been used, finishing with a layer of rice. Bake for 30 minutes. Allow to cool and then chill. Turn out when cold.

Note: This pudding is also delicious served hot, when it can be baked and served in a deep oven-to-table dish.

CHESTNUT PUDDING
pudding aux marrons

Preparation time: 30 minutes
Cooking time: 35–40 minutes
Serves 6

250 g (9 oz) sweet chestnuts
250 ml (8 fl oz) milk
60 g (2 oz) butter, softened, plus
    extra for greasing
6 eggs, separated
1 teaspoon vanilla extract
180 g (6¼ oz) caster sugar
125 g (4¼ oz) ground almonds
Pinch of salt
1 quantity Rum Sauce (p. 46)
    or redcurrant jelly

Make a slit in the skin of each chestnut, cook in a pan of boiling water for 15 minutes and peel off the shells and outer skins while still warm. If fresh chestnuts are not available, use vacuum-packed peeled chestnuts or tinned unsweetened chestnuts.

In a separate saucepan bring the milk to the boil and add the chestnuts. Simmer until soft, about 15 minutes, then transfer to a blender and process them with the milk into a smooth purée while they are still very hot. Preheat the oven to 180°C/350°F/Gas Mark 4 and grease a 20-cm (8-inch) charlotte mould or ovenproof dish with butter. Transfer the chestnut purée to a bowl and beat in the 6 egg yolks, adding these one at a time, followed by the vanilla, sugar and ground almonds. Stir in the salt and butter.

Whisk the egg whites until they form stiff peaks and fold these gently into the chestnut mixture. Transfer to the dish and place this in a roasting tin half-filled with hot water. Bake for 35–40 minutes. Turn out and serve hot, with rum sauce, or melt redcurrant jelly with a little water, and pour this all over the pudding.

POTATO PUDDING
pudding de pommes de terre

Preparation time: 20 minutes,
    plus cooling time
Cooking time: 30–35 minutes
Serves 6

185 g (6½ oz) mixed candied fruit,
    finely chopped
100 ml (3½ fl oz) rum
250 g (9 oz) floury potatoes, peeled
Pinch of salt
60 g (2 oz) butter, diced,
    plus extra for greasing
6 eggs, separated
150 g (5 oz) caster sugar
Grated zest of 1 unwaxed lemon
1 quantity Sweetened Whipped Cream (p. 38)

Place the crystallized fruit in a small bowl with the rum. Place the potatoes in a pan of boiling water and cook until soft, drain well and mash or pass through a potato ricer to make a smooth purée. Stir in the salt.

Preheat the oven to 180°C/350°F/Gas Mark 4 and grease a 1.3-litre (2½-pint) pudding basin with butter. Beat the egg yolks, butter, sugar and lemon zest into the mashed potato while it is still hot. Stir in the crystallized fruit and rum. Whisk the egg whites until they form stiff peaks and fold gently but thoroughly into the potato mixture. Transfer the mixture to the basin and place in a roasting tin half-filled with hot water. Bake for 30–35 minutes. Turn out when cold and serve with crème chantilly.

SWEET POTATO PUDDING
pudding de patates

Preparation time: 20 minutes
Cooking time: 1 hour
Serves 6

1 kg (2¼ lb) sweet potatoes
130 g (4½ oz) caster sugar
100 ml (3½ fl oz) milk
2 eggs
60 g (2 oz) butter, diced
Pinch of salt
1 teaspoon vanilla extract
1 quantity Rum Sauce (p. 46)

Peel and chop the sweet potatoes and cook in enough boiling water to cover until soft. Pass through a potato ricer or process them to a smooth purée. Mix the sweet potato purée with 80 g (2¾ oz) of the sugar, the milk, eggs, butter, salt and vanilla. Preheat the oven to 180°C/350°F/Gas Mark 4.

To make a light caramel, pour the remaining sugar into a saucepan and heat over a medium heat until the sugar is slightly melted around the edges, about 5 minutes. Using a wooden spoon, gently stir until the sugar has completed melted and is amber coloured, about 10 minutes. Coat the inside of an ovenproof dish or mould with the caramel and fill the dish with the potato mixture. Place in a roasting tray half-filled with hot water and bake for 35–40 minutes. Turn out and serve hot or cold with a rum sauce.

ROYAL PUDDING
pudding royal

Preparation time: 35 minutes, plus
   cooling and chilling time
Cooking time: 40 minutes
Serves 6

50 g (1¾ oz) butter, plus extra for greasing
100 g (3½ oz) glacé cherries
500 ml (18 fl oz) milk
100 g (3½ oz) digestive biscuits, crushed
4 eggs, beaten
200 ml (7 fl oz) rum
100 g (3½ oz) sponge fingers
100 g (3½ oz) Macaroons (p. 208)
250 ml (8 fl oz) crème fraîche
Icing sugar, to taste

Prepare the day before. Preheat the oven to 180°C/350°F/Gas Mark 4 and grease a 20-cm (8-inch) charlotte mould with butter. Chop 30 g (1¼ oz) of the glacé cherries. In a saucepan, bring the milk to the boil and stir in the digestive biscuits, 50 g (1¾ oz) of the butter, the eggs, rum and chopped cherries. Arrange alternating layers of the sponge fingers, milk mixture, macaroons and remaining cherries in the mould. Cover and place the mould in a roasting tin half-filled with hot water. Bake for 30 minutes, then uncover and bake for a further 10 minutes. Allow to cool. Turn out the next day and serve with the crème fraîche sweetened with icing sugar.

Royal Pudding

BAKED RICE PUDDING
riz au four

Preparation time: 10 minutes
Cooking time: 1 hour
Serves 6

Butter, for greasing
1.25 litres (2 pints) milk
Vanilla extract or grated lemon zest, to taste
120 g (4 oz) caster sugar
250 g (9 oz) pudding rice

Preheat the oven to 160°C/325°F/Gas Mark 3 and generously grease a 20-cm (8-inch) square ovenproof dish with butter. In a large saucepan, bring the milk and the vanilla or lemon zest to the boil, then add the sugar. Rinse the rice, drain and place it in the prepared dish. Pour over the boiling sweetened milk. Bake for 1 hour, or until the rice is tender.

RICE AND CURRANT PUDDING
pudding de riz

Preparation time: 20 minutes, plus
  cooling time
Cooking time: 15–20 minutes
Serves 6

140 g (4¾ oz) caster sugar
180 g (6¼ oz) short-grain rice
1 litre (1¾ pints) milk
Pinch of salt
2 teaspoons vanilla extract
2 eggs, separated
100 g (3½ oz) currants
1 quantity Crème Anglaise (p. 49) or
  rum for sprinkling (optional)

Preheat the oven to 200°C/400°F/Gas Mark 6. Coat the inside of a 20-cm (8-inch) charlotte mould with caramel, using 60 g (2 oz) sugar. Rinse and drain the rice. Place the milk in a saucepan with the salt, vanilla and 80 g (2¾ oz) of the sugar. Bring to the boil, then sprinkle in the rice and cook over low heat for 15 minutes or until the rice is tender, stirring occasionally. When the rice is cooked, remove from the heat and stir in the egg yolks and the currants. Whisk the egg whites until they form stiff peaks and fold this into the rice mixture. Pour into the prepared mould and bake for 15–20 minutes. When cold, turn out. This pudding can be served with crème anglaise or sprinkled with hot rum and flambéed.

RICE PUDDING WITH SABAYON SAUCE
riz au sabayon

Preparation time: 1 hour 30 minutes,
  plus cooling time
Cooking time: 20 minutes
Serves 6

Butter, for greasing
1 quantity Rice Milk Pudding (p. 265)
1 quantity Sabayon (p. 46)

Preheat the oven to 200°C/400°F/Gas Mark 6 and grease a 20-cm (8-inch) charlotte mould with butter. Pour the rice milk pudding into a buttered mould and bake for 20 minutes. Allow to cool. Turn out when cold and serve with sabayon custard.

SEMOLINA AND CARAMEL PUDDING
pudding à la semoule

Preparation time: 25 minutes, plus
    cooling time
Cooking time: 30 minutes
Serves 6

1 litre (1¾ pints) milk
2 teaspoons vanilla extract
salt
120 g (4 oz) caster sugar
125 g (4¼ oz) semolina
40 g (1½ oz) butter
3 eggs, lightly beaten
100 g (3½ oz) skinned almonds, chopped

Preheat the oven to 160°C/325°F/Gas Mark 3. In a large saucepan, heat the milk with vanilla extract, a small pinch of salt and 60 g (2 oz) sugar until it comes to the boil. As it reaches boiling point, sprinkle in the semolina, stirring continuously. Cook over low heat, stirring at intervals, until it has thickened. Remove from the heat and stir in the butter, the eggs and the almonds.

To make a light caramel, place the remaining 60 g (2 oz) sugar into a saucepan and heat over medium heat until the sugar is slightly melted around the edges, about 5 minutes. Using a wooden spoon, gently stir until the sugar has completely melted and is amber coloured, about 10 minutes. Coat the inside of a mould with the caramel.

Transfer the semolina mixture to the mould and bake for about 30 minutes. Turn out when cold.

SEMOLINA WITH CRÈME ANGLAISE
semoule à la crème

Preparation time: 30 minutes,
    plus cooling time
Cooking time: 15 minutes
Serves 6

1 litre (1¾ pints) milk
120 g (4 oz) caster sugar
125 g (4¼ oz) semolina
50 g (1¾ oz) candied fruit, finely chopped
2 eggs, separated
1 quantity Crème Anglaise (p. 49)

Place the milk in a saucepan with 60 g (2 oz) of the sugar. Heat gently to boiling point and sprinkle in the semolina stirring continuously. Cook gently for 15 minutes, stirring frequently. Remove from the heat and stir in the candied fruit and egg yolks. Allow to cool. Whisk the egg whites until they form stiff peaks, then fold gently into the semolina.

To make a light caramel, pour the remaining sugar into a saucepan and heat over medium heat until the sugar is slightly melted around the edges, about 5 minutes. Using a wooden spoon, gently stir until the sugar has completely melted and is amber coloured, about 10 minutes. Coat the inside of a charlotte or savarin mould with the caramel.

Preheat the oven to 180°C/350°F/Gas Mark 4. Fill the dish with the semolina mixture and bake for 15 minutes. Once cold, dip the base of the mould in hot water and turn out the dessert into a serving dish. Serve the dessert with crème anglaise poured over it.

VERMICELLI PUDDING
pudding au vermicelle

Preparation time: 20 minutes,
  plus cooling and chilling time
Cooking time: 30 minutes
Serves 6

1 litre (1¾ pints) milk
80 g (2¾ oz) caster sugar
Grated zest of 1 lemon
150 g (5 oz) vermicelli
3 eggs, separated
60 g (2 oz) ground almonds
60 g (2 oz) butter
1.5 litres (2½ pints) Crème Anglaise (p. 49)
  or Redcurrant Jelly, to serve

Prepare the day before. Preheat the oven to 180°C/
350°F/Gas Mark 4. In a saucepan, bring the milk, sugar
and lemon zest to the boil. Break up the vermicelli and
add to the milk. Simmer for 15 minutes. Remove from
the heat. Thoroughly mix in the egg yolks, almonds and
butter. Allow to cool.

Whisk the egg whites to stiff peaks and gently fold them
into the mixture. Pour the pudding into 6 individual
ramekins rinsed in water. Bake for 30 minutes. Allow to
cool and keep in the refrigerator. Serve the next day
with the crème anglaise or redcurrant jelly.

TAPIOCA PUDDING
pudding au tapioca

Preparation time: 20 minutes, plus
  cooling time
Cooking time: 40 minutes
Serves 6

550 ml (19 fl oz) milk
160 g (5½ oz) caster sugar
150 g (5 oz) tapioca
6 eggs, separated
40 g (1½ oz) butter

In a saucepan, bring the milk and 100 g (3½ oz) of the
sugar to the boil. Pour in the tapioca and simmer for
1 minute. Remove from the heat and allow to cool. Whisk
the egg whites to stiff peaks. Stir the egg yolks and butter
into the tapioca, then gently fold in the egg whites.

Preheat the oven to 160°C/325°F/Gas Mark 3. To make
a light caramel, pour the remaining sugar and 1 tablespoon
water into a saucepan and heat over a medium heat
until the sugar is slightly melted around the edges,
about 5 minutes. Using a wooden spoon, gently stir
until the sugar has completed melted and is amber
coloured, about 10 minutes. Coat a 1.25-litre (2-pint)
mould to coat the insides.

Pour the pudding into the mould and place in
a roasting tin half-filled with hot water. Bake for
40 minutes. Allow to cool, then turn out and serve.

Vermicelli Pudding

BREAD PUDDING
pudding au pain

Preparation time: 20 minutes, plus
soaking time
Cooking time: 1 hour
Serves 6

500 ml (18 fl oz) milk
160 g (5½ oz) caster sugar
3 eggs, beaten
500 g (1 lb 2 oz) crustless stale bread, diced
1 teaspoon vanilla extract or lemon zest

In a large saucepan, bring the milk and 100 g (3½ oz) of the sugar to the boil. Remove from the heat and whisk the eggs into the hot milk. Stir in the bread and vanilla extra or lemon zest and leave to soak until the bread is soft.

Preheat the oven to 160°C/325°F/Gas Mark 3. To make a light caramel, pour the remaining sugar and 1 tablespoon milk into a saucepan and heat over medium heat until the sugar is slightly melted around the edges, about 5 minutes. Using a wooden spoon, gently stir until the sugar has completely melted and is amber coloured, about 10 minutes. Carefully pour into a 20-cm (8-inch) charlotte mould to coat the insides.

Pour the bread pudding mixture into the mould and bake for 1 hour. Allow to cool a little and turn out to serve.

Note: The vanilla can also be replaced with 125 g (4¼ oz) chopped candied fruit or prunes.

BREAD PUDDING WITH ALMONDS
pudding au pain et aux amandes

Preparation time: 15 minutes,
plus cooling time
Cooking time: 40–50 minutes
Serves 6

250 g (9 oz) butter, well softened,
plus extra for greasing
250 g (9 oz) ground almonds
100 ml (3½ oz) white wine
2 eggs, plus 3 egg yolks
125 g (4¼ oz) caster sugar
200 ml (7 fl oz) crème fraîche
30 g (1¼ oz) potato flour
60 g (2 oz) fine breadcrumbs from
a stale loaf
Orange flower water or grated nutmeg,
to taste

Preheat the oven to 160°C/325°F/Gas Mark 3 and grease a 1.3-litre (2½-pint) pudding basin with butter. Place the ground almonds in a bowl. Stir in the soft butter, followed in order by the white wine, whole eggs and egg yolks, the sugar, crème fraîche, potato flour and the breadcrumbs. Mix very thoroughly. Flavour either with orange flower water or with a pinch of nutmeg. Transfer this mixture to the pudding basin and place in a roasting tin half-filled with hot water. Bake for 40–50 minutes. Wait until the pudding is cold before turning it out.

Bread Pudding

Chestnut Cake

CHESTNUT CAKE
gâteau de marrons

Preparation time: 1 hour, plus cooling time
Cooking time: 1½–1¾ hours
Serves 6

1 kg (2¼ lb) chestnuts
250 ml (8 fl oz) milk
170 g (6 oz) caster sugar
1 teaspoon vanilla extract
4 egg whites
500 ml (18 fl oz) Crème Anglaise (p. 49),
  to serve

Make a slit in the skin of each chestnut, cook in a pan of boiling water for 15 minutes. Drain and allow to cool slightly, then peel off the shells and outer skins while still warm.

Preheat the oven to 160°C/325°F/Gas Mark 3. Put the chestnuts, milk, 100 g (3½ oz) sugar and vanilla in a saucepan and simmer for 15 minutes. Remove from the heat, cool a little and then sieve or process the chestnut mixture in a blender until smooth. Whisk the egg whites to stiff peaks and fold gently into the purée.

To make a light caramel, pour the remaining 70 g (2½ oz) sugar into a saucepan and heat over a medium heat until the sugar is slightly melted around the edges, about 5 minutes. Using a wooden spoon, gently stir until the sugar has completely melted and is amber coloured, about 10 minutes. Coat a 20-cm (8-inch) charlotte mould with the light caramel.

Pour in the chestnut mixture. Bake for 1½–1¾ hours. Serve with the crème anglaise.

BREAD AND CURRANT PUDDING
pudding au pain et aux raisins

Preparation time: 25 minutes
Cooking time: 40–45 minutes
Serves 6

500 g (1 lb 2 oz) stale white bread or
  brioche, crust removed
100 g (3½ oz) butter, softened, plus
  extra for greasing
200 g (7 oz) currants
750 ml (1¼ pints) milk
150 g (5 oz) caster sugar
Pinch of grated nutmeg
4 eggs
Pinch of salt

Slice the bread or brioche thinly and evenly. Spread the slices with butter. Grease a high-sided ovenproof dish with butter and place a layer of the buttered slices in it. Sprinkle with currants. Repeat this layering process until all the bread and currants have been used, finishing with a layer of bread.

Preheat the oven to 180°C/350°F/Gas Mark 4. In a saucepan, bring the milk to the boil with the sugar and a pinch of nutmeg. Beat the eggs lightly in a bowl with the salt. Slowly whisk the hot milk on to the eggs in a thin stream. Pour this mixture over the bread in the dish and bake for 40–45 minutes.

Note: Currants may be replaced with 500–700 g (1 lb 2 oz–1½ lb) fresh seasonal fruit.

DESSERTS

— BY —

CELEBRATED CHEFS

Sadaharu Aoki (France)
Maison Bertaux (United Kingdom)
Arnaud Delmontel (France)
Laurent Duchêne (France)
Gale Gand (United States)
Phillipa Grogan (Australia)
Pierre Hermé (France)
Michael Laiskonis (United States)
Gerard Mulot (France)
François Payard (United States)

SADAHARU AOKI

Boutique Port Royal, 56 boulevard de Port Royal , 75005, Paris, France

Sadaharu Aoki trained in both Japan and France, and by 1999, he was making pastries for prominent fashion houses such as Kenzo, Chanel and Christian Dior. Two years later he set up his first pastry boutique where he introduces Japanese flavours to his French pastries. Some specialities include Opéra cake with Matcha Tea, Yuzu Tartlet and Pistachio Fruit Tartlet.

SALTED CARAMEL TART
tarte au caramel salé

Preparation time: 1 hour, plus cooling time and
   30 minutes chilling time
Cooking time: 30 minutes
Serves 4

For the chocolate mousse:
115 g (4 oz) milk chocolate, broken into pieces
60 ml (2 fl oz) single cream
85 ml (3 fl oz) whipping cream, whipped

For the sweet pastry:
100 g (3½ oz) butter
20 g (¾ oz) ground almonds
60 g (2¼ oz) icing sugar
¼–½ teaspoon salt
½ egg
175 g (6 oz) plain flour

For the caramel:
75 ml (2½ fl oz) cream
25 g (1 oz) salted butter
75 ml (2½ fl oz) liquid glucose
½ teaspoon Guérande salt
2 vanilla pods
70 g (2½ oz) sugar

Cocoa powder, to decorate

For the chocolate mousse, put the chocolate pieces into a heatproof bowl. Pour the cream into a small saucepan and heat until boiling, then pour the hot cream over the chocolate pieces and mix. Blend in the whipped cream and leave to cool in the refrigerator for 3 hours.

Meanwhile make the pastry. Add the butter, ground almonds, icing sugar, salt, egg and flour to a medium-sized bowl and briefly mix until the ingredients are combined; take care to avoid over-mixing. Wrap with clingfilm and chill in the refrigerator for about 30 minutes until firm.

Preheat the over to 175°C/345°F/Gas Mark 3–4. Line a 20-cm (8-inch) round flan tin with the pastry. Line the pastry with greaseproof paper and fill with baking beans. Blind bake in the oven for about 20 minutes until a pale golden brown in the centre with slightly darker sides. Remove the paper and beans, return the pastry case to the oven and bake for 10 more minutes.

To make the caramel, put the cream, butter, glucose, salt and vanilla pods into a saucepan and bring to the boil. Put the sugar into a separate saucepan and heat until it reaches 170°C/340°F, then stir in the cream mixture and heat until this mixture reaches 105°C/220°F. Remove and discard the vanilla pods. Pour the caramel into the pastry case, smooth over and leave to cool and set.

Put the chocolate mousse into a piping bag fitted with an 8-mm (⅓-inch) nozzle and, starting from the centre pipe the mousse in a spiral pattern over the cooled caramel. Finally, cocoa powder can be dusted top of the tart, if desired.

MAISON BERTAUX

28 Greek Street, London, W1D 5DQ, United Kingdom

*Established in 1871 by a group of Communards who
fled Paris to London, Maison Bertaux is London's oldest pâtisserie
and serves up some of the city's finest pastries. The recipes have
been passed down to each generation of chefs and everything is
freshly made daily on the premises.*

MONT BLANC
mont blanc

Preparation time: 15 minutes, plus cooling time
Cooking time: 1 hour
Makes 12–15

For the meringue:
6 egg whites
350 g (12 oz) caster sugar

For the topping:
250 g (9 oz) tin chestnut spread
1 tablespoon rum
25 g (1 oz) icing sugar
300 ml (10 fl oz) whipping cream
25 g (1 oz) caster sugar
Freshly whipped cream, to decorate

Preheat the oven to 150°F/300°F/Gas Mark 2. Line a baking tray with greaseproof paper. To make the meringue bases, whisk the egg whites and 225 g (8 oz) of the caster sugar together in a grease-free bowl until they form stiff peaks. Add the remaining sugar and whisk for a further 30 seconds. Place the mixture in a piping bag with a large nozzle, and pipe 12–15 ovals of the mixture onto the prepared tray, or alternatively use a spoon to form the ovals. Bake in the preheated oven for about 1 hour, until the meringues peel away easily from the lining paper. Allow to cool.

To make the topping, beat the chestnut spread, rum and icing sugar together in a bowl until smooth. Whip the cream and the caster sugar together in a separate bowl, then gently fold into the chestnut mixture. Pipe or spoon the topping onto the cooled meringue bases and decorate with freshly whipped cream.

ARNAUD DELMONTEL

Pâtisserie Arnaud Delmontel, 39 rue des Martyrs, Paris, 75009, France

Arnaud Delmontel offers some of the finest pastries in Paris and has received numerous accolades for his breads and desserts. Known for offering seasonal variations of classic desserts, his specialities include Le Royal, layers of chocolate whipped cream, crispy praline and marzipan sponge covered in a thin layer of dark chocolate, and La Framboisine, a flavourful raspberry mousse confection.

KERALA-STYLE DESSERT
le kerala

Preparation time: 20 minutes
Cooking time: 25 minutes, plus 12 hours for chilling
Serves 8

For the macaroon base:
2 medium egg whites
50 g (1¾ oz) caster sugar
40 g (1½ oz) ground almonds
40 g (1½ oz) icing sugar
10 g (¼ oz) plain flour

For the fried pears:
2 firm Williams pears
Knob of butter
1 tablespoon clear honey
½ vanilla pod, halved lengthways
   and seeds removed

For the cardamom crème brûlée:
210 ml (7 fl oz) double cream
2 pinches of ground cardamom
1 Ceylon tea bag
2 egg yolks
20 g (¾ oz) caster sugar
2 pinches of X58 pectin (powdered
   pectin-based gelling agent)
2 pinches of powdered gelatine

½ canned pear half in syrup, to decorate

Preheat the oven to 180°C/350°F/Gas Mark 4. Line a baking tray with a sheet of greaseproof paper. Beat the egg whites in a grease-free bowl until they form stiff peaks, then whisk in the sugar. Sprinkle the ground almonds, icing sugar and flour into the mixture, and stir carefully with a spatula. Transfer the mixture to a piping bag with an 8-mm (⅓-inch) nozzle. Pipe out a macaroon on to the prepared baking tray, starting in the middle and working outwards in a spiral, to make a disc 18 cm (7 inches) in diameter. Bake in the oven for 5 minutes, then set aside.

Peel the pears and cut into dice. Add the butter, honey and vanilla seeds to a small saucepan over medium-low heat, and when the butter has melted, add the pear dice and heat for 2–3 minutes. Set aside. Put the cream and ground cardamom into a saucepan and heat until almost scalding, with bubbles appearing just around the edge of the pan. Remove from the heat and add the tea bag. Allow to infuse for 10 minutes, then remove the tea bag.

Beat the egg yolks with half the sugar in a bowl until pale and fluffy. Reheat the flavoured cream, then add the egg yolk mixture, stirring constantly. Do not allow the heat to exceed 85°C/180°F or the mixture may curdle. When this temperature is reached, remove the pan from the heat. Mix the pectin with the remaining sugar and stir into the custard, followed by the diced pears. Add the powdered gelatine and stir. Pour into an 18-cm (7-inch) moule à manquér tin. Allow to cool, then place in the refrigerator overnight, or until firm.

Place the smooth side of the macaroon on the surface of the crème brûlée, invert the mould and turn out. Slice the canned pear and fan this out on top.

LAURENT DUCHÊNE

Laurent Duchêne, 2 rue Wurtz, 75013, Paris, France

Laurent Duchêne taught pastry arts at Le Cordon Bleu in Paris and worked with Raymond Blanc before establishing his first shop on rue Wurtz. Duchêne believes in combining rigour and creativity in desserts while preserving the balance of textures and traditions. He is known for his classic pastries and cakes as well as his specialities such as Le Carré Chocolat, a decadent chocolate sponge cake.

STRAWBERRY SORBET WITH LAVENDER CRÈME BRÛLÉE
vacherin fraise, crème brûlée à la lavande

Preparation time: 30 minute
Cooking time: 10 minutes
Serves 4

For the strawberry sorbet:
150 ml (5 fl oz) water
50 g (1¾ oz) caster sugar
300 g (10½ oz) strawberries, hulled
Juice of 1 lemon

For the lavender crème brûlée:
125 ml (4 fl oz) milk
1 teaspoon dried lavender
6 egg yolks
100 g (3½ oz) caster sugar
350 ml single cream

To decorate:
4 meringue shells
400g (14 oz) strawberries

To make the sorbet, bring the water and sugar to the boil and then allow to cool completely. Liquidize and strain the strawberries, then add to the syrup mixture. Add the lemon juice. Process in an ice-cream maker, following the manufacturer's freezing instructions.

To make the crème brûlée, preheat the oven to 120°C/250°F/Gas Mark 1. Bring the milk to the boil. Turn off the heat, add the lavender, cover and leave to infuse for 10 minutes. Beat the egg yolks with the sugar until pale and fluffy. Stir in the single cream, followed by the scented milk. Strain.

Pour a shallow layer of the custard, about 2 cm/¾ inch deep, into four ovenproof ramekins. Bake at 120°C/250°F/Gas Mark 1 for 10 minutes.Sprinkle the surfaces of the baked custards with sugar and caramelize under the grill or with a blow torch. Allow to cool completely, then chill.

Place two quenelles (oval-shaped scoops) of sorbet on each plate, on top of the crème brûlée. Cover the sorbet with a meringue shell. Decorate with strawberries, cut in half lengthways.

Tip: Before placing the sorbet on the plate, make sure that the crème brulée is chilled to avoid melting the sorbet.

GALE GAND

Tru, 676 North Saint Clair Street, Chicago, IL, 60611

Gale Gand attended culinary school at La Varenne in Paris before opening Trio, Brasserie T, Vanilla Bean Bakery and later Tru in the USA. She was recognized as Outstanding Pastry Chef in 2001 by The James Beard Foundation and Pastry Chef of the Year by Bon Appétit *magazine. By 2006, she had opened Gale's Coffee Bar, Osteria di Tramonto, Tramonto's Steak & Seafood and RT Lounge with Rick Tramonto.*

RASPBERRY RHUBARB PIE
tarte framboise et rhubarbe

Preparation time: 45 minutes, plus at least
  1 hour chilling time
Cooking time: 1 hour
Serves 8

For the sour cream ice cream:
475 ml (16 fl oz) sour cream
250 ml (9 fl oz) single cream
2 tablespoons freshly squeezed lemon juice
225 g (8 oz) caster sugar
½ vanilla pod, halved lengthways
  and seeds removed, or
  ½ teaspoon vanilla extract

For the baked rhubarb filling:
8 stalks rhubarb, trimmed and washed
450 g (1 lb) raspberries
Juice of 1 orange
½ vanilla pod, halved lengthways
  and scraped
100 g (3½ oz) caster sugar
4 teaspoons cornflour

For the glacé kumquat vanilla syrup:
300 ml (10 fl oz) simple syrup
¼ vanilla pod, halved lengthways
¼ orange, peel and juice
10 kumquats, sliced and deseeded

For the pâte bric:
6 sheets pâte bric or filo pastry, thawed
120 g (4 oz) butter, melted
Caster sugar
Kosher salt

Icing sugar, to decorate

To make the ice cream, whisk all the ingredients together, then allow to chill, covered, for at least 1 hour or overnight. Process in an ice-cream maker, following the manufacturer's freezing instructions.

Preheat the oven to 180°C/350°F/Gas Mark 4. Split the bigger stalks of rhubarb in half, then cut into 12-mm (½-inch) slices and put into a large bowl. Put half of the raspberries into a food processor with the orange juice and process to a purée, then strain it over the sliced rhubarb. Add the vanilla pod scrapings, sugar and cornflour and toss well to mix in and distribute the vanilla seeds. Place in a 20-cm (8-inch) square baking tin and bake for 30 minutes, carefully stirring halfway through. Allow to cool. Do not turn off the oven.

Meanwhile, add the simple syrup, vanilla pod and orange peel and juice to a saucepan and bring to the boil. Reduce the heat, add the kumquat slices and simmer for about 20 minutes until the kumquat is tender. Allow to cool, then chill in the refrigerator.

For the pastry, working with one sheet at a time, brush a sheet of pâte bric or filo pastry lightly with melted butter. Sprinkle evenly with sugar and a tiny pinch of salt. Cut 2 of the sheets into quarters for the bases, gathering up each piece to form a cup-like shape. Cut the remaining 4 sheets into halves for the tops, gathering up each piece to form a mound. Use flan rings for both types to hold the shapes in place while baking. Bake in the oven for 7 minutes.

To serve, gently fold 6 of the remaining raspberries into 60 g (2 oz) of the warm baked rhubarb filling, then spoon the mixture into the cup-shaped bases and add the top (the thicker pastry). Add the kumquat slices on the plates and then add a scoop of ice cream next to each pastry. Sprinkle the plates lightly with icing sugar.

PHILLIPA GROGAN

Phillippa's Bakery and Provisions Store, 1030 High Street, Armadale VIC, 3143, Australia

Phillippa Grogan cultivated her baking skills in France and England, working at the award-winning restaurant Clarke's. Convinced that there would be a similar demand in Melbourne, she set up a wholesale bakery, which doubled in size within five years. The philosophy behind her success is to use traditional methods and natural ingredients to keep alive the time-honoured arts of pastry, bread and preserve-making, always with the emphasis on great flavour.

LEMON CURD TART
tarte au citron

Preparation time: 20 minutes
Cooking time: 1 hour 20 minutes
Serves 8–10

For the shortcrust pastry:
180 g (6½ oz) butter, plus extra for greasing
240 g (8½ oz) flour, plus extra for dusting
Pinch of salt
70 ml (2½ fl oz) cold water

For the lemon tart filling:
9 eggs
375 g (13 oz) caster sugar
200 ml (7 fl oz) fresh lemon juice
250 ml (9 fl oz) whipping cream
Zest of 2 lemons

For the pastry, cut the butter into pea-sized pieces with two knives using a scissor-like action, then add the flour and salt and use your fingertips to rub the mixture together. Combine the ingredients until the mixture resembles breadcrumbs (do not over-mix or the crumb will be greasy). Add enough cold water to mix until the dough comes together. Wrap firmly in clingfilm and chill in the refrigerator for 30 minutes.

Preheat the oven to 190°C/375°F/Gas Mark 5. Grease a 25-cm (10-inch) flan tin. Roll out the pastry on a lightly floured work surface to a thickness of 2–3 mm (about ⅛ inch), then use it to line the flan tin. Trim the edges neatly and prick the base all over with a fork. Line the pastry with a sheet of baking parchment, fill with baking beans and bake blind in the oven for 15 minutes. Remove the lining paper and beans, then return to the oven for 5 minutes until the base is a pale golden-brown. Remove from the oven and allow to cool. Reduce the oven temperature to 120°C/250°F/ Gas Mark ½.

For the filling, whisk the eggs until frothy in a large bowl. Add the sugar and lemon juice, mix to combine, then add the cream and mix again until just combined. Pass the mixture through a sieve, then stir in the lemon zest. Pour the mixture into the tart case and bake for about 1 hour and 10 minutes until just set – the filling should still wobble a bit.

Note: There will be some leftover pastry, which can be rolled out thin, cut into bite-sized pieces, sprinkled with salt and chopped nuts or spices such as cumin, sesame seeds or cracked black pepper, baked in a hot oven for 5–10 minutes and served with drinks.

PIERRE HERMÉ

72 rue Bonaparte, 75006 Paris, France

Known as 'the Picasso of Pastry', Pierre Hermé began his career at the age of 14 at Gaston Lenôtre, and has invented a world of tastes, sensations and pleasures by revolutionizing established traditions. In 1998, he opened his first shop in Tokyo, then another in Paris in the heart of Saint Germain. By 2010, he had eight outlets in Tokyo, nine in Paris, one in Strasbourg, two in London, a factory in Alsace and an online shop.

ISPAHAN
ispahan

Preparation time: 1¼ hour, plus 30 minutes standing and cooling time
Cooking time: 25–30 minutes
Serves 6–8

For the pink macaroon:
250 g (9 oz) icing sugar
250 g (9 oz) ground almonds
6 egg whites
1 teaspoon red food colouring
65 ml (2¼ fl oz) still mineral water
250 g (9 oz) caster sugar

For the Italian meringue:
75 ml (2½ fl oz) still mineral water
265 g (9½ oz) caster sugar
4 egg whites

For the cream:
90 ml (3 fl oz) fresh full-fat milk
3 egg yolks
90 g (3¼ oz) caster sugar

To assemble:
450 g (1 lb) unsalted butter, room temperature
1 teaspoon rose essence
30 ml (1¼ fl oz) rose syrup
250 g (9 oz) fresh raspberries
200 g (7 oz) tinned lychees, drained, stoned and cut into thirds, and chilled in the refrigerator for 24 hours
Fresh rose petals and liquid glucose, to decorate

To make the pink macaroon, sift the icing sugar and ground almonds together into a bowl. Add 3 egg whites (about 90 g/3¼ oz) to a separate bowl, lightly stir together, then mix in the red food colouring. Pour the coloured egg whites into the icing sugar and almond mixture but do not stir yet.

Meanwhile bring the water and sugar to the boil: it will eventually need to reach a temperature of 118°C/244°F. When it reaches 110°C/230°F, quickly whisk the remaining egg whites until stiff.

When the syrup reaches 118°C/244°F, whisk it into the stiffly beaten egg whites and allow to cool to a temperature of 50°C/122°F before combining this meringue with the icing sugar, ground almond and unwhisked egg white mixture, folding it in.

Transfer the mixture into a piping bag fitted with a smooth 12-mm (½-inch) nozzle. Line two baking trays with greaseproof paper. Pipe out the mixture in a spiral to form two 20-cm (8-inch) discs on the baking trays. Allow the discs to stand and develop an outer crust for at least 30 minutes at room temperature.

Preheat the oven to 180°C/350°F/Gas mark 4. Put the baking trays in the oven and bake for 20–25 minutes, opening the oven door twice, very briefly, during the cooking time. Take the trays out of the oven and allow to cool before decorating.

For the Italian meringue, put the water and 1 tablespoon of the sugar in a saucepan and bring to the boil. When the boiling point is reached, clean off any sugar deposits from the upper, inner sides of the saucepan with a damp pastry brush. Cook until a temperature of 118°C/244°F is reached. Beat the egg whites in a grease-free bowl until soft peaks form. Drizzle the sugar syrup over the beaten egg whites. Continue whisking until cool.

To make the cream, bring the milk to the boil in a saucepan. Beat together the egg yolks and sugar in a mixing bowl, then stir in the hot milk. Stir over medium-low heat until a temperature of 85°C/185°F is reached and cool quickly in a food processor with the whisk attachment.

To assemble, beat the butter in the bowl of a food processor with first the blade, then the whisk attachment. Stir in the cooled cream, then fold in 175 g (6 oz) of the Italian meringue, the rose essence and rose syrup with a spatula. Use immediately.

Place the first pink macaroon disc upside down on a serving plate and use a piping bag fitted with a 10-mm (3/8-inch) nozzle to pipe out a rose petal cream spiral to cover the surface of the macaroon. Reserve 3 raspberries and arrange the remainder in a circle around the outermost edge of the filling so that they will still be visible after assembly, then arrange two more concentric circles of raspberries inside the first circle, leaving some space between these in which to arrange the lychees.

Pipe another layer of rose petal cream on top and cover with the second pink macaroon disc, pressing gently into place. Decorate the surface of the dessert with the 3 fresh raspberries and 5 fresh red rose petals, each of the latter enhanced by a drop of 'dew' in liquid glucose, made using a paper cone.

Note: It is advisable to make this dessert the day before, so it is soft. It is also better to use egg whites stored for several days at room temperature and avoid using almonds that are too oily, which will make the mixture heavy and leave an oily trail on the surface of the dessert. Fresh lychees can be substituted for tinned lychees but may not have the same consistent flavour.

MICHAEL LAISKONIS

Le Bernardin, 155 West 51st Street, New York, NY, 10020

Michael Laiskonis, executive pastry chef of Le Bernardin, earned the titles of Bon Appétit's Pastry Chef of the Year in 2004 and Outstanding Pastry Chef in 2007 from the James Beard Foundation. His work in refining and updating classic French desserts has helped the restaurant maintain its constellation of starred reviews.

CANNELÉS
cannelés

Prepation time: 10 minutes, plus 12 hours resting time
Cooking time: 1 hour
Makes: 36

500 ml (17 fl oz) full-fat milk
50 g (2 oz) unsalted butter
250 g (9 oz) granulated sugar
Pinch of salt
1 vanilla pod, split lengthways and seeds removed
2 eggs
2 egg yolks
100 g (3½ oz) plain flour
Generous 2 tablespoons dark rum
Non-stick spray (optional)

Add the milk, butter, 125 g (4½ oz) of the sugar, the salt and vanilla pod to a medium saucepan and bring to a boil over high heat. Remove from the heat and discard the vanilla pod.

Meanwhile, put the eggs, egg yolks and remaining sugar into a bowl and, using an electric whisk, beat for about 5 minutes until light and frothy. Add the flour to the egg mixture followed by the warm milk and the rum. Pass the contents of the bowl through a fine-mesh sieve and allow to chill in the refrigerator overnight.

To bake, preheat the oven to 180°C/350°F/Gas Mark 4. Lightly spray the holes of a flexible silicon cannelé mould and fill with the mixture. (You may have to do this in batches, depending on the number of cannelés your mould can make.) Bake the cannelés for about 50–60 minutes, or until deep golden brown. Allow to cool slightly before unmoulding.

GERARD MULOT

Gerard Mulot, Magasin Saint Germain, 76 rue de seine
2, rue Lobineau, 75006, Paris, France

Gerard Mulot is a house renowned for exquisite fruit tarts, buttery
pastries and chocolate collections. His goal has always been to produce
the highest quality pastries by using the best ingredients and combining
unusual tastes and textures from crusty and creamy to sweet and fruity.
Today, there are four boutiques with pastries and chocolates made at
Mulot's second shop in Paris.

CHOCOLATE TART
tarte chocolat

Preparation time: 25 minutes, plus 2½ hours
   resting time
Cooking time: 20 minutes
Serves 6

For the chocolate rich sweet pastry:
300 g (11 oz) butter, at room temperature
190 g (6¾ oz) icing sugar
25 g (1 oz) cocoa powder
½ teaspoon salt
65 g (2¼ oz) ground almonds
1 teaspoon vanilla powder
2 eggs
450 g (1 lb) plain flour

For the chocolate and coffee ganache:
175 g (6 oz) plain chocolate, 55% cocoa solids
175 g (6 fl oz) single cream
Scant 1 teaspoon instant (freeze-dried) coffee
   (optional)
35 g (1½ oz) butter, cut into small pieces

In a large mixing bowl, use your hands to quickly combine the butter, icing sugar, cocoa and salt. Work in the ground almonds and the vanilla powder, followed by the eggs and, finally, the flour. Stop kneading the dough as soon as it comes away cleanly from the sides of the bowl. Shape it into a ball, wrap in clingfilm and allow to rest for 1 hour in the refrigerator. When the pastry has rested, take it out of the refrigerator and leave it at room temperature for 10 minutes before rolling it out on a lightly floured work surface to a thickness of 3 mm (⅛ inch).

Butter a round, straight-sided 22-cm (8½-in) tart or cake tin and line it with the pastry to form a case with 2-cm (¾-inch) sides. Trim the edges neatly and prick the base with a fork. Chill in the refrigerator for at least 30 minutes.

Preheat the oven to 180°C/350°F/Gas Mark 4. Take the lined tart tin out of the refrigerator, cover the base with a sheet of greaseproof paper and add enough baking beans to fill the pastry case. Bake blind for 20 minutes, until the chocolate pastry is well cooked. Allow to cool completely before unmoulding.

To make the ganache, chop the chocolate with a knife and place in a heatproof bowl. Heat the cream in a small saucepan and add the instant coffee when it comes to the boil. Pour the hot, coffee-flavoured milk over the chocolate and stir very slowly with a wooden spoon to avoid incorporating any air, which would make the ganache less glossy. Allow to cool to lukewarm before adding the butter, still stirring slowly. Pour this mixture into the pastry case, tapping the base very gently to level out the filling and leave to harden for 1 hour at room temperature.

FRANÇOIS PAYARD

François Payard Bakery, 116 West Houston Street, New York, NY, 10012

François Payard honed his skills and passion for the pastry arts at his grandfather's revered shop, Au Nid des Friandises on the French Riviera. Since moving to Paris to learn the artistry of modernizing traditional desserts, Payard has achieved success in some of the world's best restaurants, including La Tour d'Argent and Le Bernardin, and earned several titles for Best Pastry Chef. Payard – his eponymous bakery and Café – is located in New York City and Las Vegas.

CHOCOLATE RASPBERRY CAKE
gâteau au chocolat et framboises

Preparation time: 1 hour, plus cooling time and
    20 minutes chilling time
Cooking time: 30–35 minutes
Serves 8

For the chocolate génoise:
125 g (4½ oz) cake flour, sifted,
    plus extra for dusting
55 g (2 oz) cocoa powder, sifted
6 eggs
200 g (7 oz) caster sugar
2 tablespoons unsalted butter, melted and cooled

For the raspberry sauce:
2 tablespoons eau-de-framboise or other
    raspberry liqueur
125 g (4½ oz) sugar syrup

For the whipped chocolate ganache:
100 g (3½ oz) plain chocolate with
    70% cocoa, finely chopped
125 ml (4 fl oz) double cream
150 g (5½ oz) unsalted butter, softened
2 tablespoons eau-de-framboise or other
    raspberry liqueur

For the filling:
150 g (5½ oz) raspberry jam

To make the chocolate génoise, preheat the oven to 180°C/350°F/Gas Mark 4. Butter a medium-sized loaf tin. Dust the tin with flour and tap out the excess. Whisk together the flour and cocoa powder in a medium-sized bowl and set aside.

Fill a large saucepan one-third full with water and bring to a simmer. Whisk together the eggs and sugar in a heatproof bowl, place it over the simmering water and whisk constantly until the eggs are warm to the touch. Remove the bowl from the heat and, using an electric whisk, beat on medium speed for about 8 minutes until the mixture trebles in volume, forms a thick ribbon when you lift the whisk, and is cool to the touch.

Using a large rubber spatula, gently fold the whisked eggs into the flour mixture. Place the melted butter in a small bowl and stir in a large spoonful of the egg and flour mixture until well blended. Gently fold this mixture into the remaining mixture. Scrape the batter into the prepared tin and smooth the top with a spatula.

Bake in the preheated oven for 30–35 minutes until the cake has pulled away from the sides of the tin and the top springs back when lightly touched. Allow the cake to cool in the tin on a wire rack for 10 minutes. Unmould the cake and allow to cool completely.

Meanwhile, to make the raspberry sauce, stir the eau-de-framboise or raspberry liqueur into the sugar syrup, then set aside.

To make the whipped chocolate ganache, place the chocolate in a medium-sized heatproof bowl. Bring the cream to the boil in a small saucepan over medium-high heat. Immediately pour the hot cream over the chocolate. Gently whisk until the chocolate is completely melted and smooth. Cool to room temperature.

Using an electric whisk, beat the butter in a bowl at high speed for about 3 minutes until fluffy. Beat in the chocolate mixture and eau-de-framboise until combined, scraping down the side of the bowl as necessary.

With a long serrated knife, carefully slice off the domed top of the cake so that it is level. Slice the cake horizontally into three even-sized layers. Place the bottom layer back in the clean loaf tin. Brush the cake generously with the raspberry syrup. Spread half of the raspberry jam over the bottom cake layer.

Scrape one-third of the whipped ganache on to the jam and and cover with the next cake layer. Brush with raspberry syrup. Spread the remaining jam over the cake, then scrape over another third of the whipped ganache over the layer. Top with the remaining cake layer, pressing it down gently. Brush with the remaining syrup. Put the cake into the refrigerator to chill for 20 minutes until it firms up.

Invert the cake on to a serving platter and remove the tin. Spread the remaining ganache over the top and sides of the cake. The cake can be made up to a day ahead and refrigerated. Bring the cake to room temperature before serving.

GLOSSARY

Angelica
A leafy plant used in cooking for its flavour. It is often used in candied form as a decoration for cakes and pastries.

Baba mould
A traditionally shaped, round metal mould used for making rum babas.

Bain marie
The vessel used for a gentle method of heating in which the dish to be cooked is placed in, or over, a pan of hot water, which is then placed in the oven or simmered very gently on the stove.

Baking beans
Small ceramic beans that are placed in pastry-lined tart tins when baking blind to help the pastry cook evenly and prevent it from rising.

Bake blind
To bake the raw pastry in a pastry-lined tart tin before adding the filling, to ensure that the pastry remains crisp.

Barquette mould
A small rounded metal mould with pointed ends in the shape of a boat. It is often used to make petits fours or small tartlets. Other small metal moulds can be substituted.

Blanch
To cook ingredients briefly in boiling water. Usually followed by 'refreshing', or plunging straight into cold water to stop the cooking. In pastry, it is often done to help remove the skin of nuts more easily.

Caramelize
To cook until the sugars turn brown. Also to heat sugar until it becomes a caramel. In pastry, it can mean to coat something such as the insides of a mould with a layer of caramel.

Charlotte mould
A deep circular mould, usually made from non-reactive metal, used for many French cakes and puddings. It tapers towards the bottom and is sometimes gently fluted. A deep round dish can usually be substituted.

Coat
To cover a dish with a substance, often, a sauce.

Couverture
A type of chocolate often used in professional cooking that is high in cocoa solids and cocoa butter but low in sugar, and which, when melted, is used to cover confectionery and some cakes.

Cream
To mix sugar and egg yolks until very pale and thick (as for custard or pastry cream), or to beat an ingredient such as butter until very soft and light in texture.

Double boiler
Another term for bain marie.

Double cream
Cream with a high fat content of around 48 per cent, which makes it suitable for cooking and whipping.

Flour
To sprinkle flour over a greased tin or mould, in order to prevent the mixture from sticking. It is best to tap the tin or mould against a surface to get rid of any excess flour.

Ganache
A soft mixture made with chocolate and cream, which is used to fill and ice cakes and tarts.

Glaze
To coat the surface of a tart or pastry with milk, beaten whole egg or just the yolk beaten with a little water, or to brush a liquid such as syrup over a dish to make it glossy (see also *Coat*). Also, the liquid used for glazing.

Grease
To brush or smear the inner surfaces of baking trays, cakes tins or tart tins with butter or oil, using a pastry brush or kitchen paper.

Grind
To crush an ingredient such as nuts finely or coarsely.

Guérande salt
A type of highly prized sea salt from the Guérande region in western France.

Ice
To cover a pastry or cake with icing or frosting.

Kirsch
A clear, eau-de-vie (liqueur) made with cherries, used frequently in cakes and puddings.

Knead
To work a dough against a work surface by hand until it is smooth.

Kugelhopf mould
A large, traditionally shaped metal mould with a hole in the middle and fluted sides, used to make kugelhopfs.

Line
To cover the inside of a mould or tin; this is often done with greaseproof paper smeared with melted butter, or sometimes with sponge fingers or sponge cake, or thin slices of fruit.

Line with pastry
To cover the inside of a mould or tin with pastry dough.

Moule à manqué
A round, shallow metal mould with sloping sides, used for baking cakes. Ordinary round metal cake tins can be substituted.

Orange flower water
A liquid distilled from orange blossoms and used as a flavouring.

Pâte bric
A thin pastry, somewhat similar to filo, that originated in north Africa and is often used in French pastries. Also known as *feuilles de brick*.

Prick
To make small holes in the surface of a dish, often of a pastry-lined tin, to prevent it from puffing up during cooking, using the tines of a fork.

Quenelle
A small oval shape with pointed ends. Ice cream, cream or other soft substances are often shaped into quenelles.

Ramekin
A small ovenproof ceramic dish with fluted sides.

Savarin mould
A large, traditionally shaped metal mould with a hole in the middle, used to make savarins. Any large mould with a hole can be substituted.

Simple syrup
A sugar syrup made from equal quantities of sugar and water.

Single cream
Cream with a fat content of around 18 per cent, which is suitable for pouring but is less suitable for cooking.

Well
A hollowed-out depression in a mound of flour into which ingredients such as eggs or milk are poured.

Whipping cream
Cream with a fat content of around 35 per cent, which makes it suitable for cooking and whipping but is less heavy than double cream.

Whisk
To whisk egg whites or a mixture to introduce air and make it softer and lighter.

Zest
The thin outer layer of a citrus fruit, on top of the white pith. The zest is often grated or cut into thin strips. Also, the act of removing the layer of zest.

INDEX

RECIPE NOTES

- Unless otherwise specified, use a light olive oil, or a flavourless oil such as sunflower or canola.

- All crème fraîche is full-fat; if you cook with low-fat crème fraîche it may split. Double cream can always be substituted for crème fraîche.

- All flour is plain white flour, unless otherwise specified.

- Eggs are medium size and butter is unsalted, unless otherwise specified. Milk is full-cream.

- Always use the freshest eggs and cream possible.

- Some recipes call for fresh yeast. If unavailable, substitute 1 teaspoon fast-action yeast for ¼ oz fresh yeast.

- All citrus fruits should be unwaxed when zest is required.

- Plain, dark chocolate with a high cocoa content should be used for chocolate recipes, unless otherwise specified.

- Cooking times and temperatures are for guidance only, as individual ovens vary. If using a fan oven, follow the manufacturer's instructions to adjust the oven temperatures as necessary.

- Some recipes include raw or very lightly cooked eggs. These should be avoided by the elderly, infants, pregnant women, convalescents and anyone with an impaired immune system.

- All spoon measurements are level unless otherwise stated. Australian standard tablespoons are 20 ml. Australian readers are advised to use 3 teaspoons in place of 1 tablespoon when measuring small quantities.

- Both metric and imperial measures are used in this book. Follow one set of measurements throughout, not a mixture, as they are not interchangeable.

Ginette Mathiot
Ginette Mathiot (1907 – 1998), legendary French food writer and the foremost authority on home cooking in France, taught three generations of French families how to cook. Author of more than 30 best-selling cookbooks covering every aspect of French cuisine, she brought together recipes for classic French dishes in her definitive works, including *Je sais cuisiner* and *Je sais faire la pâtisserie*.

Clotilde Dusoulier
Parisian Clotilde Dusoulier is a food writer and an expert on French home cooking, who specializes in adapting traditional French dishes for modern readers. She is the author of two cookbooks and her vast knowledge of French food has led many fans to her 'Chocolate & Zucchini' website. She has adapted this English edition in consultation with a team of international cookery experts. By preserving the book's authenticity, they reveal to us all the secrets of simple, delicious French desserts.

Phaidon Press Limited
Regent's Wharf
All Saints Street
London N1 9PA

www.phaidon.com

© 2011 Phaidon Press Limited

ISBN: 978 0714 8 6240 8
(UK edition)

The Art of French Baking originates from *Je sais faire la pâtisserie*
© Éditions Albin Michel S.A., 1938, 1966, 1991, 2003; and *Je sais cuisiner*,
© Éditions Albin Michel S.A., 1932, 1959, 1965, 1984, 1990, 2002, 2003

A CIP catalogue for this book is available from the British Library.

Commissioning Editor: Laura Gladwin
Project Editor: Michelle Lo
Production Controller: Gary Hayes

Designed by BLOK
Photography by Yoko Inoue
Illustrations by Sara Mulvanny

The Publisher would like to thank Solène Chabanais, Clotilde Dusoulier, Sophie Hodgkin, Sachie Inoue, Yuki Matsuo and Yuriko Yamamoto for their contributions to the book.

Printed in China